Microsoft® Windows® 2000 Registry Handbook

Microsoft® Windows® 2000 Registry Handbook

Jerry Honeycutt

A Division of Macmillan USA
201 West 103rd Street, Indianapolis, Indiana 46290

Microsoft® Windows® 2000 Registry Handbook

International Standard Book Number: 0-7897-1674-7

Library of Congress Catalog Card Number: 99-63037

Printed in the United States of America

First Printing: May 2000

02 01 00   4   3   2   1

Trademarks

Warning and Disclaimer

ASSOCIATE PUBLISHER
Tracy Dunkelberger

ACQUISITIONS EDITOR
Jenny Watson

DEVELOPMENT EDITOR
Valerie Perry

MANAGING EDITOR
Thomas F. Hayes

PROJECT EDITORS
Natalie Harris
Tricia Sterling

COPY EDITORS
Michael Dietsch
Julie McNamee

INDEXER
Mary SeRine

PROOFREADER
Megan Wade

TECHNICAL EDITOR
Art Brieva

TEAM COORDINATOR
Vicki Harding

INTERIOR DESIGNER
Anne Jones

COVER DESIGNER
Anne Jones

COPYWRITER
Eric Borgert

PRODUCTION
Heather Hiatt Miller
Ayanna Lacey
Stacey Richwine-DeRome

Contents at a Glance

Table of Contents

About the Author

Jerry Honeycutt empowers people to work and play better by helping them use popular technologies such as the Internet and the Windows product family. Jerry graduated from the University of Texas at Dallas in 1992 with a B.S. degree in computer science. Prior to attending UTD, he spent three years at Texas Tech University in Lubbock, Texas. In his spare time, Jerry plays golf, dabbles with photography, and travels.

Dedication

For Jo and Paul

Acknowledgments

Books like this don't happen by accident; they involve a lot of work by people in a variety of disciplines. First and foremost is Jenny Watson, who stuck by this book until we got it finished. Jenny was my acquisitions editor and, in case you've ever wondered what such an editor does, she drove me to the finish line with her gentle yet firm prodding.

Valerie Perry was this book's developer. In conjunction with numerous other editors, including copy editors who seldom get enough credit for the work they do, Valerie polished the gibberish that I submitted into something that you could follow. Many other people made similar contributions to the book, and you find their names in the beginning of it. I owe Valerie a debt of gratitude and a public apology for insisting her name was something other than Valerie on more than one occasion.

Last but not least, this book's technical editor, Art Brieva, tested each and every fact to ensure its accuracy. I've worked with this talented fellow on more than one occasion.

I'd also like to thank Microsoft and all the people who worked tirelessly to bring you the next great operating system. Windows 2000 beats anything that the company has ever produced, and I'm convinced you're going to be immensely satisfied with your experience.

Tell Us What You Think!

As the reader of this book, *you* are our most important critic and commentator. We value your opinion and want to know what we're doing right, what we could do better, what areas you'd like to see us publish in, and any other words of wisdom you're willing to pass our way.

As an Associate Publisher for Que, I welcome your comments. You can fax, email, or write me directly to let me know what you did or didn't like about this book—as well as what we can do to make our books stronger.

Please note that I cannot help you with technical problems related to the topic of this book, and that due to the high volume of mail I receive, I might not be able to reply to every message.

When you write, please be sure to include this book's title and author as well as your name and phone or fax number. I will carefully review your comments and share them with the author and editors who worked on the book.

Fax: 317-581-4666

Email: consumer@mcp.com

Mail: Associate Publisher
          Que
          201 West 103rd Street
          Indianapolis, IN 46290 USA

Introduction

The Registry is the most important part of Microsoft Windows 2000. Bold statement, true, but the operating system just doesn't work without it. I'll go further.

The heart and soul of Windows 2000?

Yes, it is. Windows 2000 does little without consulting the Registry. It's the only major component that isn't code. Look at many of Microsoft's architecture diagrams, and you see the Registry smack dab in the middle with lines drawn to various components scattered around it like minions at their lord's feet.

Given the Registry's importance to Windows 2000, it's worth spending a few weeks learning about it. This book is your guide. If you are a user, it teaches you how to customize your computer more than you ever thought possible. If you are an administrator, you'll learn how to take control of your network. ■

How to Use This Book

This is not a tell-all book about Windows 2000. It doesn't cover the entire depth and breadth of the operating system like *Special Edition Using Windows 2000* (Macmillan, 1999). It does cover the Registry in more detail than you'll find in any other source, however. It provides useful tips for personalizing the operating system and overcoming its more annoying quirks. It helps administrators bring the full power of the Registry to bear on one of their biggest problems, controlling desktops in the organization.

The secrets you're looking for are in this book.

Administrator or power user, no matter, read all of Part I, "Overview," and Part II, "Management." The information in these parts shows you how to manage the Registry on a day-to-day basis, protect your computer's configuration as you learn the Registry, and edit the Registry. Take a look at the following sections to learn which parts will be most valuable to you after you've finished the first two parts of this book.

Administrators

Sometimes, Microsoft can't win. For the most part, administrators ignore features that might reduce support costs. Few use policies to control their networks or use the Registry to administer computers remotely.

If you want to make a difference in your organization, reduce support costs by learning how to administer the network using the Registry. Start by diving into Part II. It shows administrators how to use policies to control users' privileges and how to administer the Registry. Part III, "Customization," shows how to distribute customizations to numerous users on a network, which is a real timesaver. Part IV, "Troubleshooting," shows how to fix problems when solutions are in the Registry.

Power Users

If you're a power user who wants to learn more about Windows 2000, personalize or troubleshoot the operating system, or protect yourself from the many problems the Registry creates, you're reading the right book. Here are some suggestions to get you started:

- For help protecting your computer's configuration, see Chapter 5, "Safeguarding Configurations."

- For information about customizing Windows 2000 or writing scripts to customize Windows 2000, see Part III. Chapter 9, "Tracking Down Registry Settings," helps you develop your own customizations, too.

- For help fixing problems that might be in the Registry, see Part IV. If troubleshooting fails, see Chapter 5 to learn how to restore a backup Registry.

- For a reference to the contents of the Registry, a good guide that helps you learn more about Windows 2000, start with Part V, "Reference."

How This Book Is Organized

Microsoft Windows 2000 Registry Handbook covers the Registry in depth. It has 5 parts, 15 chapters, and an index.

The first two parts teach you the basics. Parts III and IV show you how to customize and troubleshoot Windows 2000 using the Registry. Part V explores the Registry so that you know exactly what's in it. More information about each part appears in the following sections.

Part I, "Overview"

Chapter 1, "Understanding Registries," is Registry 101. It describes the purpose of the Registry, important terminology, and key concepts that you must know to understand the rest of this book.

Chapter 2, "Accounting for Registry Changes," describes the operating system's new features and their impact on the Registry. If you're already familiar with Microsoft Windows NT 4.0, read this chapter to catch up quickly.

Part II, "Management"

Chapter 3, "Editing with Regedit," teaches you how to use Regedit.exe.

Chapter 4, "Editing with Regedt32," is similar to Chapter 3 except that it shows you how to use Regedt32.exe.

Chapter 5, "Safeguarding Configurations," shows you how to protect your configuration and how to restore it if something terrible happens; and, it sometimes does.

Chapter 6, "Administering Registries," is for administrators who need to use remote administration and need to secure the Registry beyond the default security settings that Windows 2000 provides.

Part III, "Customization"

Chapter 7, "Customizing Windows 2000," is like TV's *Inside Edition* for Windows 2000. It exposes some of the operating system's deepest, darkest secrets so that you can customize it to suit your needs.

Chapter 8, "Using Microsoft Tweak UI," introduces you to this remarkable program that helps you and the Registry live together.

Chapter 9, "Tracking Down Registry Settings," shows you how to locate changes in the Registry. It introduces numerous programs that help you monitor the Registry and teaches you undocumented techniques for isolating changes.

Chapter 10, "Scripting Customizations," escalates things. Not only can you customize Windows 2000 using the Registry, but you can also distribute customizations using different types of scripts.

Part IV, "Troubleshooting"

Chapter 11, "Diagnosing Registry Errors," is a complete list of error messages, event log entries, and related errors along with their solutions.

Chapter 12, "Repairing Damaged Registries," empowers you to fix problems that have annoyed you for months and problems you don't even know about yet.

Part V, "Reference"

This portion of the book explores the contents of the Registry in detail. You find three chapters in Part V, each of which covers specific portions of the Registry:

- Chapter 13, "File Associations"
- Chapter 14, "Per-User Settings"
- Chapter 15, "Per-Computer Settings"

Special Features in This Book

This book has some special features designed to help you get the information you need—fast.

Chapter Roadmaps

Each chapter begins with a brief list of the topics that it covers. You know what you'll be reading before you start. Think of the roadmap as my promise to cover those topics in the chapter.

Tips, Notes, and Cautions

Notes, Tips, and Cautions give you useful information that applies to the passage you're reading. Following are samples of each element. Each sample describes the type of information you'll find it that element.

 TIP Tips enhance your experience with Windows 2000 by providing hints and tricks you won't find elsewhere.

N O T E Notes provide useful information that's not necessarily essential to the discussion. They usually contain more technical information, but can also contain interesting but non-vital technical or non-technical information. ■

> **CAUTION**
>
> Cautions warn that a particular action can damage your configuration. Given the consequences of editing the Registry, you shouldn't skip the cautions in this book.

TROUBLESHOOTING

I have a problem; what's the solution? Troubleshooting sections anticipate problems and provide solutions.

▶ Cross-references point to a chapter where you can learn more about the topic at hand.

Nuggets of Information

Sidebars are detours from the main text. They provide background or interesting information that is relevant but not essential reading. You might find information that's a bit more technical than the surrounding text or a brief diversion into the historical aspects of the surrounding text.

Keyboard Conventions

The keyboard conventions listed here help you better understand what the instructions are telling you to do. They help you understand the key combinations and menu commands that you are supposed to type or choose.

Hotkeys	Underlined characters are hotkeys. For example, the *F* in File is a hotkey. To use a hotkey, press Alt and the underlined letter.
Key combinations	Key combinations are separated by plus signs. For example, "Press Ctrl+Alt+D" means hold down the Ctrl and Alt keys and then press and release the D key.
Dialog boxes	In general, instructions won't tell you to click OK to close a dialog box, saving your changes, except when necessary. All other instructions are explicit: "In the Scheme list, click Windows Standard."
Menu commands	Instructions for menus are explicit. "On the File menu, click New" is an example. So is "On the Start menu, click Programs, point to Accessories, and then click Notepad." When instructions tell you to point to a submenu, pointing the mouse at it is enough to open it.

Note that Windows 2000 has an option to disable the underlined character in hotkeys until you press Alt. To display hotkeys all the time, click the Effects tab on the Display Properties dialog box and click the Hide Keyboard Navigation Indicators Until I Use the Alt Key option.

Typeface Conventions

This book uses some special typeface conventions that make it easier to read:

Italic	Italic indicates new terms. It also indicates placeholders in commands, addresses, and code. You replace the placeholder with your own text. On occasion I use italic for emphasis.
Bold	Registry keys and values are bold.
`Monospace`	Monospace (or computer type) represents code, in general. Filenames also appear in monospace.

Code Continuation

When a line of code is too long to fit on one line of this book, we break at a convenient place and continue it on the next line. The code on the next line begins with the code continuation character (➥).

Special Directories

Using Windows 2000 environment variables as the standard, I use the following placeholders throughout this book:

UserProfile	Represents the directory in which Windows 2000 stores user profiles. Generally, this is C:\Documents and Settings, but administrators change the location in setup scripts.
SystemDrive	Represents the drive on which you install Windows 2000. Usually C.
SystemRoot	Represents the drive and directory that contain Windows 2000. By default, this is C:\Winnt.
WinDir	Same as *SystemRoot*, but I seldom use it in this book.

Abbreviations

The following are common abbreviations for root keys in Windows 2000's Registry, and I use them in subkeys but not by themselves:

HKCR	**HKEY_CLASSES_ROOT**
HKCU	**HKEY_CURRENT_USER**
HKLM	**HKEY_LOCAL_MACHINE**
HKU	**HKEY_USERS**
HKCC	**HKEY_CURRENT_CONFIG**

Overview

Understanding Registries

In this chapter

What Is the Registry?

Young technology companies start with little or no organization—a bunch of computer geeks sitting around a table piled high with pizza and computers. As those companies leave their kitchens and enter the real world, they must add hierarchy to their structure chart to handle the complexities of doing business. And so it is with Microsoft Windows. In the operating system's nascent years, it put settings in INI (Configuration Settings) files, as did most Windows-based applications. Windows is all grown up now, and its INI files no longer make the grade. Enter the Registry, which introduces the hierarchy necessary to manage such a complex system.

The Registry is the heart and soul of Windows. That's my favorite way to describe the Registry, but Microsoft calls it the central repository for configuration data. *Configuration database* is better. Indeed, the Registry is a *hierarchical database*—it stores data in a hierarchy like an outline or a company's structure chart. This structure enables you to locate any setting with a simple notation, which is similar to a path in the MS-DOS file system. Each setting in the Registry is an ordered pair that has a name and a value, much like banks associate account numbers with balances. You've just read my one paragraph description of the Registry; now, take a look at Figure 1.1 to get a good overview of how Windows uses the Registry.

The Registry serves dozens of innovative purposes, enabling features that were, at best, difficult in earlier versions of Windows. It makes possible intimate relationships between the operating system, applications, and user interface. The computer's hardware configuration resides in the Registry, including Plug and Play devices. It supports multiple hardware configurations, and multiple users can share a single computer but keep their personal preferences. The Registry also supports remote administration. With few exceptions, programs designed for Microsoft Windows 2000 store all their settings in the Registry. The list of technologies that the Registry enables goes on, and you learn about many of them in this chapter.

The Registry's Strengths and Weaknesses

Caught between a rock and a hard place, the Registry's primary role is also its Achilles' heel. Rather than scatter configuration settings willy-nilly across hundreds of INI files, the Registry provides a central place to store all settings. Sharing is simpler. Organization is standard. Technical knockout.

Oh, yes, but central storage makes the Registry a weak link, a single point of failure upon which stability depends. Because everything relies on settings in the Registry, if the Registry fails, a single program can fail or possibly the entire system can fail. If you're stuck between a rock and a hard place and you purchased this book for help, read this chapter and Chapter 5, "Safeguarding Configurations."

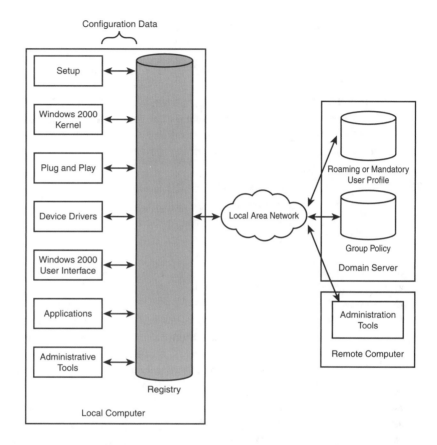

FIGURE 1.1
Most Windows 2000 components use the Registry.

What's So Important About the Registry?

Why do you care about the Registry? What is so important about the Registry that I suggest you spend the next few days or weeks plowing through this book? Let me explain.

The Registry is a central place to store all settings, reducing the INI-file hell that was characteristic of earlier versions of Windows. It's like having a hundred-dollar bill in your wallet rather than a pocket full of one-dollar bills. This has advantages. It makes backing up settings easier. Instead of looking for numerous INI files, back up the Registry and you're done. Central storage means administrators have one place to go to secure settings, which they do in Windows 2000 by changing access control lists (ACLs) for each group of settings in the Registry. One more thing: Microsoft defines clear standards for where programs put particular types of settings—application, user, hardware, and otherwise. Predictability like this makes settings easier to find and innovative technology more common because, among many reasons, developers can build applications that work well together.

Sounds dandy, but *customizing* Windows 2000 is probably the reason you purchased this book. I'm here to tell you that you can customize the heck out of the operating system using the Registry. Make the user interface snappier, add commands to shortcut menus, slim down the Start menu (shown in Figure 1.2), tweak your Internet connection, and add new commands to Microsoft Internet Explorer 5. For an abundance of customizations you can use to make Windows 2000 suit your needs, see Chapter 7, "Customizing Windows 2000." Other parts of this book show you how to ferret out your own customizations, too. For example, Chapter 9, "Tracking Down Registry Settings," shows you how to use numerous common tools to locate changes that the operating system and other applications make in the Registry.

FIGURE 1.2
Administrators can
strip the Start menu
of most commands.

Administrators get the best deal—wouldn't you like to spend more time at your desk and less time wandering the halls? Through use of the Registry, remote administration enables administrators to change a networked computer's configuration settings. The Registry supports varieties of other remote administration tools, too, including remote performance monitoring and policies. *Policies* are the greatest thing since sliced bread, because they give administrators more control over what users can do on their computers, not just on the network. Administrators aside, remote administration helps businesses reduce the total cost of owning Windows 2000. Chapter 6, "Administering Registries," tells you more about remote administration and policies.

If configuration settings are trees, then configuration profiles are forests. Enabled by the Registry, *profiles* allow Windows to apply different groups of settings in different situations. Two types of profiles are visible in the Registry, user profiles and hardware profiles, but Windows keeps others without actually calling them such. For example, each time a user logs on to a computer, the operating system loads the user's settings into the Registry. Each user's profile is separate from other user profiles, so users can change preferences without affecting others. One user can have a purple desktop while another has a lime-green desktop, for example, all on the same computer.

Hardware profiles work similarly to user profiles, except the operating system loads a different hardware profile depending on the computer's configuration. The most common cases are mobile computers. Windows keeps one profile for when users dock the computer, in which case additional PC Card slots are available, and one for when they undock the computer, without the additional slots.

Life as a Registry

You've just read a brief introduction to the Registry, but following Windows 2000 through a typical day gives you a better idea about what is in this vast tome. The following sections, which comprise a journal of sorts, does just that. It kicks off by describing how the operating system uses the Registry to start the computer. Then it describes how the operating system uses the Registry at strategic points throughout the day, including when an imaginary user, Fergus, logs on to the computer, double-clicks a file, or installs a new program.

Fergus Starts Windows 2000   As Windows 2000 starts, it reflects the computer's configuration in the Registry. This data includes the number of CPUs; the amount of RAM; and the configuration of bus controllers in the computer. It also updates information about each device on those bus controllers, including the resources it uses (DMA, interrupts, and I/O addresses). Next, using the Registry, Windows 2000 configures the computer. It initializes device drivers, opens the computer's network connections, and starts services, such as Task Scheduler. In short, it loads the configuration data required to start the computer from the Registry to the Log On to Windows dialog box. It doesn't load per-user configuration data, however; that process begins when Fergus (the imaginary user) logs on to the computer.

Fergus Logs On to Windows 2000   After Fergus types his name and password in the Log On to Windows dialog box and presses Enter, Windows 2000 validates his credentials. You correctly guessed that the Registry plays a key role in this process. After approving his credentials, the operating system loads his settings into the Registry. That is, the operating system keeps users' settings separate and loads their settings only when they log on to Windows 2000. Examples of per-user settings are color schemes, folder options, and the Start menu's sort order.

Fergus Double-Clicks a File   When Fergus double-clicks a file in Microsoft Windows Explorer, Windows 2000 looks up the file's extension in the Registry. It does this to find a program that can open the file. The operating system runs the program, passing the name of the file to it as a command-line option. When the program starts, it reads its per-computer settings and its per-user settings from the Registry. Per-computer settings apply to all users and per-user settings apply to the current user. Not only does the program read its own settings from the Registry, it also reads data from the Registry that describes the computer's configuration. Examples include information about fonts and the location of folders, such as the user's desktop.

Fergus Installs a New Program   When Fergus installs a new application, the setup program adds the application's settings to the Registry. Some settings are per computer and other settings are per user. The configuration data that the setup program puts in the Registry enables Fergus to open a file by double-clicking it, using the Add/Remove Programs dialog box to uninstall the application, and pointing at a file in Windows Explorer to display more information about it. Importantly, the setup program also adds settings that enable an application's components to work together and with other applications.

Fergus Opens a File's Properties Dialog Box   Windows 2000 goes through all sorts of gyrations when Fergus clicks Properties on a file's shortcut menu. First, it loads the shortcut menu's commands from the Registry. That one sentence sounds easy but requires the operating system to read tons of data from the Registry. When he clicks Properties, the operating system displays a dialog box that it customizes for that file using data it finds in the Registry. Again, simple sentence but the operating system puts a lot of work into it.

Keep in mind that I've grossly generalized the concepts depicted in Fergus' adventures to focus on helping you understand why the Registry is the heart and soul of Windows 2000. Where in the Registry the operating system stores this data isn't important at the moment.

Other Incarnations

Microsoft's earliest operating system, MS-DOS, had no Registry. Users specified the computer's configuration using a murky soup including Config.sys, Autoexec.bat, and varieties of other configuration files, environment variables, and command-line options. Each program kept its own settings. The operating system provided few device drivers, not even a mouse driver. Specialized hardware—devices other than communication ports and disks—required users to install device drivers provided by the manufacturer and usually also required programs that were explicitly built for use with the device. Examples are scanners and tape drives. Programs did not work well together; they couldn't even share settings well. I've painted a fairly bleak picture and many people still favor MS-DOS over Windows, but MS-DOS is a dinosaur.

Microsoft Windows 3, not much higher than MS-DOS on the evolutionary ladder of operating systems, added INI files to the mix. INI files are simple ANSI text files that contain one setting per line. Each setting looks like *name=value*. They group settings into different sections using headings that look like [*section-name*]. A handful of INI files (Win.ini, System.ini, Progman.ini, Control.ini, and Protocol.ini) provided central storage for many settings. These include hardware and device driver settings and many other settings that are common to all programs. Plus, most programs kept private INI files, and most computers contained thousands of those files. INI files were great, giving users numerous ways to customize their computers, but these goblins caused the following problems, too:

- Programs scattered private INI files all over the computer's disk. Not a big problem until users try troubleshooting or customizing the computer. Also, this didn't help programs share or synchronize settings. A similar setting might change in one INI file but not in another, causing all sorts of havoc if synergy is important.

- INI files are plain ANSI text files, which made customizing the computer easy for anyone who knew how to use Notepad. Support costs sailed as users broke their computers regularly while trying to "customize."

- The types and size of data that programs could store in an INI file were limited. Programs were limited to text, requiring programmers to invent all sorts of interesting ways to represent data, and INI files were limited to 64KB.

- INI files didn't provide methods for the operating system to communicate changes to programs, such as when the user adds new hardware or installs new fonts. Programs usually didn't reflect all the computer's configuration changes, requiring users to reinstall the program in some cases.

- INI files did not support the concept that more than one user might want to use a single computer, not to mention that a user might want their settings to follow them around as they use multiple computers. Along the same vein, INI files made remote administration totally impractical.

- Microsoft defined no standards for how programs store settings in central or private INI files. This is probably the most severe limitation. Figuring out the resulting spaghetti is almost impossible and, in fact, a handful of computer books were popular due to this fact.

Along comes the original Registry (or registration database as it was first called), which Windows 3.1 introduced. Microsoft created it to enable OLE (Object Linking and Embedding) and the operating system's drag-and-drop features. These technologies required an accurate database that contained the location of each program as well as the various parameters each program required to communicate with others. Parameters included information about the types of data with which each program could work and what the program could do with that data. The database also provided a way for File Manager to associate file extensions with programs so that double-clicking a file opened it in the appropriate program. (This is still the primary purpose of the Registry, although it's a bit more elaborate now.) The Windows 3.1 Registry was limited. It had only a single branch, which was limited to 64KB of data, and it didn't address the INI file's limitations because all the old INI files were still required by the operating system. Still, the Registry you see in Windows 2000 looks similar to the original Registry.

The Registry as a cornerstone started with Microsoft Windows NT 3.5 and Microsoft Windows 95. With those two operating systems, the Registry became a key component in everything the operating systems do. From the time it first boots to the time it shuts down, every task the operating system performs uses the Registry's configuration data in one way or another. With these two operating systems, most of the INI file's limitations are gone. The 64KB size limit is gone. The Registry supports multiple hierarchies. All configuration data can go into the Registry. Multiple users can easily share a single computer and users' settings can follow them around from computer to computer. For that matter, look at the list of INI file limitations you saw earlier in this section, and most of those go away. Windows NT even supported security in the Registry, similar to NTFS security, but Windows 95 didn't. Windows 95's Registry supported something that Windows NT didn't, however, and that's Plug and Play. The Registry is one of the key components that enables Plug and Play. Although Windows 95 still relied somewhat on INI files and many Windows 95 programs still used private INI files, making it somewhat difficult for multiple users to keep all their settings separate from each other, Windows NT didn't.

Microsoft Windows NT 4 didn't make any fundamental changes to the Registry, but it did catch up with Windows 95 when it adopted Windows 95's new look and feel. The most prominent addition was the support of policies and settings that Windows Explorer and the new desktop used. Windows 98 didn't make many changes, either. The organization was the same. Everything else about it looked the same. Microsoft did optimize the code that provides programs access to the Registry, however, and they added a great new program called Registry Scanner. Registry Scanner, not available in Windows 2000, is able to scan the Registry for errors, repair any errors it finds, and back up the Registry. Users can run Registry Scanner manually, but the operating system runs the program once each time it starts.

Fear Not the Cult

The cult-like mystery that surrounds the Registry has many causes. Programmers and geeks mystify the Registry to secure their positions at the upper echelons of geekdom—job security, as it were. Microsoft produces little documentation for the Registry. The Registry is only accessible via a specialized API (Application Programming Interface) and specialized tools, tools that aren't on the Start menu. The message is *don't touch*.

Everyone makes repeated warnings about the dangers of messing around with the Registry. Microsoft is the worst about using scare tactics to dissuade people from entering dark territory. Look at every Microsoft document that discusses the Registry, and it starts with a warning about the dire consequences of changing the Registry. Every book on the subject, including all my previous books, plastered warnings on every other page. Well, I don't want you to believe that tinkering with the Registry is certain death for your computer's configuration. Take a few commonsense precautions, and you and your computer's configuration will be just fine. To that end, here is the last warning you'll see in this book other than more specific warnings about steps that might damage your computer.

> **CAUTION**
>
> Changing the Registry can damage your computer's configuration. Be careful. Before making any change, particularly if you're not sure of the consequences, back up all or part of the Registry. When making any change that you fear could prevent Windows 2000 from starting properly, update your Emergency Repair Disk. For more information about how to back up the Registry, see Chapter 5, "Safeguarding Configurations." This chapter describes many techniques for tinkering with the Registry safely, such as making temporary copies of individual settings.

Registry Bits and Pieces

Throughout this section, while learning about the Registry's anatomy, I compare the Registry to Windows 2000's file system. This analogy works, because the operating system organizes the Registry similar to how it organizes files on the computer's disk. In fact, Figure 1.3 shows

Microsoft Registry Editor, the program you use to edit the Registry, and Windows Explorer side by side, comparing what you see in each.

FIGURE 1.3

Windows 2000 organizes the Registry similarly to how it organizes files on the computer's disk.

Folders and Subkeys   Files and Values

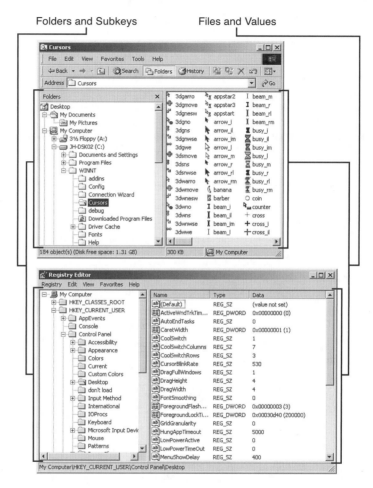

Registry Editor's left pane, the *key pane*, displays the Registry's hierarchy. Registry Editor displays My Computer at the top of the key pane, and everything you see underneath My Computer is in the local computer's Registry. Just as Windows Explorer displays each of the computer's disks underneath My Computer, Registry Editor displays five *root keys* underneath My Computer. That is, our analogy continues by comparing root keys in Registry Editor to disks in Windows Explorer. Table 1.1 shows the name of each root key in the Registry Editor and the common abbreviations, which I use to make this book more readable.

Table 1.1   Root Keys and Their Abbreviations

Name	Abbreviation
HKEY_CLASSES_ROOT	HKCR
HKEY_CURRENT_USER	HKCU
HKEY_LOCAL_MACHINE	HKLM
HKEY_USERS	HKCU
HKEY_CURRENT_CONFIG	HKCC

N O T E   Within most code, Microsoft uses Hungarian notation to name variables, among other things. *Hungarian notation* is a simple way to describe what a variable contains by beginning its name with a descriptive prefix. They used this same notation to name each root key. The prefix **HKEY** indicates that it's a handle to a key—not the most meaningful thing to users, but useful information for programmers. ■

Per-User, Per-Computer, Per-Me

Throughout this chapter, you've seen two conspicuous looking adjectives that sound important: per-user and per-computer. Well, they are important.

Per-computer configuration data are settings that apply to the computer and all users who use that computer, not individual users. Another common term for per-computer is *computer-specific*.

Per-user configuration data are settings that apply to individual users. Each user who logs on to the computer has his or her private, per-user settings, and Windows 2000 takes responsibility for matching users to their settings by storing them in user profiles. The operating system prevents users from using or changing settings that don't belong to them. Another common term for per-user is *user-specific*.

I mention these now because within the Registry, per-user and per-computer settings live in different places. Per-user settings are in **HKEY_USERS** and per-computer settings are in **HKEY_LOCAL_MACHINE**.

Keys

If root keys in Registry Editor are like disks in Windows Explorer, then subkeys are like folders. In fact, subkeys have many characteristics in common with folders. You can nest subkeys and, visually, you can tell whether a subkey contains nested subkeys because you see a plus sign to the left of its name. Registry Editor even uses the same icon for subkeys as Windows Explorer does for folders. Names can contain up to 256 characters and they can use any combination of ASCII characters, other than a backslash (\), asterisk (*), or question mark (?). Also, Microsoft reserves all names that begin with a period.

You must get acquainted with the notation that most sources use to describe fully qualified names. The fully qualified name of a subkey contains the name of each key in the subkey's hierarchy, and you separate each part with a backslash, similar to separating each part of a file path. For example, **HKCU\Software\Honeycutt** is a fully qualified name of a subkey called **Honeycutt**. This notation simply says that **Honeycutt** is in **Software**, which is in the root key **HKCU**. Just remember that the fully qualified name of any subkey starts with the name of the root key and contains the name of every subkey all the way down the hierarchy to the topic of conversation.

To recap the terminology you've learned thus far, take a look at the following list:

- **Key**   In the Registry, a key is a folder that can contain subkeys, similar to how folders in Windows Explorer can contain subfolders.

- **Root Key**   You see five root keys, sometimes called subtrees, at the top of the Registry's hierarchy. **HKEY_USERS** is a root key, for example.

- **Subkey**   Subkey is the term I typically use to describe any key other than root keys. When a parent-child relationship between two subkeys is important, I call the parent a *key* and the child its *subkey*. Unless the location of a subkey is abundantly clear, you see the fully qualified name of the subkey, which includes the root key and each subkey all the way down the hierarchy. Here's an example: **HKCU\First\Second\Subkey**.

Some root keys and subkeys are links, or aliases. Within a key that's a link, you see an exact replica of the data in the subkey to which it is linked. Links make programming and editing the Registry easier, but that's not their primary purpose. Their primary purpose is to maintain compatibility with earlier versions of Windows by making the Registry look similar to an earlier version of the Windows Registry. Think of links as a folder shortcuts that you put on your desktop. For example, **HKCR** is a link to **HKLM\SOFTWARE\CLASSES**. That means you see the exact same subkeys and values under both of these keys. Note that users can't create links in the Registry, but third-party Registry editors, such as Norton Registry Editor, enable you to simulate links, making the Registry easier to navigate.

Values

In addition to containing nested subkeys, each of the Registry's keys can contain zero or more settings. The correct term for these settings is *values*. Values are like files. Click a folder in Windows Explorer and it displays the folder's files in the right pane; similarly, click a key in Registry Editor's key pane and it displays the key's values in the *value pane*, the right pane. Refer to Figure 1.3 again to see the relationship.

You see three columns in the value pane:

- **Name**   Each value has a name. You see its name in the value pane's first column. Just like subkey names, value names can contain any combination of ASCII characters other than a backslash (\), asterisk (*), or question mark (?). Also, Microsoft reserves all names that begin with a period. Within each subkey, value names must be unique. No such requirement exists for values in two different subkeys, however. That means a single subkey can't contain two values, both named **Example**; however, two different subkeys can both contain a value named **Example**.

- **Type**   A value's type, which is in the value pane's second column, indicates the type of data in the value. For example, a **REG_SZ** value contains a string and a **REG_BINARY** value contains binary data. More information about each type of data that Windows 2000 supports can be found in the "Types" section later in this chapter.

- **Data**   Each value contains data, which you see in the value pane's third and last column. Previous versions of Windows limited this data to 64KB; Windows 2000 doesn't have the same limitation, but that doesn't change the fact that the practical limit for data is 2KB. Although the value's data usually matches its type, this isn't always the case. For example, storing strings as binary values is common practice.

Wondering about our file system analogy? Yup, it's still working. A value's name serves a similar purpose as a file's name, to uniquely identify it within a folder. The analogy you read earlier between a value's data and a file's contents is obvious, but what about the value's type? A value's type is similar to a file's extension; they both indicate the type of data in the value or in the file.

Every subkey contains at least one value, its default value. Registry Editor names each subkey's default value **(Default)** or **<No Name>**, depending on which of Windows 2000's Registry editors you're using. This is usually a **REG_SZ** value, but dimwitted programs can change its type to something else. In many cases, a subkey's default value is null—empty—and in those cases Registry Editor displays **(value not set)** in the value pane's third column.

Remember the earlier discussion in the "Keys" section about a subkey's fully qualified name? Values fit into this notation in a sick and twisted way. In most cases, the value isn't part of the name. For example, you'll read something that says, "Change InfoTip in HKCR\.txt." **HKCR\.txt** is the fully qualified name of the subkey and **InfoTip** is the name of the value to change. In other cases, "Change the value of HKCR\.txt\InfoTip" makes clear the fact that the name includes a value, **InfoTip**, which is in the subkey called **HKCR\.txt**. Whether reading this book or another source, pay close attention to the text to make sure you know whether the fully qualified name contains the name of a value or not. The intention is usually quite clear.

Figure 1.4 illustrates the important concepts about subkeys and values that you've learned to this point.

Types

Windows 2000 supports a plethora of value types in the Registry. Many of these types are highly specialized, especially when you consider that programmers can represent any possible type of data using binary data. Note that the value's type means little to Windows 2000 or the Registry. Windows 2000 just reads and writes the data without regard for its type, making the code that's using the value responsible for figuring out what it represents. Here's a description of each type:

FIGURE 1.4
Subkeys and values
are similar to folders
and files.

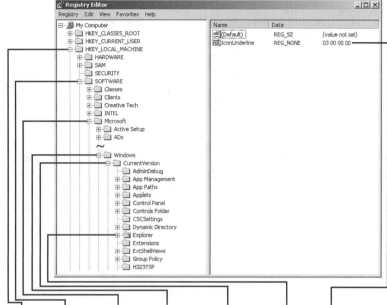

HKLM\SOFTWARE\Microsoft\Windows\CurrentVersion\Explorer\IconUnderline

- **REG_BINARY** This is raw binary data. What goes in, comes out. Registry Editor displays binary data in hexadecimal notation only; decimal notation is not even an option. All binary data in the Registry must contain even numbers of bytes, meaning the data can contain any multiple of 16-bit words. **01 BD 42 65 13 31 00 00** is an example of what a binary value looks like in Registry Editor.

- **REG_DWORD** As the second common type of data in the Registry, **REG_DWORD** is a 32-bit, double-word value. That means it can hold values as large as 2^{32}. Registry Editor displays **REG_DWORD** values in both hexadecimal and decimal notation. You can edit these values either way, too. **0x01ACEF10**, **0xC10005AA**, and **0x00000001** are examples.

- **REG_DWORD_BIG_ENDIAN** A *big-endian* value is one whose most significant byte is first in memory, followed by the less significant bytes. Registry Editor doesn't provide a way to create values of this type, but you can edit them.

- **REG_DWORD_LITTLE_ENDIAN** A *little-endian* value is one whose least significant byte is first in memory, followed by the more significant bytes. Registry Editor doesn't provide a way to create values of this type, but you can edit them.

- **REG_EXPAND_SZ** Underused, **REG_EXPAND_SZ** is a powerful enhancement to **REG_SZ**. Programs that read a **REG_EXPAND_SZ** value expand any environment variables they find in the string. For example, programs that read **%SystemRoot%\ System32** from a **REG_EXPAND_SZ** value expand **%SystemRoot%** with the path of Windows 2000's system files, usually **C:\Winnt**, yielding the string **C:\Winnt\ System32**. Unfortunately, Windows 2000 doesn't expand these strings itself, relying on programs' wits to know the difference between **REG_EXPAND_SZ** and **REG_SZ**. **REG_EXPAND_SZ** is usually no better than **REG_SZ**.

■ **REG_FULL_RESOURCE_DESCRIPTOR**   This is a useful but complicated type of binary data that stores lists of the resources a device uses. Although users can't add this type of value to the Registry, they are able to display those that already exist.

■ **REG_LINK**   Some subkeys are nothing more than aliases for other parts of the Registry. The exact same data appears within two different subkeys. Similar to short-cuts you create to a file, links join one subkey to another subkey in the Registry. In the Registry, **HKEY_CLASSES_ROOT** is a link to the subkey **HKLM\SOFTWARE**. Users can't create links using Registry Editor.

■ **REG_MULTI_SZ**   A multiple string (see **REG_SZ** later in this list). This is a list of zero or more strings. Internally, the Registry separates each string with a zero, but when editing **REG_MULTI_SZ** values in Registry Editor, you separate each string with a carriage return.

■ **REG_NONE**   My favorite type of value, **REG_NONE** indicates a value that contains no data at all—like my brain first thing in the morning. I've never seen this type in the Registry.

■ **REG_QWORD**   Soon, Microsoft will produce a version of Windows 2000 for 64-bit processors. When that day comes, the Registry is ready, because it supports **REG_QWORD**. This type of value is a 64-bit quadruple-word, which is similar to **REG_DWORD** only twice the size. Currently, Registry Editor makes no provision for editing this type of data.

■ **REG_QWORD_BIG_ENDIAN**   This is similar to **REG_DWORD_BIG_ENDIAN** except that it contains the big-endian form of a 64-bit quadruple-word. This is advanced planning for future versions of Windows 2000 that support 64-bit processors. Currently, Registry Editor doesn't enable users to edit this type of data.

■ **REG_QWORD_LITTLE_ENDIAN**   This contains the little-endian form of a 32-bit quadruple-word, but is similar to **REG_DWORD_LITTLE_ENDIAN.** Like **REG_DWORD_BIG_ENDIAN**, Microsoft added this value type in anticipate of support for 64-bit processors. Currently, Registry Editor doesn't support editing this type of data.

■ **REG_RESOURCE_LIST**   This groups together as one block of binary data, one or more **REG_FULL_RESOURCE_DESCRIPTOR** values. Users can't edit this type of data but they can display the data. This is the common way Windows 2000 represents a device's configuration.

■ **REG_RESOURCE_REQUIREMENTS_LIST**   Uncommon but sometimes used type of value, this is a binary list of resources that a device requires. Users can't edit these values, but they can display them.

■ **REG_SZ** **REG_SZ** are string values, the most common type of data and the simplest type of values in the Registry. **Windows 2000, %SystemRoot%\System32**, and **Jerry Honeycutt** are examples of strings you might see in the Registry. Internally, the Registry terminates each string with a zero, but you never see it. Note that earlier versions of Registry Editor displayed strings within quotation marks, but the current version does not.

Of the types you just learned, three are pervasive in the Registry. **REG_BINARY**, **REG_DWORD**, and **REG_SZ** are the most common. The remaining types are seldom used, if at all.

Root Keys in the Registry

Part V, "Reference," is your complete reference to the contents of the Windows 2000 Registry. This section provides an overview of its contents, however, so you can navigate the Registry until you hike deeper into its dark forests.

As noted earlier, in Registry Editor you see five root keys. Two of these root keys have special prominence because Windows 2000 actually saves their contents as files. Those are **HKEY_LOCAL_MACHINE** and **HKEY_USERS**. The location of these files isn't important at the moment; you learn about that in the "Registry Files on Disk" section at the end of this chapter.

The remaining root keys are links, about which you've already learned. **HKEY_CURRENT_USER** is a link to a subkey in **HKEY_USERS**. **HKEY_CLASSES_ROOT** and **HKEY_CURRENT_CONFIG** are links to subkeys in **HKEY_LOCAL_MACHINE**. To make abundantly clear the relationship between the primary two root keys and the three links to their subkeys, take a gander at Figure 1.5. This diagram shows **HKEY_LOCAL_MACHINE** and **HKEY_USERS** with lines drawn from the appropriate subkeys to each of the remaining root keys. What this diagram also shows is a brief glimpse of each root key's subkeys.

HKEY_USERS

Abbreviated **HKU** when it's part of a subkey's fully qualified name, **HKEY_USERS** contains per-user settings. Normally, this root key has three subkeys, one for the computer's default user settings and two for the current user. Settings that Windows 2000 applies prior to any user logging on to the computer are in **HKU\.DEFAULT**. Contrary to most other sources, even Microsoft documentation, the operating system does not apply these settings to users the first time they log on to the computer.

FIGURE 1.5
Links provide a convenient way for programmers and users to access important subkeys buried within the Registry.

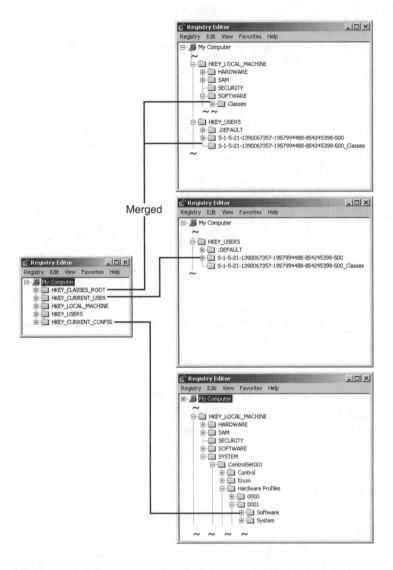

The remaining two subkeys have funky names. The first is *SID*, in which *SID* is the current user's security identifier (see the following sidebar, "Those Insidious SIDs"). **HKU*SID*** contains the current user's per-user settings, which run the gamut from desktop preferences to software settings for applications such as Microsoft Office 2000. All the settings in **HKU*SID*** apply to the user whom the SID uniquely identifies and no other user. The second subkey is ***SID*_Classes**, which contains per-user file associations and COM (Component Object Model) classes that Windows 2000 merges with **HKLM\SOFTWARE\Classes** to form **HKEY_CLASSES_ROOT**, a subkey you learn about in "HKEY_CLASSES_ROOT," later in this chapter.

One situation exists in which **HKEY_USERS** has more than three subkeys, and that's when multiple users log on to the computer at once. What? Yes, Windows 2000 allows programs to run in different security contexts, a feature that Microsoft calls *secondary logon*. For example, if Fergus (whom you met earlier in this chapter) logs on to the computer using a regular account, he can't run programs that require administrative rights. Instead of logging out and back on to the computer under an account that does have administrative rights, he clicks Run A̲s on the program's shortcut menu and runs the program using an account that does have those rights, such as Administrator. In this case, Windows 2000 loads the secondary user account's settings into the Registry and you see two more subkeys in **HKEY_USERS**; thus, the secondary logon feature causes another user to log on to the computer and the operating system to load that user's settings into the Registry.

Those Insidious SIDs

SIDs are odd looking and lengthy alphanumeric strings that uniquely identify local and domain user accounts as well as local and domain user groups. A SID's structure is similar to that of a telephone number. The first part uniquely identifies the authority, usually a domain, that issued the SID, and the second part uniquely identifies the account within that domain.

S-1-5-21-553393301-1521681255-927750060-1004 is an example of a SID.

SIDs have three important characteristics. First, they are globally unique, and the operating system *never* reuses a SID. Also, by using SIDs to identify users, groups, and domains, Windows 2000 does not rely on names, which change frequently, for authentication.

The last characteristic is the most important, particularly for administrators collapsing domains when migrating from Windows NT Server 4 to Windows 2000 Server. Encoded within each SID is the domain that issued the SID. When moving users and groups from one domain to another, Windows 2000 must assign a new SID to them, one that identifies the new domain. Here's the rub: Those same users and groups will lose access to resources that give permission to the original SID. Because the consequences of restructuring your domain without careful consideration are severe, make sure you read about domain restructuring in *Windows 2000 Resource Kit* (MS Press, 2000).

HKEY_CURRENT_USER

HKEY_CURRENT_USER, abbreviated **HKCU** when part of a subkey's fully qualified name, contains the current user's per-user settings. This root key is a link to **HKU*SID***, where *SID* is the security identifier of the user who logged on to the computer using the Log On to Windows dialog box. It'll never link to any subkey of **HKEY_USERS** that Windows 2000 creates to support a secondary logon. Don't confuse **HKU*SID*** with **HKU*SID*_Classes**, either, which contains per-user file associations and COM classes.

Here is an overview of what's in **HKEY_CURRENT_USER**:

- ■ **Appevents** Associates sounds with events, such as logging on to the computer, opening a menu, or closing a window. Users configure sounds using Control Panel's Sound icon.

- **Console**   Contains properties for a console window, such as the MS-DOS command prompt. Users change these settings by clicking Properties on the Control menu.
- **Control Panel**   Contains settings that users change in the Control Panel. Examples are power options, desktop appearance, and accessibility options. Not all the settings in this subkey are controllable via Control Panel icons and not all Control Panel settings are in this subkey.
- **Environment**   Contains environment variables that users define using Control Panel's System icon.
- **EUDC**   Associates an End User Defined Characters font with a specific codepage.
- **Identities**   Contains a subkey for each identity users create in Microsoft Outlook Express 5. Identities make sharing a single mail client easier by associating a mail store, address book, and other settings with each identity. Users configure identities by clicking Identities on the File menu in Outlook Express 5.
- **Keyboard Layout**   Defines the current keyboard layout. Users change the keyboard layout using the Keyboard icon in Control Panel.
- **Network**   Contains a subkey for each persistent network connection. That is, each subkey represents a mapped network drive. To create a network connection, users click Map Network Drive on a shared folder's shortcut menu.
- **Printers**   Describes the printers to which the user is connected. Users configure printers using Control Panel's Printers icon.
- **RemoteAccess**   Defines the dial-up settings that users configure using the Connections tab of the Internet Options dialog box, which is the Internet Options icon in Control Panel.
- **Software**   Contains per-user settings for each application, including Windows 2000 itself. Other than a few rogue Microsoft applications that don't follow Microsoft's own rules, most applications store settings in *Vendor\Application*, where *Vendor* is the name of the vendor and *Application* is the name of the application. Those vendors following the rules to the T add an additional subkey called *Version*, enabling each of an application's versions to keep their settings separate.
- **UNICODE Program Groups**   Stores program group settings from earlier versions of Windows NT that used Program Manager. On clean installations, this subkey is always empty.
- **Volatile Environment**   Contains environment variables used during the logon process.
- **Windows 3.1 Migration Status**   Indicates the migration status of Windows 3.1 program groups and INI files after upgrading from Windows 3.1. This subkey is always present but doesn't make much sense, because Microsoft doesn't support an upgrade path from Windows 3.1 to Windows 2000.

HKEY_LOCAL_MACHINE

Abbreviated as **HKLM** when part of a subkey's fully qualified name, **HKEY_LOCAL_MACHINE**, contains per-computer settings such as its hardware and network configuration. Here's an overview of the five subkeys you see in it:

- **HARDWARE**   Describes the hardware that Windows 2000 detects in the computer. Aside from describing the computer's processors and memory, this subkey describes the resources each device uses and maps devices to device drivers, with the advent of Plug and Play in Windows 2000. Note that Windows 2000 builds this subkey as the operating system boots.

- **SAM**   Contains the local security database (Security Accounts Manager). Windows 2000 stores local users and groups in **SAM** and Windows 2000 Server stores domain users and groups in the same subkey. Permissions prevent most users, even with administrative rights, from viewing this subkey. Use Control Panel's Users and Passwords icon to manage the local security database. Note that **SAM** is a link to **HKLM\SECURITY\SAM**.

- **SECURITY**   Contains the local security database, **SAM**, as well as local policies and other secrets. Windows 2000 prevents users from viewing this subkey, but you learn about its contents in Part V.

- **SOFTWARE**   Contains per-computer settings for each application, including Windows 2000. Just like **HKCU\Software**, a few misbehaved Microsoft applications don't follow the rules, but most applications put settings in **Vendor\Application**, where **Vendor** is the name of the vendor and **Application** is the name of the application. Those vendors following the rules add an additional subkey called **Version**. The most interesting, useful, and customizable subkey of **HKLM\SOFTWARE** is **Classes**. This subkey defines the computer's file associations and COM classes. The Registry makes accessing this easier, because the root key **HKEY_CLASSES_ROOT** is a link to **Classes**.

- **SYSTEM**   Contains control sets, which describe the device drivers and services that Windows 2000 loads when it starts. Additionally, control sets define every aspect of the computer's system-level configuration. Each control set is in a subkey called **HKLM\SYSTEM\ControlSet**nnn, where nnn is a three digit number beginning with 000. The subkey **CurrentControlSet** is a link to the current control set that Windows 2000 is using. **HKLM\SYSTEM\Select** contains a value called **Current** that indicates which of the control sets Windows 2000 is using.

N O T E   **HKEY_CURRENT_CONFIG** is a link to the current hardware profile, which is in Hardware Profiles under the current control set, **HKLM\SYSTEM\CurrentControlSet\ Hardware Profiles\Current**. The abbreviation for this root key is **HKCC**. ■

HKEY_CLASSES_ROOT

HKEY_CLASSES_ROOT, abbreviated **HKCR** when part of a subkey's fully qualified name, contains file associations and COM classes. This root key is a bit more complicated than in previous versions of Windows.

HKEY_CLASSES_ROOT is no longer just a link to **HKLM\SOFTWARE\Classes**. Windows 2000 merges the contents of **HKCU\Software\Classes** and **HKLM\SOFTWARE\Classes** to form **HKEY_CLASSES_ROOT**. **HKEY_CURRENT_USERS** contains per-user file associations and COM classes. Per-computer life associations and COM classes are in **HKEY_LOCAL_MACHINE**. Delve deeper into Microsoft's lair by tracing to its source: **HKCU\Software\Classes**. This subkey is actually a link to **HKU*SID*_Classes**, in which *SID* is the security identifier of the current user. Per-user settings have priority over per-computer settings, so any time a file association or COM class is in both **HKEY_LOCAL_MACHINE** and **HKEY_CURRENT_USER**, the operating system uses one in **HKEY_CURRENT_USER**.

This new way of doing business complicates things for programmers and users alike. If you change a file association in **HKEY_LOCAL_MACHINE**, the change affects all users who log on to the computer because it contains per-computer settings. If you change a file association in **HKEY_CURRENT_USER**, the change affects only that user. What happens when you change a file association in **HKEY_SOFTWARE_CLASSES**, however? The results can be unpredictable. The rule is that if the subkey or value exists in **HKCU\Software\Classes**, that's where Windows 2000 changes it. If not, Windows 2000 changes it in **HKLM\SOFTWARE\Classes**. The best thing for you to do is consciously choose to change per-user or per-computer file associations and COM classes and make those changes in **HKEY_LOCAL_MACHINE** or **HKEY_CURRENT_USER**.

> **N O T E** **HKEY_CLASSES_ROOT** is the largest part of the Registry. It represents 78% of the Registry on the computer I'm using to write this chapter. I figured that percentage by saving the entire Registry to a file and then saving just **HKEY_CLASSES_ROOT** to a file. Divide the size of **HKEY_CLASSES_ROOT** by the size of the entire Registry to get the percentage. ▪

Registry Files on Disk

To programs, you, and the rest of the world, Windows 2000 presents the Registry as one big glob of configuration data. To this point, I've presented it to you that way. This is the *logical* structure of the Registry, but a different *physical* structure stores different parts of the Registry in different files. Each file is a *hive file*, and each part of the Registry that Windows 2000 saves in a separate file is a *hive*.

Figure 1.6 shows the relationship between a hive and its hive file. *SystemRoot*\System32\ Config is the directory shown in the figure, and it contains per-computer hive files. What this shows is that Windows 2000 stores the contents of **HKLM\SOFTWARE** in a hive file called Software.

FIGURE 1.6
Microsoft saves
each subkey of
**HKEY_LOCAL_
MACHINE** as a hive
file in *SystemRoot*
System32\Config.

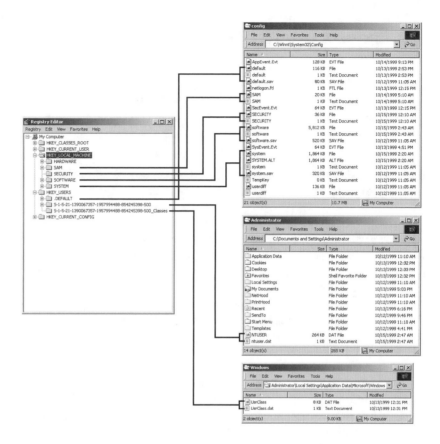

For a list of all the hives that Windows 2000 supports, including per-user hives, see Table 1.2. There are a few surprises in this table. First, **HKLM\HARDWARE** doesn't have a hive file. Why? Windows 2000 dynamically creates this hive each time the operating system starts and it doesn't save the hive to disk when it shuts down. **HKU\.DEFAULT** is the hive that the operating system uses prior to any user logging on to the computer, and it stores its hive file with all the other per-computer hive files. **HKU*SID*** and **HKU*SID*_Classes** are per-user hive files. The surprise here is that the operating system doesn't store both of them in the same place. It puts **HKU*SID*** in *UserProfile***Ntuser.dat**. **HKU*SID*_Classes** is in *UserProfile***Local Settings\Application Data\Microsoft\Windows\UsrClass.dat**. The difference makes sense, however. If the user profile is a roaming profile (see Chapter 6, "Administering Registries"), Windows 2000 synchronizes Ntuser.dat with the network copy of the user's profile, but it won't synchronize UsrClass.dat because Local Settings is a non-roaming folder.

Table 1.2   Hives and Hive Files

Hive	Hive File
HKLM\HARDWARE	
HKLM\SAM	SystemRoot\System32\config\Sam
HKLM\SECURITY	SystemRoot\System32\config\Security
HKLM\SOFTWARE	SystemRoot\System32\config\Software
HKLM\SYSTEM	SystemRoot\System32\config\System
HKU\.DEFAULT	SystemRoot\System32\config\Default
HKU\SID	UserProfile\Ntuser.dat
HKU\SID_Classes	UserProfile\Local Settings\Application Data\ Microsoft\Windows\UsrClass.dat

Windows 2000 backs up each hive file with two other files. Files with the .log file extension are transaction logs of all the changes to a hive. Also, at the end of the text-mode portion of the setup process, Windows 2000 saves a copy of each hive file using the .sav file extension. Windows 98 users can draw a parallel between System.1st and files with the .sav file extension. **HKLM\SYSTEM** is such an important hive that it's the only one for which Windows 2000 creates a backup copy using the .alt file extension.

N O T E   I would love to tell you that Microsoft had some grand scheme in how it chose the different hives, such as it better separates different kinds of data. I would be lying, however. The truth is that Windows 2000 stores all subkeys of **HKEY_LOCAL_MACHINE** in a hive file without regard to any sort of grand scheme. In other words, it just worked out that way. Of note is the fact that Microsoft capitalizes the name of each hive in the Registry. ▪

Resource Kits

Some of the more useful Registry tools are in the Windows 2000 Professional CD-ROM in Support\Reskit. It includes tools like Reg.exe, which is a command-line Registry editor you can use to edit the Registry from within batch files. The official resource kits, one for Professional and one for Server, contain the same Registry tools. Neither has anything extremely useful other than Regentry.chm, a good reference for useful Registry values.

Some of the utilities that were in earlier versions of the resource kits are no longer in them. For example, Compreg.exe and Regback.exe aren't in the Windows 2000 Resource Kit. You won't miss them, however, because Reg.exe combines the features of all the missing utilities in a single package. Better yet is the fact that Microsoft Press cleaned up Reg.exe so that it works better.

2

Accounting for Registry Changes

Registry Editors

Both Registry editors, *Regedit* and *Regedt32*, are almost identical to the earlier versions in Microsoft Windows NT 4.0. Microsoft Windows 2000 introduces just a few new features, however:

- *Regedit* has a new menu, Favorites, which works similarly to the same menu in Microsoft Internet Explorer 5. Save frequently used subkeys in this menu and then return to them quickly by clicking their names on the menu. For more information, see Chapter 3, "Editing with Regedit."

- Reflecting changes to Windows 2000's user security user interface, *Regedt32* has new dialog boxes for changing permissions, auditing, and so on. See Chapter 4, "Editing with Regedt32."

The bottom line is that if you're familiar with the Registry editors from other versions of Windows, you'll have no problem using them in Windows 2000. Neither editor has any major changes.

Registry Content

After a quick inspection, you'll think that rather little has changed in the Registry, which is mostly true. Although a few changes are relatively earth shattering, most changes are subtle and support new features in Windows 2000: new settings, new objects, and so on. **HKCR** is more complicated. It's no longer just a link to **HKLM\SOFTWARE\Classes**. Windows 2000 merges the contents of **HKCU\Software\Classes** and **HKLM\SOFTWARE\Classes** to create **HKCR**. Settings in **HKCU** take precedence over settings in **HKLM**. For more information, see Chapter 13, "File Associations."

This change represents a difference in how the operating system stores class information as hive files on disk. All the user settings are no longer in a single hive file, Ntuser.dat. Windows 2000 still stores most of the user settings in Ntuser.dat, just as it always did, but it stores per-user class information in a hive file in *UserProfile*\Local Settings\Application Data\Microsoft\Windows\UsrClass.dat. Why it stashes this file so deeply in users' profile folders when Ntuser.dat is at the root of the profile folder is beyond me.

Registry Security

Three changes to security significantly affect Windows 2000:

- **Permissions** Windows 2000 has new security dialog boxes, and you see those dialog boxes in *Regedt32*. Figure 2.1 is an example.

- **Remote Access**   Whereas Windows NT Workstation 4.0 allowed anyone on the network to connect to the Registry, Windows 2000 Professional limits access to administrators and backup operators. Windows 2000 still uses `winreg` to control remote access to the Registry, however. For more information about `winreg`, see Chapter 6, "Administering Registries."

- **HKLM\SAM**   Two things here. First, domain controllers store security information in Active Directory now, and they only store it in **SAM** for use in Active Directory Restore Mode or in mixed-mode environments. Second, by default, Windows 2000 now encrypts the contents of **HKLM\SAM** using *Syskey*, a utility you learn about in Chapter 6.

FIGURE 2.1
Windows 2000 has new security dialog boxes.

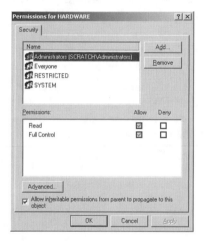

Secondary Logon

Secondary Logon is a unique new feature that enables you to run a program as a different user. This is a great and long overdue feature. On a daily basis, you can use your computer with an account that has limited rights. This prevents some viruses from inflicting their damage and prevents human error from damaging the configuration. When you need to administer the computer, run the utility as Administrator.

I mention this because you might see something strange in the Registry. Normally, you only see three subkeys in **HKU**: **.DEFAULT**, *SID*, and *SID*_**Classes**. If you run a program as a different user, you'll see two additional subkeys: *SID* and *SID*_**Classes**. You'll see the same set of two subkeys for each account under which you're running a program.

Disaster Recovery

Backing up the Registry and recovering from disasters is similar in Windows 2000 to Windows NT Workstation 4.0. Two things move around a bit and there is one new feature:

- Windows 2000 supports a boot menu, called Advanced Options Menu, which is similar to Windows 98. The most important thing about this menu is that you can start Windows 2000 in Safe Mode, which frequently allows the operating system to start when it won't start normally. After starting in Safe Mode, you can diagnose the problem (it always seems to be a video driver), fix it, and then start the computer normally. Chapter 12, "Repairing Damaged Registries," tells you more about the boot menu.

- Making an Emergency Repair Disk is different in Windows 2000 than in Windows NT Workstation 4.0. Instead of using *Rdisk*, which doesn't even exist in Windows 2000, you use Microsoft Windows Backup. The contents of an Emergency Repair Disk are a bit different, too. For more information, see Chapter 5, "Safeguarding Configurations."

- Recovery Command Console is a long-awaited new feature. The problem with NTFS is that you couldn't access the disk if Windows NT 4.0 wouldn't start. That means that you had to install a dual copy of the operating system to repair a problem. Recovery Command Console provides limited access to the disk if Windows 2000 won't start. It has a command-line interface similar to the MS-DOS command prompt and also has commands that allow you to enable and disable device drivers and servers. For more information, see Chapter 12.

Resource Kit Tools

Administrators will be most affected by the changes in the lineup of tools included in *Microsoft Windows 2000 Resource Kit* (MS Press, 1999). Most of the tools with which administrators are familiar are now gone. Those include

- **Compreg.exe**
- **Delsrv.exe**
- **Regback.exe**
- **Regchg.exe**
- **Regdel.exe**
- **Regdir.exe**
- **Regkey.exe**
- **Regread.exe**
- **Regrest.exe**
- **Secadd.exe**

A handful of Registry utilities is left, including **Dureg.exe**, **Reg.exe**, **Regdmp.exe**, **Regfind.exe**, **Regini.exe**, and **Scanreg.exe**. You won't miss the others.

The biggest surprise in the resource kit is *Reg* (**Reg.exe**). Dust off this old utility and give it a second chance (earlier versions never worked properly) because it has a whole new interface and a whole new attitude. The darned thing works now. Every command passed my tests. The best part is that each command has consistent command-line options and is more intuitive and easier to use.

One notable change is that you specify subkey and value names as separate options, making the utility less likely to be confused as to whether you're changing a subkey's default value, and so on. It's a great utility to use to make script changes to the Registry and includes the following commands:

- Add
- Compare
- Copy
- Delete
- Export
- Import
- Load
- Query
- Restore
- Save
- Unload

Part

I

Ch

2

Management

Editing with Regedit

Introducing Regedit

Remember the *Newhart* TV show with the brothers Larry, Darryl, and Darryl? Each time they introduced themselves, Larry would say, "This is my brother Darryl and this is my other brother Darryl." Likewise, Registry Editor is the name of two different programs—both have the same name, both have similar features, but each has unique capabilities. Regedit is the program you learn about in this chapter; Microsoft Windows 3.1, Microsoft Windows 95, and Microsoft Windows 98 also include it. This basic Registry editor is easier to use and has a better search feature than its sibling, Regedt32. Regedt32 is the other Registry editor, which every version of Microsoft Windows NT includes. Regedt32 can change subkeys' permissions, can edit advanced data types such as REG_MULTI_SZ, and has other features that make it more of a power tool than Regedit. Despite that, Regedit is still the appropriate choice for most editing jobs because it's quicker and easier to use.

N O T E Throughout this book, I distinguish between the two registry editors only when necessary to avoid confusion or whenever you must use a particular program to perform a task. In most cases, when you read *Registry Editor*, you can use either Regedit or Regedt32. Regedit and Regedt32 aren't arbitrary names; they are the names of each program's executable file. ▪

Microsoft doesn't treat all users equally. The company's attitude about Regedit is that if users don't know about it, they won't miss it. When users install Microsoft Windows 2000, the setup program doesn't copy a shortcut for Regedit to the Start menu, and Microsoft doesn't say much about it. For that matter, Windows 2000 Help contains barely a handful of screens that describe how to use Regedit. That's probably just as well; Microsoft wants to prevent inexperienced users from accidentally harming their configurations by tampering with the Registry, so the company doesn't provide encouragement by over-documenting it. Administrators and power users can't avoid Regedit, however. It's their window into their computer's configuration—Windows 2000's heart and soul—allowing them to fix many problems and customize the operating system in a variety of ways. Use Regedit to customize Windows Explorer, for example, or use it to customize files' shortcut menus. Many articles in Microsoft's Knowledge Base require you to use Regedit to make subtle changes to the registry.

Regedit is a powerful but simple program. It has no toolbar; its menus are straightforward. It has two panes, displaying the registry's organization on the left side of the window and actual configuration data on the right side—not too complicated. This is the program you learn to use in this chapter. You also learn varieties of helpful tips that come from my own agonizing experiences with Regedit. The program is so simple, however, that it's not useful for certain tasks. If you must change subkeys' permissions or edit data types other than REG_BINARY, REG_DWORD, and REG_SZ, use Regedt32, which you learn about in Chapter 4, "Editing with Regedt32."

▶ For more information about Regedt32, **see** Chapter 4, "Editing with Regedt32."

▶ To learn how to protect yourself from human error, **see** Chapter 5, "Safeguarding Configurations."

Starting Regedit

Regedit isn't on the Start menu, but it is in SystemRoot, with the filename Regedit.exe. On the Start menu, point to Programs, click Run, and then type regedit in the Run dialog box. Typing the path is not necessary. You can drag Regedit.exe from SystemRoot to the Start button to create a shortcut for it. For even quicker access to the Registry, drag Regedit.exe to the Quick Launch toolbar.

Administrators can stop users from starting or using Regedit. First, they can prevent the setup program from copying Regedit.exe to the computer. How? Burn a new CD-ROM that doesn't contain Regedit.exe. Second, create setup scripts—answer files that allow users to run the setup program unattended—that remove Regedit.exe during the last steps of the setup process. Last, copy the source files sans Regedit.exe to a network share from which users install Windows 2000. Administrators can also use Group Policy to prevent users from editing the Registry, even though Regedit.exe is on the computer. The policy, called Disable Registry Editing Tools, causes Regedit to close after displaying a message that says Registry editing has been disabled by your administrator. This policy works for Regedt32, too.

Administrators should rely on neither restriction to guard the gates, however. They are deterrents that restrict Registry access to the most determined users, but those users can easily circumvent both restrictions. If Regedit.exe is missing, copy it from the I386 directory of a Windows 2000 CD-ROM. Grab the help file, too. If the policy Disable Registry Editing Tools is preventing access through Regedit, use a script to remove it from the Registry. Chapter 12, "Repairing Damaged Registries," shows you one. Last, if you don't have access to the CD-ROM or you're unable to use the script shown in Chapter 12, download any of the shareware Registry editors, few of which honor Disable Registry Editing Tools. ZDNet Downloads is a good source, and the address is http://www.zdnet.com/swlib. Symantec's Norton Registry Editor, which you learn about in the sidebar called "Norton Registry Editor," is a good third-party Registry editor that doesn't honor Disable Registry Editing Tools.

▶ For more information about security, including assigning permissions to individual subkeys, **see** Chapter 6, "Administering Registries."

▶ To learn how to customize registries with scripts, **see** Chapter 10, "Scripting Customizations."

▶ To learn how to circumvent Disable Registry Editing Tools using a script, **see** Chapter 12, "Repairing Damaged Registries."

Part

II

Ch

3

Norton Registry Editor

Chapter 1, "Understanding Registries," introduces you to Symantec Norton Registry Editor, part of Symantec's popular Norton Utilities. The company sells versions for Windows 98 and Windows NT 4.0 and hasn't yet said a word about a version of the utilities for Windows 2000. You can borrow Norton Registry Editor from existing versions of Norton Utilities, however. Chapter 1 describes the files you must copy from the Norton Utilities CD-ROM to use it. You can also download an evaluation copy of the utilities at http://www.symantec.com.

continues

continued

Norton Registry Editor is more powerful than Regedit or Regedt32. It looks similar to Regedit, as you can see in Figure 3.1, except that it uses different icons to represent each data type and has an area at the bottom of the window for displaying output such as search results and recent changes that you can undo. In Windows 2000, Norton Registry Editor adds Security to the menu bar. It supports the same security features as Regedt32.

FIGURE 3.1

Norton Registry Editor is a must-have utility if you spend a lot of time editing the Registry.

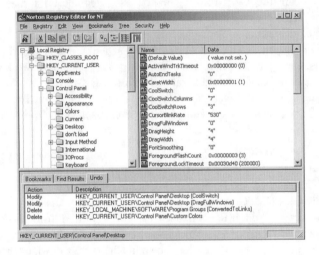

Some of Norton Registry Editor's advanced features make it the ultimate tool for power users and administrators. Its search feature is useful, allowing you to choose from a list of matches rather than pressing F3 to search again, and it has a search-and-replace feature that's missing in Regedit. The editor allows you to create shortcuts to subkeys that it displays under My Computer in the key pane, a nifty way to make sure your most-often-used subkeys are available at the root of the hierarchy. And I saved the best for last. Norton Registry Editor has an undo feature. You can undo recent changes in any order or undo the most recent change by pressing Ctrl+Z.

Navigating Regedit

Figure 3.2 shows what Regedit looks like on your desktop. You see its menu bar across the top of the window and its status bar across the bottom. The status bar displays the fully qualified name of the selected subkey. You're familiar with most of the items you see in the program's window because you know how to use Windows Explorer. You can certainly use Regedit with its default window size, but maximizing the window makes viewing subkeys and values much easier.

Part

II

Ch

3

FIGURE 3.2
Navigating Regedit's window is much like navigating folders and files in Windows Explorer.

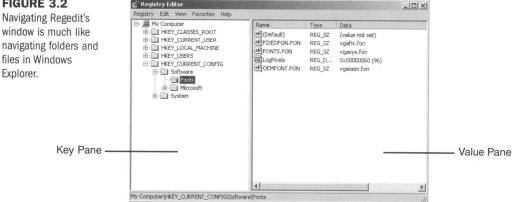

Key Pane ——————————————————————— Value Pane

Within the window, you see two panes, which Regedit separates with a divider that you can drag to change the size of both. The left pane is the *key* pane and contains the Registry's hierarchy. The right pane is the *value* pane, and it contains the values in the selected subkey. In the key pane, click a subkey and then Regedit displays its values in the value pane. Drag the divider to the left to make the key pane smaller and the value pane larger, or drag it to the right to make the key pane larger and value pane smaller. I prefer a larger key pane so that I can easily see the Registry's hierarchy. The following sections describe each pane in more detail.

 TIP   If the key pane isn't big enough to see the subkey's fully qualified name, look at its full name in the status bar. To copy to the Clipboard the subkey's fully qualified name, click Copy Key Name on its shortcut menu.

Key Pane

The key pane shows the organization of the Registry—its hierarchy. Regedit displays subkeys immediately under their parent keys and indents them to show their parent-child relationship. It looks similar to an upside-down tree or an outline. Even though Windows 2000 stores the Registry in separate hive files, Regedit displays the entire Registry as one logical unit. When you update a subkey in Regedit, the operating system automatically updates the appropriate hive file. Changes to HKU are in users' hive files, `UserProfile\Ntuser.dat`, and changes to HKLM are in the appropriate per-computer hive file, `SystemRoot\System32\config`. For more about hive files, see Chapter 1.

The first item in the key pane is My Computer. Its children are the root keys in the local computer's Registry, and Regedit represents them as folders. Each root key contains subkeys, which Regedit also represents as folders. Click plus signs (+) to expand subkeys, or click minus signs (-) to collapse subkeys. If you'd rather use the keyboard to explore the Registry, use the shortcuts listed in Table 3.1 to move around Regedit. These keyboard shortcuts are often the quickest way to navigate because using Regedit can be a mouse-intensive activity that's likely to wear out your wrist. Collapse an entire branch by pressing the left-arrow key, for example, and press the left-arrow key again to select the parent key.

Table 3.1 Keyboard Shortcuts

Key	Description
Searching	
Ctrl+F	Opens the Find dialog box
F3	Repeats the previous search
Miscellaneous	
Delete	Deletes the selected subkey or value
F1	Displays Registry Editor Help
F2	Renames the selected subkey or value
F5	Refreshes the key and value panes
F10	Opens the main menu of Regedit
Shift+F10	Displays the shortcut menu (right-click) for the selected subkey or value
Alt+F4	Closes Regedit
Navigation	
Keypad +	Expands the selected subkey's children
Keypad -	Collapses the selected subkey's children
Keypad *	Expands all the selected subkey's children
Up-arrow	Selects the previous subkey
Down-arrow	Selects the next subkey
Right-arrow	Expands the selected subkey if collapsed; otherwise, selects its first child
Left-arrow	Collapses the selected subkey if expanded; otherwise, selects the subkey's parent
Home	Selects the key pane's topmost subkey
End	Selects the key pane's bottommost subkey
Page Up	Moves up one page in the key pane
Page Down	Moves down one page in the key pane
F6	Toggles between the key and value panes
Tab	Toggles between the key and value panes

Regedit has one feature that makes navigating much quicker, particularly in subkeys with a lot of children or values. In the key pane, begin typing the name of a subkey. Regedit selects the first open subkey that matches the characters you've typed. It won't match subkeys that are hidden beneath others, however; it just matches subkeys that are visible in the key pane. For example, open HKCR, type .ba, and Regedit selects the first matching subkey, HKCR\.bat.

You mustn't dawdle; pause too long and Regedit assumes you're starting over. This feature is an incremental search, and it works equally well in the value pane of Regedit. In a long list of values, you can press the down-arrow key as many times as it takes to get to a value, mouse around the scrollbars, or press one or two letters—take your pick.

▶ **See** Chapter 1, "Understanding Registries," to learn more about hive files. Windows 2000 stores major portions of the registry in hive files.

▶ **See** Chapter 7, "Customizing Windows 2000," to learn how to change keyboard mappings. For example, you can swap the Ctrl and Alt keys.

Value Pane

The value pane shows the selected subkey's values. Each row is a single value. The Name column contains each value's name, the Type column contains each value's type, and the Data column contains each value's data. Regedit usually but not always presents data in a format suitable to the value's type. Resize columns by dragging the dividers between them left and right. To see more of each value's name and data, for example, drag the divider between the Type and Data columns to the left so that the Type column disappears. To restore the Type column, drag the same divider to the right.

Part

II

Ch

3

Regedit supports editing only REG_BINARY, REG_DWORD, and REG_SZ values. Try editing any other type of value, and it opens the value in the Edit Binary Value dialog box. In this particular arena, Microsoft made a big mess. The Type column is new. Earlier versions of Regedit didn't have it, so users relied on the icons shown in Table 3.2 to determine values' types. Beside the names of REG_SZ values, Regedit displayed the icon shown in the first row of Table 3.2. Beside the names of all other values, it displayed the icon in the second row. Users knew that Regedit supported only the big three, so they expected to edit values other than REG_DWORD and REG_SZ using the Edit Binary Value dialog box. Now, the Type column shows the names of all the types that the Registry supports. This leads users to believe they can edit values such as REG_FULL_RESOURCE_DESCRIPTOR and REG_MULTI_SZ in Regedit, but they can't. To make matters more confusing, Regedit displays the icon shown in the first row of Table 3.2 next to REG_MULTI_SZ values, but it opens them in the Edit Binary Value dialog box. Give me a break!

Icon	Description
Table 3.2	**Icons in the Value Pane**
[ab]	String values (REG_SZ, REG_MULTI_SZ, and so on)
[011 110]	Binary values (REG_DWORD, REG_BINARY, and so on)

The first value in the value pane is always (Default). It's the selected subkey's default REG_SZ value that you learned about in Chapter 1. All subkeys have it, whether it contains data or not, but some subkeys don't contain additional values. Including the default value, each subkey can have one or more values that have names, types, and data. To edit any value, double-click its name in the value pane or, on the Edit menu, click Modify. Note too that you can choose a variety of commands from each value's shortcut menu.

TIP Regedit gets confused. Columns sometimes disappear and you can't restore them through the user interface. You must restore them by removing the program's configuration from the Registry. To do so, close Regedit and use Regedt32 to remove `HKCU\Software\Microsoft\Windows\CurrentVersion\Applets\Registry` from the Registry. You must use Regedt32 to remove this subkey because Regedit saves its configuration each time you close it.

▶ To learn more about the different types of values, **see** Chapter 1, "Understanding Registries."

▶ **See** Chapter 4, "Editing with Regedt32," for more information about using Regedt32. Regedt32 is the Registry editor you should use to edit values other than `REG_BINARY`, `REG_DWORD`, and `REG_SZ`.

Working with Keys and Values

The following sections show how to use Regedit to search, add, change, delete, and print configuration data. Before continuing, heed this advice: Back up the Registry before making changes that might harm the computer.

As is the case with most Microsoft programs, Regedit provides numerous ways to access each feature. Subkeys' shortcut menus have commands to rename, delete, and create new subkeys under them. Values' shortcut menus have commands to change, delete, and rename them. The main menu has similar commands that apply to the selected subkey or value. Of course, you can always edit a value by double-clicking its name in the value pane, and you can always use the keyboard shortcuts you learned about in Table 3.2, earlier in this chapter.

▶ **See** Chapter 5, "Safeguarding Configurations," to learn how to back up the Registry before making changes to it or, at the very least, back up the portion of the Registry in which you're working.

Searching

Regedit searches for subkeys, value names, and value data that match the text for which you're looking. It searches for full and partial matches. For example, `Windows 2000` and `Windows 98` both match the search string `Windows`. Use the search feature to find values relating to a specific product, find all values that reference a specific file, or locate values related to a particular device. Users frequently send me messages asking what value contains a particular bit of configuration data, such as usernames. My reply is usually to search the Registry for their names, and they're likely to find it. Here's how to search subkeys, value names, and value data for a particular string:

1. On the Edit menu, click Find.

Regedit opens the Find dialog box in Figure 3.3.

FIGURE 3.3

In the Look At area, deselect the portions of the Registry in which you don't want to search.

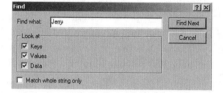

2. In Find What, type text for which you're looking.

If you're searching for numbers in string values, try the decimal and hexadecimal notations because both formats are common in the Registry.

3. Click Find Next, and Regedit begins searching beginning with the selected subkey.

This sometimes takes a while—up to several minutes on slower machines. Regedit displays an hourglass while it's searching. If it finds a matching subkey, it selects that subkey in the key pane. If it finds a matching value, it opens in the key pane the subkey containing the value and selects the value in the value pane.

4. Press F3 to continue searching.

Regedit looks for the next matching subkey or value. When Regedit reaches the bottom of the Registry, it displays a message that says `Finished searching through the Registry`.

You can hasten the search if you know what portion of the Registry contains the string for which you're searching: subkeys, value names, or value data. In the Look At area, clear the Keys, Values, or Data check boxes if you don't want to search in one or more of those places. If you're pretty certain that the string you're finding is in a value's name, for example, deselect Keys and Data to limit Regedit to value names, speeding up the search. Limiting a search to subkeys can cut by half the amount of time the search takes. Also, selecting the Match Whole String Only check box when you don't want Regedit to search for partial matches speeds up the search, or so you'd think. But timing searches using this check box, I found otherwise. It makes no appreciable difference in the time Regedit takes to search the registry, so use this check box only to limit the number of matches. The following table illustrates some of my tests searching for a bogus string that's not in my computer's Registry:

Time	Description
150 seconds	Searching subkeys, value names, and value data for full and partial matches
75 seconds	Searching subkeys for full and partial matches
75 seconds	Searching subkeys for full matches only

Part
II

Ch
3

A limitation of Regedit is that it only searches string values, not REG_BINARY, REG_DWORD, or other binary values. You simply can't search for 0x000000001 and expect Regedit to find matching REG_DWORD values. You can still locate these values, however, by exporting the Registry to a text file and searching the text file with your favorite editor. See the later section "Exporting and Importing" to learn how to export the Registry to Registration Entries (REG) files. What you need to know is how those values look in a REG file so you can search for them using a text editor. The only drawback is that you must convert strings to hexadecimal before searching binary values for strings. The following table shows the format of REG_BINARY, REG_DWORD, and REG_SZ values in the registry and in REG files:

Type	Format in Regedit	Format in REG File
REG_BINARY	a0 00 00 01	hex:a0,00,00,01
REG_DWORD	0x00000054	dword:00000054
REG_SZ	Jerry Honeycutt	"Jerry Honeycutt"

For example, if you were searching for the REG_DWORD value 0xA0B0C0D0, you would search the REG file for dword:A0B0C0D0. If you were searching for the binary value 0x052059021465, you would search the REG file for the string hex:05,20,59,02,14,65. To search for the string "Hi" in binary values, you would search for the string hex:48,69, its hexadecimal equivalent. Note that Regedit exports values other than REG_BINARY, REG_DWORD, and REG_BINARY as binary values, so search for strings in those types of values as though they were REG_BINARY.

▶ For more information about locating values in the registry, **see** Chapter 9, "Spying on the Registry."

▶ To learn how different values look in REG files, **see** Chapter 10, "Scripting Customizations."

Search Techniques

After getting to know the Registry, you should be able to predict where to find certain subkeys and values. With that knowledge, you can select a subkey somewhere near where you think you'll find the item and then use the search feature to find it. This takes much less time than searching the entire Registry for the item.

Here's an example. If searching for a file extension, open HKCR and do an incremental search to locate it more quickly. You can locate the *program identifier* associated with a file extension, which defines the commands available for the file, by looking at the file extension's default value.

Finding a program's configuration data is straightforward because most programs store the same types of data in similar places. File associations are in HKCR. Programs store settings in Software\Vendor\AppName\Version under HKLM and HKCU, where *Vendor* is the name of the company that produced the software, *AppName* is the name of the application, and *Version* is the version number of the program, CurrentVersion in many cases.

Recall that per-computer configuration data is in HKLM, and per-user data is in HKCU. Use that information to your advantage. If you're certain that the configuration data for which you're searching is computer-specific, select HKLM before searching. You'd search for any information about a particular device in this root key, for example. Otherwise, if you're certain the data is user-specific, select HKCU before searching.

Changing Values

To change a value, double-click it in the value pane, or select it and then click Modify on the Edit menu. When you open a value, Regedit displays a different dialog box, depending on the value's type. Regedit opens REG_BINARY, REG_DWORD, and REG_SZ values in the Edit Binary Value, Edit Dword Value, and Edit String dialog boxes, respectively. For values of types other than REG_DWORD and REG_SZ, Regedit opens them in the Edit Binary Value dialog box, so you're better off editing those values using Regedt32. The remainder of this section describes how to edit each type of value.

Using the Edit String dialog box to edit REG_SZ values is uneventful. In Value Data, change the string. Select the entire string and type over it to replace its contents. Also, the cut-and-paste feature is available in Value Data. Don't add quotation marks to the value unless you want to embed them in the actual string.

Regedit opens REG_DWORD values in the Edit DWORD Value dialog box, shown in Figure 3.4. Know the hexadecimal value? Type it in Value Data. If you want to enter the hexadecimal value 0x1234, type 1234, omitting prefixes that typically identify hexadecimal values. If you don't know the hexadecimal value, click Decimal, type the value in decimal notation, and let Regedit convert it for you. Here's a bonus: In the value pane, Regedit displays REG_DWORD values using both notations (decimal notation is in parenthesis).

Part

II

Ch

3

FIGURE 3.4
Choose Decimal if your hexadecimal math is a bit rusty. Regedit will convert the value to hexadecimal notation.

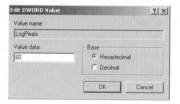

Figure 3.5 shows the Edit Binary Value dialog box, which Regedit opens when you edit anything other than REG_DWORD and REG_SZ values, including REG_BINARY values. In Value Data, you see three different columns of information. The first column shows the hexadecimal address of the first byte in that row. For instance, 0010 means that the first byte in that row of binary data is the 16th byte. The second column contains the actual binary data, which you read left-to-right and top-to-bottom. The third column shows the ASCII-character equivalent of each byte in the second column. You can edit values in either the second or third columns.

Position the cursor anywhere in the second column and type hexadecimal digits, 0 through F. Position the cursor in the third column and type ASCII characters. No matter in which column you're editing, Regedit updates the other column after each change. In either column, you can select bytes and type over them to replace them with new bytes.

FIGURE 3.5

The Edit Binary Value dialog box shows decimal values converted to hexadecimal values using Windows calculator in scientific mode.

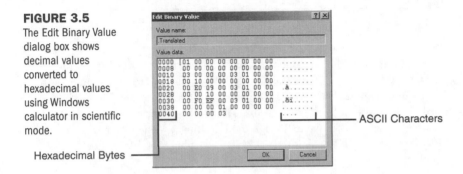

ASCII Characters

Hexadecimal Bytes

One capability—I don't call it a feature—is that you can select the value's name in Value Name and copy it to the Clipboard. This works for each of the Edit Type dialog boxes and is a useful sanity-saver when writing about the Registry. It ensures that I get value names correct. It's also useful to make sure you spell value names correctly when creating scripts. If you missed the tip about copying subkey names to the Clipboard, you do so by clicking Copy Key Name on the shortcut menu. The sidebar, "Clipboard Techniques," later in this chapter, describes other ways to use the Clipboard in Regedit.

Windows 2000 or running programs might not immediately reflect changes you make to the Registry. To make sure they do reflect your changes, cause them to reread those values from the Registry. If you change values in HKLM, for instance, you might have to restart the computer in order for Windows 2000 to recognize them. If you change values in HKCU, you might have to log off and back on again. You can make most programs recognize changes by closing and restarting them. This is true except for services that start when the operating system starts. In those cases, you must stop and start the services or restart the computer to see your changes at work.

CAUTION

Use a bit of caution when changing values. The later sidebar "Protecting Yourself" provides some good tips for backing up the portions of the Registry in which you're working. This helps you recover from any problems that your edits might cause. The best I can offer when editing a value is to copy it by giving the original value an obscure name. Then add a new value that has the original name and value. If things go awry, you can remove the new value and restore the original from the backup.

▶ To learn how to do hexadecimal math manually, **see** Chapter 1, "Understanding Registries."

▶ **See** Chapter 4, "Editing with Regedt32," for more information about editing other types of values using Regedt32. Regedit can only edit REG_BINARY, REG_DWORD, and REG_SZ values.

Creating Keys and Values

Creating new subkeys or values is generally harmless and equally useless, unless, of course, you know for sure that Windows 2000 or another program will use them. It's the equivalent of an Easter egg hunt. You wouldn't hide Easter eggs in places that nobody will look because they won't find them. Likewise, don't hide subkeys and values in places that no programs will look because it's a futile exercise. So why create new subkeys or values? Microsoft's Knowledge Base frequently instructs users to create new values to fix varieties of problems. Chapter 7, "Customizing Windows 2000," describes a plethora of subkeys and values you can add to the Registry. Valid reasons for adding subkeys and values abound.

When you create new subkeys, Regedit creates a subkey called New Key #N, where N is a number starting with 1, and selects its name so you can rename it. When you create a new value, Regedit creates a value called New Value #N and also selects its name so you can rename it. In both cases, Regedit increments N to ensure that the subkey or value is unique within its scope, its parent subkey. Regedit sets the initial value of new REG_SZ values to an empty string, REG_BINARY values to an empty binary string, or REG_DWORD values to zero. Change the value as described in the preceding section.

To create new subkeys or values, do one of the following:

- Select the subkey under which you want to create a new subkey. On the Edit menu, point to New, and click Key; then, type the name of the subkey.

- Select the subkey under which you want to create a new value. On the Edit menu, point to New and then click String Value, Binary Value, or DWORD Value. Type the name of your new value. Edit the value as described in the preceding section.

Clipboard Techniques

Use the Clipboard to make tasks easier. You can copy to and paste from the Clipboard whenever you edit a subkey's name or value's name or data. Thus, consider these different ways to use the Clipboard in Regedit:

- To copy the fully qualified name of a subkey to the Clipboard, click Copy Key Name on the subkey's shortcut menu.

- To copy a value's name to the Clipboard, double-click the value to edit it. In Value Name, select the value's name and then press Ctrl+C to copy it to the Clipboard. Click Cancel to avoid changing the value accidentally.

- To copy a value's data to the Clipboard, open the value to edit it. In Value Data, select the data, and then press Ctrl+C to copy it to the Clipboard. Click Cancel to avoid changing it accidentally.

- To paste data from the Clipboard into a value, double-click the value to edit it, select the data you want to replace, and then press Ctrl+V.

- To copy a subkey or value's name to the Clipboard, click Rename on the item's shortcut menu, and then press Ctrl+C to copy it to the Clipboard.

continues

The third item in the list tells how to copy a value's data to the Clipboard. Use this technique to back up a value before changing it. Copy the value's data to the Clipboard and paste that data into a new value that has a bogus name. If you want to restore the original value, copy the backup data to the Clipboard and paste it back into the value.

Deleting Keys and Values

Be careful about deleting subkeys and values. You'll likely prevent Windows 2000 from working properly by deleting configuration data carelessly. To remove a subkey or value, follow these steps:

1. Do one of the following:
   - In the key pane, select a subkey.
   - In the value pane, select a value.

2. Press Delete.

   Regedit prompts you to confirm that you want to delete the subkey or value.

3. Click Yes to delete the subkey or value.

A common use for deleting subkeys and values is to restore programs' default settings. This doesn't always work with large programs that choke when their settings are missing but works well with small programs that re-create their settings. For example, you learned how to remove Regedit's settings from the Registry to restore its configuration. Another example is removing `.txt` from `HKCR\Software\Microsoft\Windows\CurrentVersion\Explorer\FileExts` in order to remove customizations to text files' shortcut menus.

Renaming Keys and Values

Renaming subkeys and values in Regedit is much like renaming folders and files in Windows Explorer, except you can't rename selected items by clicking their names. Instead, select the subkey or value you want to rename, click Rename on the Edit menu, and then type over the name to change it. Better yet, select the subkey or value, press F2, and then type over the name.

Renaming subkeys and values has a practical purpose. It's a good way to hide configuration data prior to deleting it permanently. Hiding items under obscure names is logically the same as removing them because no program knows to look for them if you give them funky names. If things go awry, however, you can restore items' original names to undelete them. For example, assume you want to remove `IsShortcut` from the `lnkfile` program identifier, which prevents Windows 2000 from displaying an overlay on shortcuts' icons. Instead of deleting the value, rename it to something like `MyIsShortcut` and test the change. Permanently remove `MyIsShortcut` after you're satisfied that everything works okay (seldom true in this case).

TIP Renaming subkeys and values is a smart way to document your data that you delete. If you forever leave items in the Registry with obscure names, you'll always know what those items originally contained. The same goes for changing a value. Note the value's name and data before renaming it to some obscure name. Create a new value with the name and data you noted. Now you have one copy of the value you can change and one copy of the value serving as a reminder of its original contents.

Printing Subkeys

Some folks think printing the Registry is useful as a backup tool or for reading the Registry to better understand it. Considering that a full printout of the entire Registry would occupy hundreds of pages and that you can't import a printout back into the Registry, this position is nonsense.

Printing a small subkey does have merit, however. It serves as a useful guide when working within small portions of the Registry. You can restore the original data if you foul up, and it serves as a guide for the types of data that belong in each value. Also, it is sometimes helpful to print a small portion of the Registry that you need as a reference when working in another part of the Registry. This is particularly true because you can't open two copies of Regedit to view two portions of the Registry at the same time. Having a printout of a subkey keeps you from moving hither and thither between two distant subkeys.

To print a subkey, select it in the key pane, and then click Print on the Registry menu. Regedit includes the entire branch, beginning with that subkey, and sends the print job to the spooler. The resulting output looks almost similar to a REG file, as shown in Listing 3.1. The format is slightly different, however. Regedit doesn't put quotation marks around string values, for instance. It also doesn't prefix binary values with the string hex:. The most notable difference is that it writes REG_DWORD values as REG_BINARY values, reversing the bytes as required in a little-endian architecture (see Chapter 1). The following table describes how Regedit formats each data type when it prints it:

Part

II

Ch

3

Type	Format in Regedit	Format in Printed Output
REG_BINARY	A0 00 00 00 01 23	A0,00,00,00,01,23
REG_DWORD	0x00000054	54,00,00,00
REG_SZ	"This is a string"	This is a string

Listing 3.1   Regedit Printer Output

```
[HKEY_CURRENT_USER\Control Panel\Desktop]
DragFullWindows=1
FontSmoothing=1
UserPreferencemask=a0,00,00,00
ScreenSaveUsePassword=00,00,00,00
SmoothScroll=01,00,00,00
```

continues

Listing 3.1   Continued

```
MenuShowDelay=400

[HKEY_CURRENT_USER\Control Panel\Desktop\WindowMetrics]
MenuWidth=-270
MenuHeight=-270
MinAnimate=0
Shell Icon Size=32
IconTitleWrap=0
test=01,00,00,00

[HKEY_CURRENT_USER\Control Panel\Desktop\WindowsMetrics]
MinAnimate=1
```

Bookmarking Favorite Subkeys

The Favorites feature is long in coming. Earlier versions of Regedit did not provide a way to bookmark the subkeys you use most, so you had to plow through the Registry's hierarchy every time you wanted to inspect the same old values. In Regedit, Favorites is akin to Favorites in Internet Explorer 5, which allows you to bookmark the Web sites you visit most often. Bookmark subkeys to which you want to return quickly.

Favorites works similarly in both programs and doesn't require much narrative to use it in Regedit. In the key pane, click the subkey you want to bookmark, and then click Add to Favorites on the Favorites menu. In the Add to Favorites dialog box, type a friendly name for the subkey. Regedit adds this friendly name to the Favorites menu, sorted in alphabetical order. Quickly return to the subkey by clicking its friendly name on the Favorites menu. Regedit opens the subkey in the key pane, expanding the hierarchy as necessary to reveal the subkey.

Just for grins, I include the following list, which contains the subkeys I usually bookmark and are the ones that I think are the most useful:

■ **HKCU\Software\Microsoft\Windows\CurrentVersion**

I usually bookmark Explorer and Policies under this subkey, too, keeping the Registry's most useful settings a couple of mouse clicks away.

■ **HKLM\SOFTWARE\Microsoft\Windows\CurrentVersion**

Like the previous bullet, I usually bookmark Explorer and Policies to make them accessible.

■ **HKLM\SYSTEM\CurrentControlSet**

■ **HKLM\SYSTEM\CurrentControlSet\Control\hivelist**

Regedit stores your favorite subkeys in the Registry at `HKCU\Software\Microsoft\Windows\CurrentVersion\Applets\Regedit\Favorites`. For each subkey you bookmark, it creates a REG_SZ value in Favorites. The value's name is the friendly name of the bookmark, which you typed in the Add to Favorites dialog box, and the value's data contains the fully qualified name of the subkey, including the computer's name and the root key: `My Computer\HKLM`. You can use the same bookmarks on any computer. Export this subkey to a REG file, which you learn to do later in this chapter, and then import that REG file whenever you want your favorite subkeys available.

Removing a subkey from the Favorites menu is counter-intuitive, as this is one of those features in Windows 2000 that doesn't require you to select an object before applying a command to it. Instead, click Remove Favorite on the Favorites menu and then, in the Remove Favorites dialog box, click the friendly name of the subkey you want to remove. This doesn't delete the subkey from the Registry; it only removes the subkey's bookmark from the Favorites menu.

Part

II

Ch

3

N O T E Regedit has an annoying new feature that users usually want to disable the first time they experience it for themselves. Each time users close Regedit, it saves the selected subkey's fully qualified name. The next time they start Regedit, it opens that same subkey again, restoring the key pane to the way it was before they closed the program. This is crazy if you want to start Regedit fresh each time. (I like to close and restart Regedit just to clean up my mess in the key pane.) At this moment, the only way I know to disable this feature is to change your permissions to `HKCU\Software\Microsoft\Windows\CurrentVersion\Applets\Regedit` using Regedt32 so that Regedit can't change this subkey. Doing so prevents Regedit from saving other settings, though. Alternatively, write a script that removes the REG_SZ value LastKey before launching Regedit. See Chapter 10 to learn about scripts. ▪

Exporting and Importing

Exporting the Registry creates a text file with the `.reg` extension that you can edit using any text editor. This file contains all the information required to describe the subkeys and values in the subkey you export; in fact, you can import a REG file back into the Registry. When you export a subkey, Regedit writes all of that subkey's descendent subkeys and values. No means is available to export a single subkey without its descendents.

Up to this point, you've used Regedit to work with the Registry. You can also export subkeys to a REG file and edit them using a text editor such as Microsoft Notepad. For example, use the editor's search-and-replace feature to make massive changes to the REG file. Beware, however, because you can inadvertently change values you don't mean to change. More common is editing a REG file to remove subkeys and values that you don't want in the file. If you want to create a REG file that includes a subkey without all its descendent subkeys, for example, edit the file to remove the descendent subkeys. Here's a more practical example: Fergus customized Microsoft Windows 2000 Professional on one computer and then exported the subkey `HKCU\Control Panel\desktop` to a REG file. Because Fergus is using the REG file to customize other computers and is only interested in a handful of values, he removes the values and subkeys he doesn't want to include in it.

 TIP REG files are indeed a great way to share customizations with other users. After you've edited the file to remove unnecessary subkeys and values, distribute the file. If you want to distribute the file to network users, send it to them as an attachment to a message. Better yet, you can add a command to their logon script that automatically imports the file, put a link to the file on a Web page, or create a network share that contains many REG files from which users can choose. See Chapter 10 for more information.

Aside from editing subkeys and values with a text editor and sharing customizations, exporting subkeys to a REG file has more immediate practical purposes. Export as a backup any subkey in which you're working. When confusion clouds your mind or edits get out of hand, import it back into the Registry to restore the original settings. This will restore values that you change and remove, but it won't remove values that you added to the Registry. Thus, if you added a value that prevents Windows 2000 from working properly, restoring a REG file won't fix the problem; you'll have to remove the new value yourself.

Exporting

Here's how to export all or part of the Registry:

1. In the key pane, click the subkey at the top of the branch that you want to export to a REG file.

2. On the Registry menu, click Export Registry File.

   You see the Export Registry File dialog box shown in Figure 3.6. This dialog box works like most of the other common dialog boxes.

FIGURE 3.6
The Export Registry File dialog box is similar to other common dialog boxes except for the Export Range area.

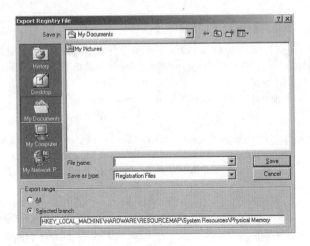

3. In File Name, type the name of the file into which you want to export the Registry.

4. In the Export range area, do one of the following:

- To export the entire Registry, click All.
- To export the subkey, click Selected Branch.

Regedit supports two formats for REG files, version 4 and version 5. Earlier versions of Regedit only supported version 4 REG files but Windows 2000's thorough support of Unicode requires the addition of version 5. Version 4 REG files are ANSI text files, whereas version 5 REG files are Unicode text files. When Regedit writes REG_EXPAND_SZ and REG_MULTI_SZ values to version 4 REG files, both of which Regedit encodes as binary in a REG file, it uses ANSI character encoding. When writing the same values to version 5 REG files, it uses Unicode character encoding.

The differences are only significant when you work with different operating systems. Version 5 REG files are only compatible with Windows 2000 and many text editors can't properly edit them. If you must create REG files that are compatible with earlier versions of Windows or your text editor doesn't support Unicode character encoding, create version 4 REG files. Note also that certain values are easier to edit in version 4 REG files. The last caveat, and the most important one for my international readers, is that you must use version 5 REG files if the registry contains multilingual data.

You specify which type of REG file you're creating in the Export Registry File dialog box. In the Save as Type list, click the type of REG file you want to create. Registration Files are version 5 REG files and Win9X/NT4 Registration Files (REGEDIT4) are version 4 REG files. Clicking All Files (*.*) creates version 5 REG files.

NOTE Make sure that you use clear 8.3 names for REG files. Clear names help you find these files at the MS-DOS command prompt, and 8.3 filenames help make sure that you can easily use the name in command-line options. ∎

▶ See Chapter 1, "Understanding Registries," for more information about Unicode and ANSI character encoding. The primary advantage of Unicode is that users can write multilingual documents using a single character set, as Unicode is big enough to represent most of the world's languages.

▶ To learn how to create REG files using a text editor, see Chapter 10, "Scripting Customizations."

Importing

Typical in Windows 2000, you can import a REG file more than one way. The first is the most useful and allows you to import the file without starting Regedit. Click Merge on the file's shortcut menu or, easier yet, double-click the file. If you use this method to import a REG file while Regedit is open, make sure you press F5 to refresh the display so that Regedit reflects changes. The second method uses Regedit:

1. On the Registry menu, click Import Registry File.
2. In the Import Registry File dialog box, select the REG file you want to import into the registry.
3. Click Open.

   Regedit displays a message that says `Information in filename has been success-fully entered into the Registry` after importing the REG file.

Import isn't the best name for this feature; *merge* is better. Regedit merges the REG file's contents into the Registry, replacing existing items and adding new ones. It does not remove subkeys or values that exist in the Registry but not in the REG file; it only adds new items and updates existing ones. Just keep in mind that importing a REG file is not the same as synchronizing a REG file with the Registry. If you must remove a subkey or value from the Registry, remove it using Regedit or write a script that removes it.

Be careful not to accidentally double-click a REG file. Regedit will automatically merge it into the Registry, as Merge is the default command for REG files. To avoid this problem, change the default command for REG files, as described in Chapter 7. You can also save REG files using a file extension other than `.reg`, preventing accidents. Also consider organizing REG files in their own folder, so that you're more inclined to be careful when working with files in that folder.

> **CAUTION**
>
> Nothing prevents you from importing a Windows 98 or Windows NT 4.0 REG file into Windows 2000, and vice versa. Don't because it might prevent either operating system from working properly. The content of each operating system's registry is sufficiently different for me to jump up and down and wave my arms madly while I give you this warning.

▶ To learn how to change the default command for REG files so that you don't accidentally import them, **see** Chapter 7, "Customizing Windows 2000."

Reading REG Files

REG files look much like classic `INI` files and are easy to inspect. Open REG files in Notepad by clicking Edit on their shortcut menus. The first line of a version 5 REG file always contains `Windows Registry Editor version 5.00`, which identifies the file as a REG file. Version 5 REG files start with `REGEDIT4`. Following a single blank line, the remainder of the file contains the keys and values Regedit exported.

Listing 3.2 shows a REG file. It contains multiple sections. Each subkey is in its own section. The fully qualified name of each subkey is between square brackets. Each subkey's values are in the subkey's section. Except for default values, values' names are in quotation marks. Regedit represents in REG files default values using a single at sign (@). Values' data look different depending on their types (see Table 3.3). Anatomy lesson over.

Listing 3.2   A Sample REG File

```
Windows Registry Editor version 5.00

[HKEY_CURRENT_USER\Control Panel\Desktop]
"DragFullWindows"="1"
"FontSmoothing"="1"
"wallpaper"=""
"TileWallpaper"="0"
"UserPreferencemask"=hex:a0,00,00,00
"WallpaperStyle"="0"
"ScreenSaveLowPowerActive"="1"
"ScreenSavePowerOffActive"="0"
"ScreenSaveActive"="0"
"ScreenSaveTimeOut"="60"
"ScreenSaveUsePassword"=dword:00000000
"SmoothScroll"=hex:01,00,00,00
"WheelScrollLines"="3"
"Pattern"=""
"DragWidth"="2"
"DragHeight"="2"
"DoubleClickWidth"="4"
"DoubleClickHeight"="4"
"HungAppTimeout"="inget"
"WaitToKillAppTimeout"="inget"
"CoolSwitchRows"="inget"
"CoolSwitchColumns"="inget"
"MenuShowDelay"="400"
"test"=dword:00000054

[HKEY_CURRENT_USER\Control Panel\Desktop\ResourceLocale]
@="00000409"

[HKEY_CURRENT_USER\Control Panel\Desktop\WindowsMetrics]
"MinAnimate"="1"
```

Part

II

Ch

3

Table 3.3   Format of Values in REG Files

Data Type	Version 4	Version 5
REG_BINARY	hex:00,00,00,01	hex:00,00,00,01
REG_DWORD	dword:00000001	dword:00000001
REG_EXPAND_SZ	hex(2):48,49,00	hex(2):48,00,49,00,00

continues

Table 3.3   Continued

Data Type	Version 4	Version 5

`REG_MULTI_SZ`
`31,00,4C,69,6E,65,20,`
`32,00,00`
	`hex(7):4C,69,6E,65,20,`
	`6E,00,65,00,20,00,31,`
	`00,00,00,4C,00,69,00,`
	`6E,00,65,00,20,00,32,`
	`00,00,00,00,00`
		`hex(7):4C,00,69,00,`

`REG_SZ`	`"A string"`	`"A string"`

▶ **See** Chapter 10, "Scripting Customizations," to learn how other value types look in REG files. You learn how values such as `REG_RESOURCE_LIST` look. Also, this chapter contains more extensive information about the format over version 4 and 5 REG files.

Protecting Yourself

I can't stress enough the importance of protecting yourself while editing the Registry. You can restore a backup copy of the Registry, but less-drastic solutions are more feasible. Create a backup copy of a value before changing it, for example, by creating a backup value and naming it whatever you like. Then copy the original value to the Clipboard and paste it to the backup value. You'll always know what data you replaced in the value.

If you're working with a number of values within a subkey, export the subkey to a REG file before editing it. If things go wrong, import the file to restore the subkey's settings. You can *replace* the mangled subkey by removing it before importing the REG file.

A sorted combination of Regedit and Regedt32 is often the best solution. Regedit is the easiest of the sibling Registry editors to use, but Regedt32 has more powerful features for backing up sub-keys. Use Regedt32 to save subkeys as hive files and use Regedit to edit the Registry. Flipping back and forth between both programs might seem silly, but you get used to the idea quickly. Just make sure you refresh either program's window if you make changes to the registry using the other.

Using Command-Line Options

Regedit provides command-line options you can use to export and import REG files. To use them, click Run on the Start menu, and then type `regedit` followed by any of the options you want to use. These command-line options are also suitable to use at the MS-DOS command prompt or within batch files. If you have a command that you want to use often, create a shortcut for it.

Regedit is the only Registry editor in Windows 98. In Windows 98, it has more command-line options than it does in Windows 2000. Users specify the location of the per-computer and per-user hive files (`System.dat` and `User.dat`) using the `/L` and `/R` options. In Windows 2000, Regedit doesn't support these options. The result is that Regedit always operates on the hive files that are loaded into the Registry. If you want to use Regedit's command line to export a hive file that's not already loaded into the Registry, you must first load that hive file using Regedt32, which you learn about in Chapter 4. An alternative is to use Microsoft Registry Console Tool, an MS-DOS–based program with features similar to Regedt32 that you learn about in Chapter 10.

The following gives you a brief summary of Regedit's command-line options, which the following sections describe in more detail:

```
REGEDIT [/S] filename
REGEDIT /E filename [subkey]
```

`filename`	Path and filename of the REG file you want to export or import
`/E`	Exports *subkey* to the REG file, *filename* (the default is to export the entire contents of the Registry)
`/S`	Imports a REG file without confirming the operation and without displaying a message when it finishes

▶ **See** Chapter 10, "Scripting Customizations," to learn more about Microsoft Registry Console Tool, a quirky MS-DOS–based program you can use to edit the registry from the MS-DOS command prompt.

▶ **See** Chapter 12, "Repairing Damaged Registries," to learn about Microsoft Recovery Console, which provides limited access to the computer when Windows 2000 doesn't start.

Exporting Registries

Use the /E command-line option to export a subkey. Omit *subkey*, and Regedit exports the entire Registry. Regedit creates version 5 REG files, which are only compatible with Windows 2000. Note that *subkey* must be a fully qualified name, and it must begin with the root key's full name, not its abbreviation. For example, the following command exports HKCU\ Control Panel\desktop:

```
regedit /E Docfiles.reg "hkey_classes_root\docfile"
```

A practical use for the /E command-line option is to back up the Registry. Create a shortcut that executes this command: regedit /E backup.reg. Just remember that it backs up the current Registry, including the current user's hive file, Ntuser.dat, but not other users' hive files. You must load those hive files using Regedt32 before trying to export them using Regedit.

Importing REG Files

To import a REG file, specify its filename without any other command-line options: regedit *filename*. Regedit imports the REG file the same way it does if you were to click Import Registry File from the Registry command.

When you import a REG file, Regedit confirms whether you really want to merge the file into the Registry. The messages says `Are you sure you want to add the information in` `filename` `to the registry?` Click Yes to complete the operation. This is an improvement over earlier versions of Regedit, which promoted accidents by blindly importing any REG files on which users accidentally double-clicked. After it finishes merging the file, Regedit displays a message that says `Information in` `filename` `has been successfully entered` `into the registry.`

You can suppress both of these messages using the `/S` command-line option. This option, which must be the first option on the command line, instructs Regedit to import the Registry file without confirming the operation and without reporting when it's finished. Although you do want to be careful with this option, you can use it in batch files so that Regedit quietly imports files without causing the batch file to pause while users close annoying dialog boxes. Great for logon scripts, it is.

> **N O T E**   Regedit cannot overwrite subkeys and values that are in use by Windows 2000 or another program. When in use, the operating system locks them. When Regedit tries merging a REG file into a subkey or value that's locked, you see a message that says `Cannot` `import` `filename`: `Not all data was successfully written to the registry.` `Some keys are open by the system or other processes.` ■

Administering Clients

The reason that Regedit is an administrator's dream is because she can use it to connect to client computers and edit the Registries on them. A few caveats, though: The administrator must have permission to edit the client computer's Registry, which Windows 2000 provides to administrators by default, and the computer must be connected to the network.

To connect to a client computer's Registry, click Connect Network Registry on the Registry menu, and then type the name of the remote computer in Computer Name. In the Connect Network Registry dialog box, you can click Browse to select a computer that's known to the network. Regedit creates a new icon at the same level as My Computer for the client computer. Under the client computer's icon are three root keys: HKCR, HKLM, and HKU. These are the only two root keys that Regedit displays for client computers because all the remaining root keys are links to these.

After you connect to a client computer's Registry, you're bound by each subkey's permissions. If you connected to the Registry with administrative rights, you have access to most of its subkeys. Otherwise, each subkey's Access Control List (ACL) determines your permissions. Keep in mind that permission to access a client computer's Registry is different than each individual subkey's permissions. Chapter 6, "Administering Registries," tells you more about securing subkeys in the Registry.

When you're finished administering the client computer's Registry, disconnect from it. On the Registry menu, click Disconnect Network Registry. When you close Regedit, it closes the connection automatically, so it won't appear again when you next start Regedit.

N O T E Regedit never updates your view of a client computer's Registry, even if the registry changes on that computer. You must manually refresh the program's window by pressing F5. ▨

▶ **See** Chapter 6, "Administering Registries," to learn how to assign permission to users that give them remote access to a client computer's Registry. Chapter 6 also shows you how to change each subkey's ACL, granting or denying access.

▶ **See** Chapter 10, "Scripting Customizations," to learn how to write scripts that change settings on client computers remotely or in logon scripts. Most of the MS-DOS–based utilities have command-line options for specifying the computer name.

Part

II

Ch

3

Editing with Regedt32

Starting Regedt32

Windows 2000 Professional has two programs called Microsoft Registry Editor. Microsoft Windows NT 3.1 introduced the first, which you learn about in this chapter, and Microsoft Windows 95 introduced the second, which you learned about in Chapter 3, "Editing with Regedit." The name of the first Registry Editor's program file is `Regedt32.exe` and the operating system hides it away in *SystemRoot*\System32. The second Registry Editor's program file is `Regedit.exe` and is in *SystemRoot*. To avoid confusion in this chapter, I'll refer to each by its filename, `Regedit` or `Regedt32`.

Regedt32 isn't on the Start menu. Run it by typing `regedt32` at the MS-DOS command prompt or in the Run dialog box. Typing `regedt32` and pressing Enter isn't much of a hassle, but if you'd like a quicker way to run the program, create a shortcut for it on the Start menu or on the Quick Launch toolbar.

If you're using a computer in a network environment or you're using a managed computer, the administrator might have disabled Regedt32. Administrators do so in different ways, which you learn about in "Securing the Registry," later in this chapter. They can edit you out of the `Regedt32.exe` file's ACL (Access Control List) or they can use policies to prevent all Registry editing tools from running. They can also prevent the setup program from installing Regedt32 or Regedit at all. If you have a good reason to edit the Registry and you can't run either Registry editor, plead your case to the administrator.

Navigating Regedt32

Regedt32 is unlike Regedit in that it presents each root key in an MDI (Multiple Document Interface) window, as shown in Figure 4.1. This user interface is an artifact of a time when MDI was new and exciting but doesn't do much for helping you administer the Registry easily. You switch between each root key's window by clicking anywhere on the window—the title bar is a good place—or by clicking the root key's name on the Window menu. Another remnant of MDI windows is the various clever ways you can arrange them in the parent window:

- On the Window menu, click Cascade to make all the windows the same size and stack one on top of the other, going from left to right and top to bottom.

- On the Window menu, click Tile to arrange all the windows within the parent window so that none overlap. This makes for some small windows that are difficult to use, however.

- On the Window menu, click Arrange Icons to arrange any minimized windows across the bottom of the parent window.

The title bar of each window indicates the name of the root key and the computer that owns the Registry you're editing. If you're editing the local computer's Registry, you see *Name* on Local Machine, where *Name* is the name of the root key, in the window's title bar.

FIGURE 4.1

Regedt32 is a simple program with no toolbar and no shortcut menus, but the MDI windows are annoying.

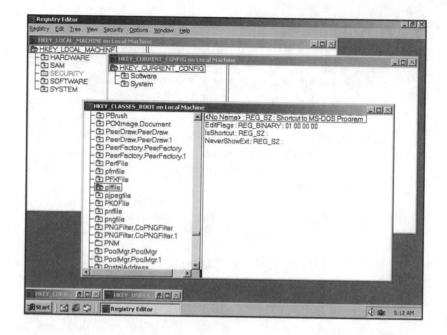

Introducing `Regedt32.exe`

Microsoft isn't as particular about editing Windows 2000's Registry as it is about editing Windows 98's Registry. In fact, Regedt32 contains extensive help as opposed to Regedit, which has only a few pages. Why? Administrators rely on the Registry to perform their job. They work with the Registry on almost a daily basis. For example, many of the fixes found in Microsoft's Knowledge Base require administrators to edit the Registry. Many suggestions that administrators find in the resource kits also require them to edit the Registry. The Registry is just one of the many tools available to administrators for diagnosing and fixing problems. That doesn't mean that Microsoft doesn't sprinkle warnings all over the place; it still does, but it recognizes the Registry's value as a tool.

Regedt32 and Regedit provide similar functions, but they're strikingly different. Aside from the obvious differences in their user interfaces—Regedit is by far the better-designed program—they have different capabilities. Regedit can search for values and exports subkeys to REG (Registration Entries) files, for example. It also makes renaming subkeys and values easy, whereas Regedt32 has no such capabilities. Regedt32 was built for administrators, however, and provides the capability to set a subkey's permissions, audit subkeys, and edit types of values that Regedit doesn't.

Both editors, Regedt32 and Regedit, have their places in your world. For day-to-day editing, you'll end up using Regedit, because the program is just too much easier to use. For serious work involving administration, you'll end up using Regedt32 out of necessity, not choice. Regardless, in the long run, you'll find yourself very comfortable with switching back and forth between both programs. Flipping between them both is as easy as pressing Alt+Tab, after all.

Part

II

Ch

4

The Key Pane

The left pane of each root key's MDI window is the *key* pane. It shows that root key's hierarchy. Although Windows 2000 stores each root key in multiple hive files, Regedt32 displays the entire root key as a logical unit. When you change anything in that root key, the operating system automatically updates the appropriate hive file.

The key pane contains several subkeys that Regedt32 represents as folders. Each subkey can contain more subkeys (also represented by folders), and each of those subkeys can contain more subkeys. Double-click a folder that contains a plus sign (+) to open it, or double-click a folder that contains a minus sign (-) to close it. A gray folder indicates that you don't have access to that particular subkey.

N O T E You can identify subkeys that are in separate hive files because Regedt32 capitalizes their names. In Figure 4.1, the subkeys of **HKLM** are all capitalized and are indeed in separate hive files. ▪

Mouse challenged? You can also use the keystrokes you see in Table 4.1 to move around windows in Regedt32. These are often the quickest way to navigate because you don't have to fumble with the mouse, trying to hit those tiny folder icons. Also, the mouse is much less useful in Regedt32 than in Regedit, because Regedt32 doesn't have toolbars or shortcut menus and all its features are quickly accessible using the keyboard (nice, eh?).

Table 4.1   Keyboard Shortcuts

Key	Description
Keypad +	Expands the selected folder one level
Keypad -	Collapses the selected folder one level
Keypad *	Expands all levels of the selected folder
Up arrow	Moves up the list one key
Down arrow	Moves down the list one key
Home	Moves to the first key in the list
End	Moves to the last key in the list
Page Up	Moves up one screen in the list
Page Down	Moves down one screen in the list
Tab	Moves the highlight to the right pane

The Value Pane

The right pane of each root key's MDI window is the *value* pane, so named because it contains the currently selected subkey's values. Each row in the value pane is a single value and looks something like ***Name : Type : Value***. ***Name*** is the value's name, ***Type*** is the value's

type (**REG_SZ**, **REG_DWORD**, and so on), and *Value* is the value's data. Regedt32 separates each part with a colon (:). **Texas : REG_SZ : "Howdy"** is a **REG_SZ** value entry called *Text* that contains the word *Howdy*—easy enough, but not presented nearly as well as values in Regedit.

Within some subkeys, you'll see a value called **<No Name>.** This is the subkey's default value and Regedit displays it as **(Default).** This is a **REG_SZ** value. All subkeys have this value, but some don't contain any additional values. Regedt32 also doesn't show default values that don't contain any data, whereas Regedit shows them as empty. Aside from **<No Name>**, each subkey can contain zero or more values that have a name, type, and data. Edit any value by double-clicking any part of it in the value pane.

Working with Keys and Values

Regedt32 is a Registry Editor. Its primary purpose is to add, remove, and change subkeys and values. You learn about these tasks in the following sections. Its secondary purpose is to administer the Registry, set permissions, load and unload hive files, and so on. You learn about these tasks later in this chapter.

Several primitive commands are useful while editing the Registry. They make the task much simpler:

- On the <u>V</u>iew menu, click Tree and Data, Tree Only, or Data Only to change how Regedt32 displays the contents in the current MDI window.

- On the <u>V</u>iew menu, click Split and drag the divider left and right to change the sizes of the key and value panes, trading space with each.

- On the <u>O</u>ptions menu, click Font and then select the font you want to use to display subkeys and values in each root key's MDI window.

- On the <u>O</u>ptions menu, click to select Auto Refresh to make sure that Regedt32 updates each window when the contents of the Registry change.

- On the <u>O</u>ptions menu, click Read Only Mode to prevent yourself from making accidental changes.

- On the <u>O</u>ptions menu, click Confirm on Delete to have Regedt32 confirm that you want to remove a subkey or value before actually doing so.

- On the <u>O</u>ptions menu, click Save Settings on Exit and Regedt32 will save changes to your preferences when it closes; otherwise, it'll forget changes to your preferences.

Part

II

Ch

4

TIP

Turn on read-only mode so that you can't accidentally change or remove a value. On the <u>O</u>ptions menu, click Read Only Mode. Regedt32 won't allow you to make any changes to the Registry. Turn off read-only mode when you're purposefully editing the Registry.

Searching for Keys

When you search the Registry, Regedt32 looks for keys that match the text you specify. It searches in the current root key's MDI window only; thus, to search in all root keys, you must repeat the search in each root key's MDI window. The search begins with the selected subkey and ends at the end of the current root key. You can't use Regedt32 to search for values, however, which makes this feature somewhat useless (you'll usually want to search for names and paths in value entries). To search for values, use Regedit, as you learned in Chapter 3. Here's how to search the Registry for matching keys:

1. On the View menu, click Find Key to open the Find dialog box you see in Figure 4.2.

FIGURE 4.2
Make sure you clear the Match Whole Word Only check box if you want to find partial matches in subkey names.

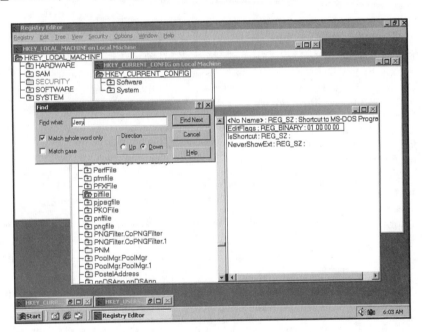

2. In Find What, type the text for which you're searching and then click Find Next.

Be patient as Regedt32 searches the Registry, particularly if you're searching a Registry to which you connected over the network. The process can take some time, up to a few minutes on slower computers. If Regedt32 finds a matching subkey, it selects that subkey in the key pane. To continue searching for the next matching subkey, click Find Next again. Regedt32 doesn't support pressing F3 to search again, so you must leave the Find dialog box open while you're searching. When Regedt32 doesn't find any matches between the current subkey and the end of the Registry, it displays the message Registry Editor cannot find the desired key.

N O T E   If you select any subkey in the key pane and press a key on the keyboard, Regedt32 selects the first subkey that starts with that character. Press the same key again, and Regedt32 selects the next subkey that starts with that character. ■

Changing Values

As a user, changing a value is probably the number-one activity you'll do with Regedt32. You might want to personalize your desktop, for example, or you might need to adjust a TCP/IP setting to work better with your network. Chapter 7, "Customizing Windows 2000," and Chapter 12, "Repairing Damaged Registries," are loaded with values that you can change to personalize or repair Windows 2000. You must have permission to change a value, or Regedt32 displays an error message.

Changing a value is easy. In the value pane, double-click the value you want to change. You see a different dialog box, depending on the value's type. Your changes might not take effect immediately. Many programs and parts of Windows 2000 poll the Registry only when they start. Thus, to see the results of some changes, you have to log off and back on to the computer, if the changes are in a **HKCU**, or restart the computer, if the changes are in **HKLM**.

Figure 4.3 shows the Binary Editor dialog box. Of all the dialog boxes that Regedt32 displays when you edit a value, this is the most complicated. Each byte in the binary string is two digits. Forget a digit, leaving an odd number of digits, and Regedt32 displays a warning and asks whether you want to pass the binary data with 0s.

Part

II

Ch

4

FIGURE 4.3
Edit **REG_BINARY** values in hexadecimal or binary notation; click either Binary or Hex.

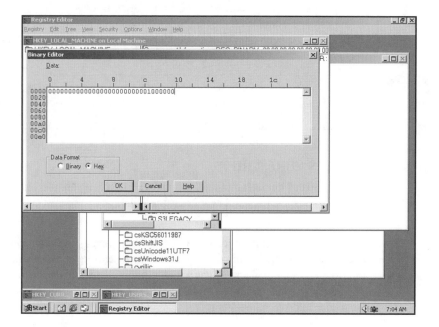

Creating Keys and Values

Creating a new subkey or value is as useless as it is harmless, if you don't know for certain that Windows 2000 or another program is going to actually use it. Creating a value called **fuzzy wuzzy wuzza bear** is useless, for example, because it's unlikely that another program would do something with the information. Creating a new value as instructed by an article in Microsoft's Knowledge Base is useful. In the key pane, select an existing subkey under which you want to create a new subkey or value and then do one of the following:

- **New Key** On the Edit menu, click Add Key, and then type the name of the subkey in Key Name.
- **New Value** On the Edit menu, click Add Value. In Value Name, type the name of the new value. In the Data Type list, click the data's type.

 TIP To quickly add a value in the value pane, press Insert. Regedt32 displays the Add Value dialog box. Do the same in the key pane to quickly add a subkey.

Deleting Keys and Values

Be very careful about deleting keys and values. You can prevent Windows 2000 from working properly by carelessly deleting keys or values from the Registry. If you don't know for sure what will happen, or you haven't been instructed to do so, *don't do it*. Otherwise, use these steps:

1. In the key pane, select the subkey you want to remove; or in the value pane, select the value you want to remove.

2. Press Delete, and then click Yes to confirm that you want to remove the subkey or value.

 TIP Before removing a subkey or a value in a subkey, save the subkey as a binary file. Then, if something goes wrong, you can restore the subkey as described later in this chapter. "Saving and Restoring Subkeys," later in this chapter, shows you how.

Renaming Keys and Values

Regedt32 provides no way to rename a subkey or value. If you need to rename a subkey or value, doing so using Regedit is generally the quickest and easiest way. You learned about Regedit in Chapter 3.

You can work around this limitation in Regedt32, however. Save a subkey to a temporary binary file, as described in the next section, "Saving and Restoring Subkeys," and then restore that temporary binary file as a new subkey with a different name. Having restored the file to a new subkey, remove the old subkey. The result is the same data with a different name: a poor man's rename feature.

Saving and Restoring Subkeys

You can save a subkey, including all its subkeys and values, to a temporary binary file. The file has the same format as any of the hive files. A frequent handle for these files is *temporary hive file*. You must have administrator rights or, at the very least, have backup rights to save and restore subkeys, which is valuable for many different reasons:

■ Save a subkey to a temporary hive file and restore it to a new subkey with a different name. The result is renaming the subkey.

■ Save a subkey to a temporary hive file and load that file on a remote computer. This is an easy way to export settings to other computers.

■ Save a subkey to a temporary hive file as a quick and easy backup in case things go wrong. If trouble arises, restore the temporary hive files, thus restoring the original settings.

To save a subkey as a temporary hive file, follow these steps:

1. In the key pane, select the subkey that you want to save.
2. On the Registry menu, click Save Key to display the Save Key dialog box.
3. Select the file in which you want to save the subkey.

Restoring a subkey from a temporary hive file replaces all that subkey's contents with the contents of the file. It doesn't merge their contents, it complete replaces the current subkey's contents. To restore a subkey from a file, use these steps:

1. In the key pane, select the key that you want to restore.
2. On the Registry menu, click Restore and then select the file that you want to restore into the selected subkey.

Part

II

Ch

4

Exporting Subkeys to Text Files

In Regedt32, saving a subkey to a text file is not like exporting a subkey using Regedit. For one, you can't import the files back into the Registry, as they weren't designed for this purpose. They are useful for browsing the contents of the Registry offline and are also easy to create:

1. In the key pane, select the subkey that you want to save in a text file.
2. On the Registry menu, click Save Subtree As, and then choose the file you want to save.

Listing 4.1 shows a sample of the text file that Regedt32 creates. It gives each subkey's name, its class (unused for the most part), and time it was last written. For each of the subkey's values, it gives the value's name, type, and data. A glimpse of this format, and you can see that it's really unsuitable for importing. It's more suitable for quick perusal.

Listing 4.1   Sample Text File

```
Key Name:          SYSTEM\ControlSet001
Class Name:        <NO CLASS>
Last Write Time:   7/17/99 - 5:56 PM

Key Name:          SYSTEM\ControlSet001\Control
Class Name:        <NO CLASS>
Last Write Time:   8/25/99 - 6:45 PM
Value 0
  Name:            CurrentUser
  Type:            REG_SZ
  Data:            USERNAME

Value 1
  Name:            SystemStartOptions
  Type:            REG_SZ
  Data:            FASTDETECT

Value 2
  Name:            WaitToKillServiceTimeout
  Type:            REG_SZ
  Data:            20000


Key Name:          SYSTEM\ControlSet001\Control\ApmActive
Class Name:        <NO CLASS>
Last Write Time:   9/21/99 - 12:15 AM
Value 0
  Name:            Active
  Type:            REG_DWORD
  Data:            0x1


Key Name:          SYSTEM\ControlSet001\Control\ApmLegalHal
Class Name:        <NO CLASS>
Last Write Time:   7/17/99 - 5:59 PM
Value 0
  Name:            Present
  Type:            REG_DWORD
  Data:            0x1


Key Name:          SYSTEM\ControlSet001\Control\Arbiters
Class Name:        <NO CLASS>
Last Write Time:   7/17/99 - 5:56 PM
```

Loading and Unloading Hive Files

Loading a hive file is very different than restoring a hive file. When you restore a hive, the contents of the hive file replace the subkey in which you restore it. When you load a hive file, Regedt32 loads that file in its own space. It doesn't replace anything. In other words, Regedt32 creates a whole new subkey under **HKLM** or **HKU**. Like saving and restoring hive files, loading hive files is very useful:

- Load a hive file from a computer that isn't working properly so that you can fix the problem. Doing so doesn't affect your computer's configuration, however.
- Load a user's individual hive file, Ntuser.dat, so that you can make changes to her user profile.
- Create a copy of a user's Ntusr.dat hive file and save it on the network as a mandatory profile.
- Load the default profile's Ntuser.dat hive file so that you can make changes that affect all users when they log on to the computer for the first time.

To load or unload a hive, you must have administrator rights or, at the very least, restore and backup rights on the computer. Also, you can't load a hive that contains a subkey in use. For instance, if you want to load the System hive from a remote computer, you must first save a copy of that hive to another file and then load it on your computer. Here's how:

1. Select either the **HKU** or **HKLM** root keys, as you can only load hive files into these two.
2. On the Registry menu, click Load Hive.
3. Choose the hive file that you want to load.
4. In Key Name, type the name of the subkey you want to create, which will hold the hive file.

After you've made any changes you like to the hive file you loaded earlier, use these steps to unload it:

1. In the key pane, select the hive you want to unload. You can only unload hive files that you yourself loaded.
2. On the Registry menu, click Unload Hive.

Administering Network Registries

Administrators have an easier time managing computers over a network with Windows 2000 than they do with Windows 98. Windows 98 requires administrators to jump through hoops to enable remote administration. Windows 2000 supports it with no effort on the part of the administrator.

Part

II

Ch

4

To connect to a remote computer and edit its Registry, follow these steps:

1. On the Registry menu, click Select Computer.
2. Do one of the following:

   - In Computer Text Box, type the name of the computer to which you want to connect.
   - In the Select Computer list, click the name of the computer to which you want to connect.

After connecting to a remote computer, you see two new MDI windows: one for **HKLM** on the remote computer and one for **HKU**. You don't see windows for the other root keys, including **HKCU** or **HKCR**. Even after connecting to a remote computer, you still see the windows for each of the local computer's root keys, unless you close them individually.

Securing the Registry

Windows 2000 makes it easy to manage the security of the Registry. You can do things as simple as blocking a user's access to Registry Editor. You can also manage the permissions of individual subkeys. That's what the remainder of this section is about. Here's what you'll learn:

- If your only concern is preventing a user from tampering with his Registry, use file permissions to prevent him from even getting at Registry Editor.
- Windows 2000 creates an ACL for each and every subkey. It determines who can and can't access each subkey. You can modify these permissions for an entire branch or just a specific subkey.
- Windows 2000 provides a mechanism to control remote access to the Registry. This mechanism is completely cryptic, but worth the work.
- Windows 2000 allows you to audit what a user does in the Registry, directly or indirectly. Audit successes and failures for different event types.

▶ **See** Chapter 6, "Administering Registries" **p. 95**, for more information about securing the Registry.

Preventing Access

The easiest way to prevent a clumsy user from messing up the Registry is to prevent him from using Registry Editor. You don't have to worry with the permissions of individual subkeys at all. If the user has no access to Registry Editor, it doesn't matter. Here are some fairly obvious methods you can use to completely prevent access to Registry Editor:

- Maintain complete control of who can log on to a computer with administrative privileges. I've worked in many shops where just about every programmer had some sort of administrative access to the server. You should maintain more control than this if you want to secure your server.

- Don't install Regedt32 or Regedit on each user's individual workstation. If she doesn't have access to Registry Editor, she can't tamper with her Registry. She could locate a copy of Registry Editor if she wanted to, but for most folks, this is entirely too much trouble. As well, if you need access to a user's computer as the administrator, you can access it remotely.

- Short of removing Regedt32 and Regedit from computers, you can place restrictions on the groups and users who can run Registry Editor. Change Regedit.exe and Regedt32.exe's permissions in *SystemRoot* and in *SystemRoot*\System32, respectively, so only administrators have access to either of these programs.

Assigning Permissions

You can control who has access to a particular subkey. For example, you can prohibit users from removing any subkeys under **HKCR** or you can allow only administrators to change a custom subkey you've added to the Registry.

In general, however, you should change the ACL only for subkeys that you've specifically added to support your own needs. In other words, I don't recommend that you tinker with the ACL for subkeys that Windows 2000 or other programs install in the Registry. Windows 2000 automatically manages those for you. Why? Changing an ACL to No Access for a subkey to which the system must have access to start can prevent the computer from starting at all.

 TIP You can change the ACL for a Registry key whether you're using NTFS or FAT. Windows 2000 stores ACLs in the Registry, so they're not depending on the file system's security.

If you really must change the ACL for a subkey, use Regedt32. Here's how:

1. In the key pane, select the subkey whose ACL you want to change.

2. On the Security menu, click Permissions. You see the Permissions for *Subkey* dialog box shown in Figure 4.4.

3. Do one of the following:

    - In the Name list, click a user or group you want to remove, and then click Remove.

    - In the Name list, click a user or group whose permissions you want to change and then, in the Permissions list, allow or deny each permission by selecting or clearing each check box.

    - Click Add, and then choose a user or group you want to add to the subkey's ACL.

Part

II

Ch

4

FIGURE 4.4

Changing a subkey's ACL is identical to changing any other object's ACL in Windows 2000.

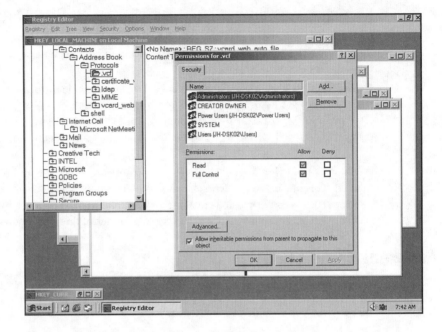

N O T E If you've changed the ACL for a subkey, turn on auditing for failures and test the system thoroughly to make sure it still works as expected. If you encounter errors, check the event log to find out why. After you're satisfied that the change didn't prevent Windows 2000 from working properly, turn off auditing. Otherwise, restore the ACL for the subkey and try again. ■

Controlling Remote Access

In the previous section, you learned how to control who can access each subkey. You can also use this ACL for a special subkey to determine who can access the Registry across the network. This method is a bit cryptic (Microsoft gets the obscure feature-of-the-decade award), but it works.

When a user tries to remotely connect to a Windows 2000 Registry, the operating system checks **winreg** in **HKLM\System\CurrentControlset\Control\SecurePipeServers**. This subkey's ACL determines who has permission to access the Registry remotely. One of two things happen:

■ If Windows 2000 finds **winreg** in the Registry and the user has permission according to the ACL for **winreg**, the user is allowed to remotely connect to the Registry. In other words, the ACL for **winreg** determines which users can remotely access the Registry. Then the ACL for each subkey the user tries to access defines what the remotely connected user can and can't do to it.

■ If Windows 2000 doesn't find **winreg** in the Registry, it allows all users to remotely connect to the Registry. The ACL for each key then defines what the remotely connected user can and can't do to it.

Change this subkey's ACL as you would any other subkey. Both Windows 2000 Professional and Windows 2000 Server create this subkey. By default, both operating systems give full control to the local Administrator's group and read control to the local Backup Operators group. This enables domain administrators to administer the computer's Registry remotely, because the Domain Admins group is a member of the local Administrators group. ●

CHAPTER 5

Safeguarding Configurations

In this chapter

Planning a Strategy

A good strategy doesn't just happen, it requires planning. I'm not suggesting that you rally the troops and spend two weeks at an offsite retreat (the definition of *planning* at more bureaucratic organizations) just to figure out how you're going to back up a bunch of Registries and protect users' configurations. I do suggest that you write some sort of minimal plan and stick to it. Anything is better than no plan at all. If you're a lone administrator, you have a lot of power to use any plan you create. Just do it. If you work with other administrators or delegate administrative tasks to other users, get those other people involved in creating the plan and, most importantly, get them to own it.

The first part of your plan is backing up computers on a regular basis. I don't need to convince you that backing up your servers is a good thing, do I? But, how often do you perform this task? Is it scheduled to occur whether you remember or not? What's amazing is that while most administrators are good about backing up servers, many almost never back up their own computers. A terrible injustice if you ask me. Downtime costs organizations vast amounts of money and could be lessened by restoring backup media. Don't be lulled into believing that all is well with your backup media, however. Test them by verifying their contents against the original files, a feature that most backup programs provide. One of the worst moments of my professional life was when a client's server failed and the backup tape was unreadable. Never again.

By using roaming user profiles, a feature you'll learn about in Chapter 6, "Administering Registries," you won't necessarily have to back up each client computer. Users' important documents and settings are in their home directories, and you can nab those each time you back up the server. Reinstalling an operating system and a few programs on users' computers is certainly easier than restoring their documents and settings, and backing up their roaming user profiles is more palatable than backing up each user's computer, particularly on large networks. Regardless of experts' sage advice, you can install Windows 2000 Professional and several applications quicker than you can restore a backup tape containing the same. You can, of course, make users responsible for backing up their computers—good luck. In large organizations, consider making each department head responsible for backing up client computers.

The next part of your strategy is to automate the process. Speaking from experience, you're not going to keep up with any plan that requires too much manual labor. With your various daily distractions, backing up computers is a task that's going to fall by the wayside. You can start a backup job from users' login scripts or by scheduling jobs on their computers. Schedule backup jobs on your servers, too. I mention this in the context of backing up a full system, but you can schedule jobs that specifically back up Registries. Schedule backup jobs during off-peak hours so that people are using fewer files, however, and the backup media more accurately reflects what's on the network. The following list shows you a possible schedule, one that I use. It's also a good start to a written plan. I use 11 tapes and rotate 4 weekly backup tapes as shown in Figure 5.1, while rotating the last tape on and off site once each month:

Daily	Update each server's emergency repair disk (ERD) and each networked computer's ERD, storing each on the server.
Daily	Back up to tape changes since the most recent backup of each server and users' home directories.
Weekly	Back up to tape each server, including users' home directories.
Monthly	Rotate the most recent full backup tape offsite, replacing it with the previous offsite tape.

FIGURE 5.1
Normal backup tapes contain all files on the computer, and differential backup tapes contain files changed since the most recent normal backup.

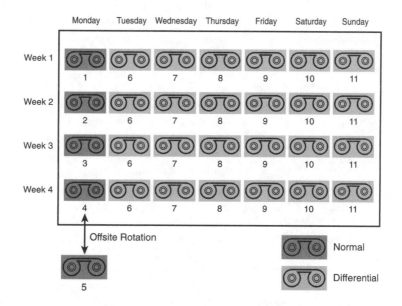

Last, the smartest and most under-used way to ensure a working configuration is creating an emergency repair disk (ERD). An ERD can fix a configuration that's so far gone that it prevents the computer from starting properly, and most administrators never bother making one. Making an ERD isn't enough, however, because the information on it is dated as soon as you make any significant change to the configuration. Thus, you must update the disk anytime you update device drivers, install a service pack, or change data in the Registry. (Even though in Windows 2000 ERDs don't contain a backup copy of the Registry hive files, the process still creates a backup copy of those files on the computer's disk and the process is still useful.) Yes, maintaining an ERD is a pain, but this chapter shows you how to use a pain reliever from Aelita Software Group called ERDisk, which helps you make an ERD for each client computer on the network, automatically.

Part
II

Ch
5

Strategy aside, working with Windows 2000's Registry requires a bit of tactical common sense:

- Stay out of the Registry if you can accomplish the same feat another way. For instance, why change file associations in the Registry, when you can safely do the same thing using the Folder Options dialog box in Windows Explorer?

- Practice a bit of self-restraint. Don't go hog wild, trying every customization you run across. If you're a certified tweaker, set up a scratch computer on which you can test settings without risking production computers. Many companies have bone yards from which you can slap together a scratch computer without the red tape.

- Make temporary backup copies of any subkey you're editing. Registry Editor, *Regedit* and its other personality *Regedt32*, both provide ways to back up a subkey before changing it. See "Saving Subkeys to Hive Files" and "Exporting Subkeys to Text Files" later in this chapter.

- Secure computers against unauthorized intrusion. That means keeping passwords secret and preventing users from logging on to computers with accounts that have rights reserved for administrators. Doing so opens their computers to opportunistic viruses that require such access to inflict their damage. Chapter 4, "Editing with Regedt32," has more suggestions for securing computer configurations.

- Practice backing up and restoring the Registry on a scratch computer. This makes sure that you're comfortable with the process and that you know what you're doing when a real crisis hits. Little else feels better than that smug feeling you get when you handle a crisis like a pro, especially if your boss is watching and you're up for a raise.

Backups Are Terrible Things to Waste

The subject of backing up the Registry is the most intense and the most read part of any Registry book. I admit to one mistake related to this topic in one of my earlier Registry books, a mistake that was not at all severe but nonetheless one that I heard about daily for the year and a half the book was on the shelf. It is on people's minds, users and administrators alike. They want to know how to protect their configurations from errant programs and, well, from themselves. Given the power that Registry books put into a person's hands, making a good backup copy of the Registry is just plain old horse sense.

The worst thing that could happen, if you're stuck without a backup copy of the Registry, is that you won't be able to start Windows 2000. Period. And, if the computer's file system is NTFS, your only hope of getting files off the computer's disk is to install another, parallel copy of the operating system or use Recovery Command Console, both of which you learn about in this chapter. If you have a good, recent backup copy of the Registry, recovery is often a snap; restore the Registry using the many techniques you learn in this chapter. The sad thing is that many users don't realize how easy recovering their configurations can be and, based on bad advice from a lazy support technician, end up reinstalling the operating system. What a waste!

Using Microsoft Windows Backup

The backup program that Windows NT 4.0 provides is serviceable, but just barely. Many administrators just swear by this program and prefer it to anything else, but I've always felt it was too limited and too difficult to use, mostly due to its poor user interface. It has one key feature, however, and that is its capability to back up the operating system's Registry, a feature lacking in many other backup programs for Windows NT 4.0.

Windows 2000 has an all-new program called Windows Backup, provided by the folks at VERITAS Software Corporation (check out the company's full line of disaster recovery products at http://www.veritas.com). And unlike other third-party programs that Microsoft includes in Windows 2000, Windows Backup is in no way crippled. To start Windows Backup, click the Start button, point to Programs, point to Accessories, point to System Tools, and then click Backup. Windows Backup has several improvements over its predecessor. First, it's tidier user interfaces, Backup Wizard and Restore Wizard, collect information about a job. It has more options that control either type of job. Best of all, selecting local and network files is much easier thanks to the Windows Explorer–like user interface. Although the power and flexibility of its predecessor remain, getting to that power is much easier.

Like many Windows 2000 system tools, users must have rights to back up or restore files on a computer. Members of the local Administrators or Backup Operators groups can back up and restore any file or folder on the local computer. Members of the domain Administrators or Backup Operators groups can back up and restore any file or folder on any computer in the domain, providing that the user has a two-way trust relationship with the domain. Users whose accounts aren't in any of those groups must have no less than read permission to any file they want to back up or must have the following rights, locally or on the domain:

- Back up files and directories
- Restore files and directories

 TIP To ensure that Windows Backup performs its best, make sure it's the only process running. More importantly, by making sure it's the only process running, you partially ensure that no other programs have a file locked, preventing Windows Backup from backing up or restoring it.

Part
II

Ch
5

Backing Up System State Data

Windows Backup lumps the Registry together with other data and calls the whole kit-and-caboodle *System State data*. Does this mean that Microsoft is minimizing the role of the Registry in Windows 2000's configuration? No. It means that the company got smart and is treating related data atomically so that related settings and files remain synchronized even after restoring them.

In Windows 2000 Professional, System State data includes the Registry, the COM+ Class Registration database, and boot files. In Windows 2000 Server, System State data also includes the Certificate Services database, Active Directory, SYSVOL directory, and various other bits of configuration data. Backing up and restoring System State data is an all-or-nothing deal. You can restore System State data to an alternative location, however, and then restore portions of it manually. Windows Backup only restores the Registry, SYSVOL directory, and boot files to an alternative location, not the remaining parts of System State data.

Windows Backup does not back up System State data on remote computers. It backs up files on remote computers via their administrative shares (ADMIN$, C$, D$, and so on), but doesn't have functionality to access a remote computer's Registry via RPC (remote procedure calls), as does Registry Editor. Don't rely on Windows Backup as a way to protect client computers' System State data unless you actually run Windows Backup on each computer locally. Many are the ways to back up System State data locally, however:

- On the Backup tab, shown in Figure 5.2, select the System State check box.
- To back up all files on the computer, including System State data, click Back Up Everything on My Computer in the Backup Wizard.
- To back up selected files on the computer, including System State data, click Back Up Selected Files, Drives, or Network Data in the Backup Wizard, and then select the System State check box on the Backup tab.
- To back up only System State data, click Only Back Up the System State Data in the Backup Wizard.

System State check box

FIGURE 5.2
To include the Registry and other System State data the backup data, select the System State check box.

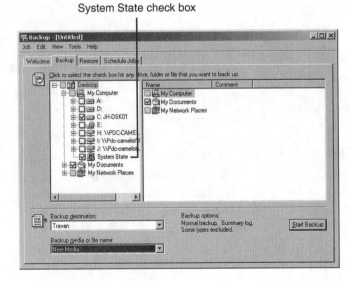

Never lull yourself into a false sense of security just because you back up the computer. Errors and bad media happen. First, make sure you verify backup data, just to ensure it matches what's on the disk. By default, Windows Backup doesn't verify backup data. To cause it to verify backup data after backing it up, click Options on the Tools menu and then, on the General tab, select the Verify Data After the Backup Completes check box.

Second, check the log file to make sure the backup data includes what you think it should. After Windows Backup finishes a job, click Report on the Backup Progress dialog box. Log files are in `UserProfile\Local Settings\Application Data\Microsoft\Windows NT\NTBackup\data`. Windows Backup opens the log file in Notepad. By default, the report contains a few measly statistics about the backup data. If you want more information, such as what files are in the backup data, click Options on the Tools menu and then, on the Backup Log tab, click Detailed.

> **N O T E**   Our primary interest is the Registry, and you'll be happy to note that Windows Backup makes a second copy of it, one that's much more accessible. **SystemRoot\Repair\Regback** contains the second copy. The only problem is that each time you back up System State data, Windows Backup replaces this backup copy of the Registry. In other words, this directory only contains a backup copy of the Registry from the most recent backup data. If you're fanatical about backups, copy this directory to another location every time you back up. ▨

Restoring System State Data

Restoring System State data is a reversal of the same processes. Use the Restore Wizard and, in the What to Restore list, select the System State check box. Otherwise, do the same on the Restore tab. Windows Backup restores System State data, including the Registry, COM+ Class Registration database, and boot files. Other backup programs require a stern warning about making sure the Registry matches the contents of other system files, particularly if you only restore the Registry. If you stick to restoring System State data the way Windows Backup does it, the Registry should stay synchronized with the rest of System State data. You might still run into problems with applications losing their settings, true only if you installed the application after the date of the backup data you're restoring, but most applications can restore their settings in the Registry.

Windows Backup does back up the entire Registry but doesn't necessarily restore it all. It identifies hives using **HKLM\SYSTEM\CurrentControlSet\Control\hivelist**. Chapter 1, "Understanding Registries," describes **hivelist**, a subkey that describes the hives comprising the Registry. An implication in the backup data includes **HKU**. The program copies hives to static files, and adds the static files to the backup data. Restoring is more complicated, however. Subkeys of **HKLM\SYSTEM** that Windows Backup will copy from the old Registry to the new are in **HKLM\SYSTEM\CurrentControlSet\Control\BackupRestore\KeysNotToRestore**. The result is that Windows Backup does not restore any subkey listed in **KeysNotToRestore**. There's more. Windows Backup doesn't restore any subkey in this

Part

II

Ch

5

list that ends with a backslash (\). If a subkey ends with an asterisk (*), Windows Backup doesn't restore it or any of its subkeys, that is, the whole subtree.

> **N O T E** To restore System State data on Windows 2000 domain controllers, start them in Directory Services Restore Mode. On the Windows 2000 Advanced Options Menu (boot menu), choose Directory Services Restore Mode. The Advanced Options Menu describes each option. ▓

Indirect Backups

Windows Backup can store backup data in a file. When doing so won't adversely affect the network's bandwidth or disk space, back up the client computer to a file on a network share. Then, pick up that file during the server's next regular backup.

Use this technique in varying degrees. Backing up every file on a client computer to the network won't be practical unless you have some grossly large disks on the server and more bandwidth than you should have. Backing up a client computer's System State data makes more sense and ensures that you can restore a computer's configuration if something goes awry.

I don't recommend this method for all situations, but in situations in which backing up a client computer isn't possible, an indirect backup is the next best thing. It's particularly useful for gathering System State data from each client computer.

Saving Subkeys to Hive Files

Using *Regedt32*, you can save any subkey as a binary file similar to hive files in **SystemRoot\System32\Config**. You can't save a root key, however, only subkeys, making this a less-than-ideal method for backing up the Registry. It is a useful way to tactically back up a subkey while you're administering the Registry, however, particularly when you're not certain whether your efforts will cripple the system and want an easy way out in such cases.

Chapter 4 shows how to save and load hive files and the difference between loading a hive file and restoring a hive file. Just for grins, here's a quick review. Loading a hive file creates a subkey under **HKLM** or **HKU** without actually replacing or changing any data in the existing Registry. Thus, you can create a new subkey called **HKLM\MyHive** and load a hive file into it. Restoring a hive file replaces the subkey you saved. For example, if you saved **HKLM\SOFTWARE** as a hive file and then restore it, *Regedt32* replaces the **SOFTWARE** subkey with the contents of the hive file. With that, here are instructions for doing each operation:

> ▓ To save a subkey as a hive file, backing up its contents, select in the key pane the subkey you want to save. On the Registry menu, click Save Key, and then type the name for the new hive file.

- To restore a hive file, replacing the current contents of the subkey with the contents of the hive file, click R̲estore on the R̲egistry menu, and then select the file you want to restore.

- To load a hive file, select in the key pane the root key, **HKLM** or **HKU**, underneath which you want to load the hive file; then, on the R̲egistry menu, click L̲oad Hive and select the hive file you want to load. In Key Name, type the name of the subkey you want to create as the subkey's temporary home.

- To unload a hive file that you loaded, select it in the key pane, and then click U̲nload Hive on the R̲egistry menu. *Regedt32* does not unload between sessions any hive files that you load.

Now, let's talk about technique. First, save a subkey as a hive file while you're fiddling with it. For example, before tweaking Windows 2000 by changing a variety of values in **HKLM\SOFTWARE\Microsoft\Windows**, save that subkey to a hive file. If you mess up, restore the hive file, replacing your mishaps with the original settings. Second, if you prefer to be more selective about the settings you restore, load the backup hive file instead of restoring it; that way, you can inspect each setting in the backup hive file and restore the ones you like. *Regedt32* doesn't have a drag-and-drop feature, but you can copy and paste values while editing them. For example, if you messed up a value called **Owner**, load the backup hive file in a subkey called **HKLM\Scratch**. Then, within **Scratch**, open **Owner**, highlight the value, and click C̲opy on its shortcut menu. Go to **Owner** in **HKML\SOFTWARE\Microsoft\Windows**, open **Owner**, and paste the contents of the Clipboard into the value.

The last technique is often the most valuable. Sadly, too many users fail to back up a subkey, change a value that they regret changing, and then find themselves unable to restore the original value. Just because they didn't explicitly create a hive file doesn't mean that a hive file isn't on the disk somewhere. Windows Backup backs up the Registry hive files to **SystemRoot\Repair\Regback** and, because these are just ordinary hive files, they can be loaded under **HKLM** or **HKU**. Be careful not to restore hive files from the repair directory, unless absolutely necessary to repair the computer, because that replaces existing settings with the hive file. This is also the way around the fact that the emergency repair process doesn't restore a subkey using the backup hive files unless it finds a physical flaw in them. You learn about the emergency repair process a bit later in this chapter.

TIP *Regedit* displays hive files that you load using *Regedt32*. If you're more comfortable editing with *Regedit*, load a hive file using *Regedt32* and then flip over to *Regedit* to copy values from the backup hive file to other values in the Registry.

Part

II

Ch

5

Copying Hive Files

Many Registry books, my titles included, describe how to manually copy hive files. This was a holdover from similar advice for Windows 95, because copying `User.dat` and `System.dat` was the best way to backup the operating system's Registry.

The technique isn't practical, however—too many steps and too many problems to overcome. First, because Windows 2000 opens the hive files for exclusive use, you can't copy the files while the operating system is running. Several ways around this problem include starting another operating system, getting an NTFS file system driver for MS-DOS, or using Recovery Command Console.

The operating system you use to copy the hive files must support the file system on the system partition. If that's FAT, you can start MS-DOS or Windows 98 and copy the hive files. If that's NTFS, the other operating system must be Windows 2000 or Windows NT 4.0 with Service Pack 3 or better.

Systems Internals sells an NTFS file system driver for MS-DOS. You can use this driver to start the computer to MS-DOS and copy the hive files. See `http://www.sysinternals.com`.

The last option, Recovery Command Console, is the easiest. Recovery Command Console provides limited access to an NTFS volume when Windows 2000 isn't actually running. It has commands that are similar to MS-DOS and a few others that are specifically useful for recovering an ill computer. For example, using Recovery Command Console, you can disable a device driver that prevents Windows 2000 from starting properly, or you can replace a file that the operating system requires to start but is corrupt. You learn how to use Recovery Command Console later in Chapter 12, "Repairing Damaged Registries."

All in all, considering the alternatives, all three methods are too much trouble.

Exporting Subkeys to Text Files

Regedit doesn't have features to load, unload, or restore hive files. As you learned in Chapter 3, "Editing with Regedit," it does have features you can use to export subkeys to REG (Registration Entries) files and import REG files into subkeys. Although these capabilities aren't as preferable as saving, loading, and restoring hive files, they're service-able, particularly if you're already comfortable using *Regedit* in Windows 98. *Regedt32* also has the capability to save subkeys as text files, but this capability is useless because you can't import that text back into the Registry.

Export a subkey using *Regedit* by selecting it in the key pane, and then choosing Export Registry File from the Registry menu. Import by selecting Import Registry File from the same menu. How *Regedit* imports a REG file is an important note, and somewhat limits its usefulness as a backup method. It doesn't replace the subkey with the contents of the REG file. It merges the REG file into the Registry and has the consequences you see in Table 5.1.

Table 5.1	Merging REG Files	
Value Exists in the Registry	Value Exists in the REG File	Action
No	No	None
No	Yes	*Regedit* adds the value found in the REG file to the Registry.
Yes	No	Nothing; *Regedit* does not remove the value from the Registry.
Yes	Yes	*Regedit* updates the value in the Registry.

Copying Users' Profile Folders

Windows 2000 stores hive files containing per-computer settings in *SystemRoot*\System32\Config. A single hive file that contains per-user settings, Ntuser.dat, is in the root of users' profile folders, *UserProfile*.

Copying hive files from users' profile folders is the easiest way to back up their settings. You can't copy hive files that are in use, because Windows 2000 locks them, but you can copy hive files that aren't in use. A user's hive file is in use when that user logs on to the computer or when you run a process in the context of that user (Secondary Logon). To quickly back up users' settings, log on to the computer as Administrator, which is usually the only account that has full access to all the profile folders, and copy Ntuser.dat from each.

When using roaming-user profiles, a feature of IntelliMirror that you learn about in Chapter 6, a copy of each account's Ntuser.dat file is in *UserProfile* and also in the user's home directory. Roaming-user profiles make backing up users' settings even simpler, because you can pick up all their profiles with a single swipe of Windows Backup. Additionally, if users' computers fail unexpectedly, restoring their configurations is a no-brainer, because Windows 2000 downloads their profiles from the network after you reinstall it. This is one of the ideas behind Microsoft's vision for a replaceable machine and is a sight to behold.

Making Emergency Repair Disks

Emergency repair disks have limited capabilities. They can help start the computer when other methods, safe mode or Recovery Command Console, fail. A computer's ERD does not contain backup copies of data, program files, or even the Registry, but it does contain enough information to make basic repairs to the system files, partition boot sector, or startup environment. Start the setup program and then use the ERD to restore these core system files. The catch is that you must create the ERD while the computer is healthy, requiring that you main-

Part

II

Ch

5

tain it on an ongoing basis. Waiting until a computer fails is not a good time to decide you need to update its ERD. Note, too, that throughout this chapter I discuss a *computer's ERD* in a possessive sense. Each computer must have its own ERD and you can't use one computer's ERD on another, no matter how desperate you are to fix it and get a raise.

Repair Disk Utility, the program you used in Windows NT Workstation 4.0 to create ERDs, is missing in Windows 2000. In its place is the ubiquitous Windows Backup, the very one that you read about earlier in this chapter. Rolling Repair Disk Utility into Windows Backup makes sense, because backing up a computer and creating an ERD are birds of a feather and should flock together (sorry). To create an ERD using Windows Backup, click E̲mergency Repair Disk on the Welcome tab. I'm not sure that you're going to like changes in the way it creates ERDs, however.

As opposed to Repair Disk Utility, Windows Backup does not create a copy of the ERD in *SystemRoot\Repair* and does not copy the Registry hive files to the ERD at all. Instead, if you choose to do so on the Emergency Repair Diskette dialog box, it backs up the Registry hive files to *SystemRoot\Repair\Regback*, the same location to which it backs them up when you back up System State data. Also, *SystemRoot\Repair* always contains a copy of the original hive files that setup created when you first installed Windows 2000. You should never change or remove these files because you might need them to get the computer working again in extreme circumstances or if you changed the administrator password and forgot it. The actual files on the ERD are meager in number and include these:

Autoexec.nt	*SystemRoot\System32\Autoexec.nt*, which Windows 2000 uses to initialize MS-DOS environments.
Config.nt	*SystemRoot\System32\Config.nt*, which Windows 2000 uses to initialize MS-DOS environments.
Setup.log	Log file indicating the files installed as well as a cyclic redundancy check (CRC) that helps the emergency repair process determine if core system files are corrupt.

CAUTION

Relying on ERDs as a method to back up the Registry is ill advised. Windows Backup does not back up the Registry hive files to the ERD. Even though the backup program does back up the Registry hive files to the disk, catastrophes can make the backup useless.

Using an ERD to repair the computer seems like a daunting task, but it's really no big deal. You must first start the setup program, Winnt.exe and not Winnt32.exe, by starting the computer with MS-DOS and running it, starting the computer with the Setup boot disks, or booting the computer with the Windows 2000 CD-ROM, which works only if you have a bootable CD-ROM drive. Note that if the computer doesn't have any disks with a FAT partition, you must use one of the latter two options, because the setup program complains that it can't find a place for its swap file if you start it from MS-DOS and don't have any FAT partitions. When the setup program first starts, it asks whether you want to set up Windows 2000 or repair a Windows 2000 installation, and that's where the following instructions start:

1. Press **R** to start the emergency repair process.

2. Press **R** again to choose the emergency repair process over the Recovery Command Console, and then do one of the following:

   - Press **M** to choose whether you want to repair the system files, partition boot sector, or startup environment (not recommended).

   - Press **F** to automatically repair the system files, partition boot sector, startup environment, and Registry, as long as a backup copy of the Registry hive files exist in *SystemRoot***Repair****Regback**.

The emergency repair process doesn't just replace the Registry with the backup copy of the hive files that are in the repair directory. It loads and unloads each subkey in the Registry and, if the subkey doesn't check out, the process restores that subkey from the backup copy. This means that you should only count on the ERD to fix physical flaws in the Registry and not to fix values that prevent the computer from starting properly. If that's the problem, you can manually restore the backup Registry hive files using Recovery Command Console. ●

Administering Registries

Security

Throughout Microsoft Windows 2000, security is the same. Every object has an access control list (ACL) that the operating system uses to determine permissions for users, individually or as a group, to use that object. Objects that are secure include files, folders, and subkeys. The benefits of tightening file and folder security using NTFS is obvious. Protect them from unauthorized access. This is particularly true on computers that multiple users share or with files in a network share.

The benefits of tightening Registry security are less obvious and equally dubious. For reasons that will become clear, I recommend that you skip this section and move right on to "User Profiles." Changing a subkey's access control list can severely cripple the computer, making it difficult for users on that computer to do their jobs. The reason is that they must have full access to the majority of the settings in the Registry, as Windows 2000 and a whole host of programs make varieties of changes to the Registry on behalf of users. If users don't have proper permission to a subkey that the operating system or applications must access, they won't be able to work properly. Registry security is thus best left to the wisdom of the operating system and not to the mercy of human error.

Still, in Microsoft Windows NT 4.0, administrators frequently had to tinker with Registry security, as it was implemented poorly. Windows 2000 improves the situation greatly, however, making it less necessary for anyone to have to change security in the Registry. In Windows 2000, **HKLM\SAM** is encrypted by default. Security on individual subkeys is more selective—full access isn't given to everyone. Access to the Registry remotely is better restricted now, too, which is a great improvement over Windows NT Workstation 4.0. New tools for security, including Security Configuration Editor, make tightening security a snap and less error prone. All in all, with regard to Registry security, administrators win out big in this release of Microsoft's flagship operating system.

▶ **See** Chapter 4, "Editing with Regedt32," **p. 65**, for more information about *Regedt32*, the preferred editor to use when administering Registry security.

Assigning Permission

You must use *Regedt32* to change permissions for subkeys. *Regedit*, *Regedt32's* younger brother, doesn't support security, but Symantec's Norton Registry Editor does. To change a subkey's ACL, click the subkey in the key pane, and then click Permissions on the Security menu. The Permissions for Classes dialog box is straightforward. In the Name list, click a name and then select Allow or Deny next to each type of permission in the Permissions list. Little reason exists to add or remove users from the Name list, but you add a user or group by clicking Add or remove one by clicking it in the list and then clicking Remove.

In the Permissions for Classes dialog box, Allow Inheritable Permissions from Parent to Propagate to This Object requires a brief explanation. Select this check box, and the subkey inherits its parent subkey's permissions; otherwise, it doesn't. This isn't the same as resetting permissions on child subkeys, which actually replaces a subkey's descendants to match its permissions. Inheritance works similarly in the Registry as it does in NTFS and enables you to make sweeping changes to a branch and then add exceptions as required. Better still, those changes are controlled from a higher point in the hierarchy, requiring less work on your behalf. For example, you can remove a user from accessing anything within a particular branch but easily allow an exception to a few particular subkeys.

You just learned the basic method for changing subkey's permissions, but a more advanced method exists. In the Permissions for Classes dialog box, click Advanced. The result is the Access Control Settings for Classes dialog box that you see in Figure 6.1. You change access permission on the Permissions tab. Do one of the following:

- To add a user, click Add.
- To remove a user, click Remove.
- To change an access control entry, click View/Edit.

When you add a user or change an access control entry, you see the Permission Entry for Classes dialog box. You can determine whether the entry applies to this subkey and all its child subkeys or just this subkey. You can change the user or group's name. Most importantly, in the Permissions list, you can select Allow or Deny next to each of the following special permissions:

- Query Value
- Set Value
- Create Subkey
- Enumerate Subkey
- Notify
- Create Link
- Delete
- Write DAC
- Write Owner
- Read Control

NOTE Windows 2000 doesn't allow you to change access control entries that it inherits from the parent subkey. To turn off inheritance for a subkey so that you can change all its access control entries, deselect Allow Inheritable Permissions from Parent to Propagate to This Object. The subkey will no longer inherit its parent subkey's permissions. ▪

Part
II

Ch
6

FIGURE 6.1

This is the same familiar dialog box that you see when changing a file or folder's access control list.

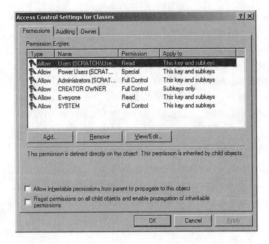

Auditing Subkey Access

Auditing subkeys helps you keep track of user access to the Registry. Honestly, I see little value in doing so unless you're specifically interested in access to particular subkeys. The impact on performance is often severe and not worth the cryptic information that you glean from it. The one exception is when you're trying to track down a setting in the Registry. As described in Chapter 9, "Tracking Down Registry Settings," you can use auditing to figure out which subkeys a program or the operating system accesses, which is good for customization.

Auditing subkeys is a two-step process. First, you must enable auditing using Group Policy, and then you must audit individual subkeys. The first step has become more complicated than with Windows NT 4.0. You don't use User Manager for Domains to enable auditing. You use Local Security Policy. In Control Panel, double-click the Administrative Tools icon and then double-click the Local Security Policy icon. In the tree pane, click Audit Policy, click Audit Object Access in the contents pane, and then click Security on the Action menu. The result is the Local Security Policy Setting dialog box, which you see in Figure 6.2. Select Success to audit successful access to objects and select Failure to audit failures. You've just completed the first step.

The second step is to audit individual subkeys:

1. In the key pane, click the subkey you want to audit.
2. On the Security menu, click Permissions.
3. In the Permissions for Subkey dialog box, click Advanced.
4. In the Access Control Settings for Subkey dialog box, click the Auditing tab.
5. Click Add to add an access control entry to the system access control list.

FIGURE 6.2
Account policy, including auditing, is more cumbersome to use in Windows 2000 than it was in Windows NT 4.0.

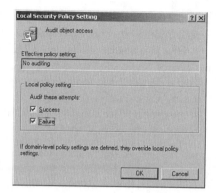

You view the results of an audit using Event Viewer. In Control Panel, double-click the Administrative Tools icon and then double-click the Event Viewer icon. Each audit event is in the security log, which you view by clicking Security Log in the tree pane.

Securing Remote Access

In Windows NT Workstation 4.0, anyone could access the Registry remotely unless someone intervened to restrict access to certain users and groups. Windows NT Server 4.0 limited access to administrators, however. The trick is a subkey under **HKLM\SYSTEM\CurrentControlSet\Control** called **SecurePipeServers\winreg**. The operating systems limited remote access to the Registry to only those users and groups given access to **winreg**. Additionally, their permissions to the Registry as a whole were limited to the permissions they had to **winreg**. Thus, by only allowing domain administrators to access **winreg**, only domain administrators could access the Registry locally.

Windows 2000 implements the same technique. The difference between it and Windows NT 4.0 is that Windows 2000 Professional restricts access to the Administrators and Backup Operators groups, which happen to include domain administrators and backup operators. Thus, by default, Windows 2000 Server and Windows 2000 Professional Registries are secure on the network, a great improvement over earlier versions of Windows NT.

You can give permission to other users by simply adding them to the access control list of **winreg**. Doing so shouldn't normally be necessary, however, because you want to limit access to remote Registries to administrators and backup operators.

User Profiles

Like Windows 98 and earlier versions of Windows NT, Windows 2000 is built for multiple users. User profiles allow more than one user to log on to a single computer and keep their settings separate from other users. Their settings, documents, favorite Web sites, and other files are separate from other users' information.

Part

II

Ch

6

Windows 2000 supports three different user profiles: local, roaming, and mandatory. Local user profiles are on the local computer. You find them in ***SystemDrive*\Documents** and **Settings\Default User**. Each user profile is in a separate folder and has the same name as the user's account name. Roaming network profiles follow users from computer to computer, as long as they're logging on to the same domain. Windows 2000 stores roaming profiles on the network. Mandatory profiles are similar to roaming profiles, except that Windows 2000 does not update the network copy of the profile when the user logs off the computer, which forces the user to start each session with the exact same settings.

By now, user profiles are probably old hat for you. A few concepts bear better explanation, however, as do the techniques you learn about in the following sections. The first concept is that of the default user profile. This is in ***SystemDrive*\Documents** and **Settings\Default User** and the operating system copies this profile to a user's profile folder the first time that user logs on to the computer, assuming that he doesn't already have a roaming profile on the network. The second concept that needs more explanation is *All Users*. This is in ***SystemDrive*\Documents** and **Settings\All Users** and applies to every user who logs on to the computer. Windows 2000 merges users' profiles with the contents of **All Users**, providing a convenient way to customize the computer in a way that affects everyone.

Copying User Profiles

The most basic thing an administrator must learn to do with user profiles is to copy them. There are many reasons for copying profiles: copy an existing user's profile to another user's profile folder; create a default profile by copying a profile that you customize; or back up a user's profile. The following section, "Configuring Defaults for New Users," shows the best reason to copy user profiles.

You can copy user profiles in Windows Explorer. Drag ***UserProfile*** from one location to another. Frequently, this works just fine. The following is an officially sanctioned way to copy profiles:

1. In Control Panel, double-click the System icon.
2. On the User Profiles tab, click the user profile that you want to copy and then click Copy To.
3. In the Copy To dialog box, shown in Figure 6.3, type the path to which you want to copy the profile in Copy Profile To.
4. Click Change and then select the user or group that you want to provide access to the user profile.

FIGURE 6.3
Using this dialog box to copy user profiles prevents errors that might occur if you copy them yourself.

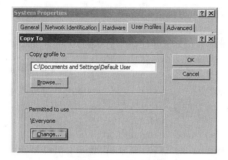

Configuring Defaults for New Users

As you read, Windows 2000 copies to the default user profiles for new users the first time they log on to the computer without already having a roaming user profile on the network. That's great, but how do you customize the default user profile?

Windows 2000 does not provide a user interface for customizing the default user profile; you must change it manually. Editing the files and folders in it is easy. You access them in Windows Explorer. To change settings in the default user profile's Ntuser.dat hive file, you must use *Regedt32*. Load the hive file, make any changes you want to make, and then unload the hive file. Because you must change settings within the Registry and not through the user interface, you must have some familiarity with how those settings are stored in the Registry.

From my experience, there is a much better way to customize the default user profile. Just copy an existing user profile, which you learned how to do in the previous section, into the Default User profile folder. For example, the first thing I do after installing Windows 2000 is log on to the computer as Administrator and customize the look and feel of the operating system. After I'm happy with the desktop's appearance and contents and have installed a bunch of common applications, I copy the profile to Default User. Every user that logs on to the computer has those same settings when they log on to the computer for the first time. A real timesaver.

Configuring the Logon User Profile

The logon user profile is a bit confusing and not really a user profile. In *SystemRoot* **System32\\config**, the location of the per-computer hive files, you find a hive file called Default. This hive file is the one you see in **HKU\\.DEFAULT**. This isn't the same thing as the default user profile that you learned about in the previous sections. This is the per-user hive file that Windows 2000 uses prior to any user logging on to the computer. In other words, when the operating system is displaying the Logon to Windows dialog box, it gets its display and other settings from this hive file.

You can customize this hive file one of two ways:

- Load the hive file in *Regedt32*, customize it, and then unload the hive file.
- Copy Ntuser.dat from an existing user profile to Default in ***SystemRoot***
  System32\config.

Allowing User Profiles to Roam

Roaming user profiles follow users from computer to computer. When they log on to the computer, the operating system checks to see if they have a profile on the network. If so, it then checks to see if the network version is more recent than the local version. If the network version is more recent, the operating system copies the network version to the local computer; otherwise, it just uses the local user profile.

When users log off the computer and they have a roaming profile, Windows 2000 copies the profile back to the network. This is assuming that they have access to the network. If they don't, the operating system can't copy the changes to the network.

If the administrator assigns a roaming profile to the user prior to the user logging on to the computer, then Windows 2000 Professional automatically creates a roaming profile for him. Otherwise, it creates a local profile. If the administrator later changes the user's profile to a roaming profile, the user must manually change his profile to roaming:

1. In Control Panel, double-click the System icon.
2. On the User Profiles tab, click the user profile that you want to copy and then click Change Type.
3. In the Change Profile Type dialog box, click Roaming Profile.

Registry Size Limit

Windows 2000 reflects the Registry in the paged pool and therefore limits its size so that it doesn't gobble up memory. If the Registry isn't large enough, you'll get frequent error messages saying so. You can change the size of the Registry, however:

1. In Control Panel, double-click the System icon.
2. On the Advanced tab, click Performance Options.
3. On the Performance Options dialog box, click Change and you see the dialog box in Figure 6.4.
4. At the bottom of the dialog box, type the new maximum size of the Registry in the Maximum Registry Size (MB) text box.

FIGURE 6.4
Most users will never
have to change the
size of the Registry.

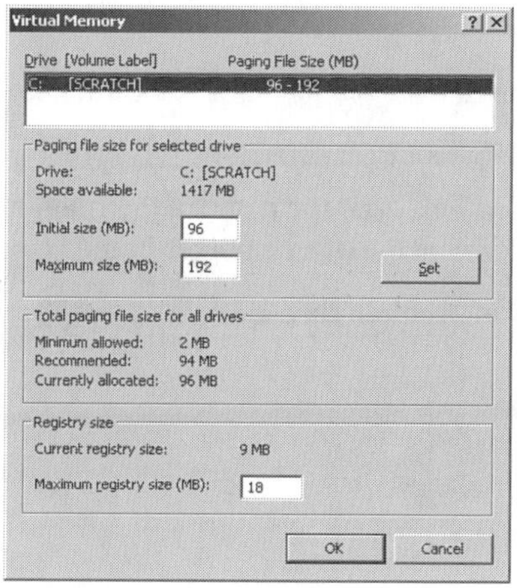

Virtual Memory

Drive [Volume Label]   Paging File Size (MB)

C: [SCRATCH]   96 - 192

Paging file size for selected drive

Drive: C: [SCRATCH]
Space available: 1417 MB

Initial size (MB):   96

Maximum size (MB):   192   Set

Total paging file size for all drives

Minimum allowed: 2 MB
Recommended: 94 MB
Currently allocated: 96 MB

Registry size

Current registry size: 9 MB

Maximum registry size (MB):   18

OK   Cancel

Remote Administration

A key part of reducing the total cost of owning any network or desktop operating system is remote administration. Remote administration enables administrators to stay at their desks, solve more problems because they're not roaming the halls, and keep computers running longer and better.

Most of the administrative tools support remote administration. Examples are Registry Editor, Microsoft Management Console, and all of its snap-ins. These tools enable users that have the appropriate rights on the remote computer to connect to the remote computer and administer it. Of course, our focus is the Registry, so the following two sections show you how to connect to a remote computer's Registry in both Registry Editors.

Regedit

Here's how to connect to a remote computer's Registry in *Regedit*:

1. On the Registry menu, click Connect Network Registry.
2. In the Connect Network Registry dialog box, type the name of the remote computer to which you want to connect or click Browse to select a computer.

When you connect to a remote computer's Registry, be aware of a few caveats. First, you only see **HKLM**, **HKU**, and **HKCR** under the computer's name in the key pane. Second, *Regedit* doesn't automatically reflect changes to the remote computer's Registry. To update the contents of the window, press **F5**.

Part

II

Ch

6

Regedt32

To connect to a remote computer's Registry in *Regedt32*, follow these steps:

1. On the Registry menu, click Select Computer.

2. In the Select Computer dialog box, type the name of the remote computer to which you want to connect or click the name of a computer in the Select Computer list.

The same caveats exist when viewing remote Registries in *Regedt32* as exist when doing the same in *Regedit*. ●

PART III

Customization

Customizing Windows 2000

In this chapter

Relocating Shell Folders

Folders that Microsoft Windows 2000 uses for special, specific purposes are *shell folders*. The Favorites, Start Menu, and My Documents folders are shell folders. Table 7.1 describes shell folders that Windows 2000 creates when you install them and includes their default paths. Their actual locations aren't important, however. That's because Windows 2000 uses their internal name to look up their paths in the Registry. You're able to change shell folder locations by pointing the operating system to their new locations.

You might want to change shell folder locations for many reasons. Share a single Favorites folder among several users, for example, by pointing Windows 2000 to a folder on the network. Maybe you prefer to put the My Documents folder in your home folder or move the Startup folder to a different location. Group Policy supports relocating most shell folders, but you can relocate shell folders without using Group Policy, which is particularly useful if you connect to a domain that's still managed by Windows NT Server 4.0.

Table 7.1   Windows 2000 Per-User Shell Folders

Name	Default Location
AppData	*UserProfile*\Application Data
Cache	*UserProfile*\Local Settings\Temporary Internet Files
Cookies	*UserProfile*\Cookies
Desktop	*UserProfile*\Desktop
Favorites	*UsreProfile*\Favorites
Fonts	*SystemRoot*\Fonts
History	*UserProfile*\Local Settings\History
Local AppData	*UserProfile*\Local Settings\Application Data
Local Settings	*UserProfile*\Local Settings
My Pictures	*UserProfile*\My Documents\Pictures
NetHood	*UserProfile*\NetHood
Personal	*UserProfile*\My Documents
PrintHood	*SystemRoot*\PrintHood
Programs	*UserProfile*\Start Menu\Programs
Recent	*UserProfile*\Recent
SendTo	*SystemRoot*\SendTo
Start Menu	*UserProfile*\Start Menu
Startup	*UserProfile*\Start Menu\Programs\Startup
Templates	*UserProfile*\ShellNew

N O T E The Local Settings folder is a new twist for Windows 2000. Chapter 6, "Administering Registries," describes how the operating system copies roaming user profiles to the network. The operating system copies everything in *UserProfile*, except the Local Settings folder, to the network each time users log off the computer. The assumption is that some settings should not follow users from computer to computer. Those settings are per-user and per-computer. ■

Per-User Shell Folders

HKCU\Software\Microsoft\Windows\CurrentVersion\Explorer\Shell Folders is the subkey from which Windows 2000 gets the location of per-user shell folders. Within this subkey are values for each shell folder, each of which has one of the names shown previously in Table 7.1. Each **REG_SZ** value is the fully qualified path of the folder's location. Notice another subkey at the same level called **User Shell Folders**, which also contains values for shell folders. The difference is that the values in **User Shell Folders** use environment variables to specify the location of users' profile folders.

To customize per-user shell folders, you update the appropriate value in both locations. For example, to change the location of Fergus' Favorites folder, change **Favorites** in both **Shell Folders** and **User Shell Folders**. In **User Shell Folders**, use environment variables to specify the location of Fergus' profile folder.

Per-Computer Shell Folders

You find similar subkeys in **HKLM**. The shell folders in **HKCU** are per-user, and the shell folders in **HKLM** are per-computer and apply to every user who logs on to the computer. The values have different names, too, including **Common AppData** and **Common Documents**. Customize per-computer shell folders the same way you do per-user shell folders, change the appropriate value in both **Shell Folders** and **User Shell Folders**, both of which are in **HKLM\SOFTWARE\Microsoft\Windows\CurrentVersion\Explorer**. Table 7.2 is similar to Table 7.1 and describes the per-computer shell folders that Windows 2000 creates.

Table 7.2   Windows 2000 Per-Computer Shell Folders

Name	Default Location
Common AppData	C:\Documents and Settings\All Users\Application Data
Common Desktop	C:\Documents and Settings\All Users\Desktop
Common Documents	C:\Documents and Settings\All Users\Documents
Common Programs	C:\Documents and Settings\All Users\Start Menu\Programs
Common Start Menu	C:\Documents and Settings\All Users\Start Menu
Common Startup	C:\Documents and Settings\All Users\Start Menu\Programs\Startup
Common Templates	C:\Documents and Settings\All Users\Templates

Part

III

Ch

7

> **CAUTION**
>
> Don't overlap shell folders. For instance, don't use the same path for the Favorites and My Documents folders. Windows 2000 creates `Desktop.ini`, a hidden file, in shell folders to add features to the folder. Overlapping shell folders causes the operating system to destroy the first folder's information in `Desktop.ini` with the second folder's information.

Working with Shell Folders

Some folders you see in My Computer or on the desktop don't actually exist on the hard disk. Windows Explorer displays them as folders and they act like folders, but they're actually objects that contain items that they display in a folder. Table 7.3 shows the unique class identifiers for many objects, which Windows 2000 defines in **HKCR\CLSID**. Thus, you find Control Panel at **{21EC2020-3AEA-1069-A2DD-08002B30309D}** and Recycle Bin at **{645FF040-5081-101B-9F08-00AA002F954E}** in **HKCR\CLSID**.

As you've learned, these folders don't exist on the hard disk; they exist in Windows Explorer's name space. *Name space* refers to the names of everything in a container—real or imaginary. I refer to My Computer's name space separately from the desktop's name space. Windows 2000 defines two different name spaces, one for each, as shown in Figure 7.1. Windows 2000 defines each namespace in **HKLM\Software\Microsoft\Windows\ CurrentVersion\explorer**. The subkey **Desktop\NameSpace** contains the name space for the desktop, and **MyComputer\NameSpace** contains the name space for My Computer.

FIGURE 7.1

The desktop and Windows Explorer use separate name spaces.

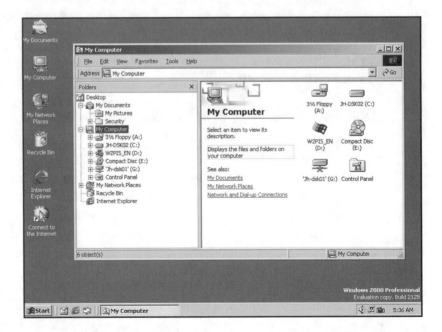

Windows 2000 adds each subkey it finds in **Desktop\NameSpace** to the desktop's name space and each subkey it finds in **MyComputer\NameSpace** to My Computer's name space. You usually see the class identifiers for the Recycle Bin and My Documents folders in the desktop's name space and My Computer's namespace is empty. What you don't see in either are subkeys for Control Panel, Printers, Network and Dial-Up Connections, and Internet Explorer. These are built-in to the operating system. You can't remove Control Panel from My Computer, but you can remove the Internet Explorer and Network and Dial-Up Connections icons from the desktop, as you will learn in "Removing a Shell Folder," later in this chapter.

Table 7.3   Useful Class Identifiers

Folder	Class Identifiers
Cabinet	{0CD7A5C0-9F37-11CE-AE65-08002B2E1262}
Control Panel	{21EC2020-3AEA-1069-A2DD-08002B30309D}
Printers	{2227A280-3AEA-1069-A2DE-08002B30309D}
My Documents	{450D8FBA-AD25-11D0-98A8-0800361B1103}
Recycle Bin	{645FF040-5081-101B-9F08-00AA002F954E}
Network … Connections	{7007ACC7-3202-11D1-AAD2-00805FC1270E}
Briefcase	{85BBD920-42A0-1069-A2E4-08002B30309D}
Internet Explorer	{871C5380-42A0-1069-A2EA-08002B30309D}
Web Folders	{BDEADF00-C265-11d0-BCED-00A0C90AB50F}
Fonts	{D20EA4E1-3957-11d2-A40B-0C5020524152}
Administrative Tools	{D20EA4E1-3957-11d2-A40B-0C5020524152}
Scheduled Tasks	{D6277990-4C6A-11CF-8D87-00AA0060F5BF}
Search Results	{E17D4FC0-5564-11D1-83F2-00A0C90DC849}

TIP

Table 7.3 listed the folders that you can put on the desktop or on the Start menu after installing Windows 2000, but other applications might provide special folders you can use as well. How do you find them? Search the Registry for any class identifiers that have a **ShellFolder** subkey with an **attributes** value entry. The default value entry of the class identifier describes the folder.

▶ **See** Chapter 13, "File Associations" **p. 257**, to learn more about class identifiers and how Windows 2000 stores them in the Registry.

Renaming Items on the Desktop

You can rename the My Computer, Network and Dial-Up Connections, and Internet Explorer icons on the desktop. Click Rename on their shortcut menus, and then type the new name of the icon. Renaming Recycle Bin and some other icons is a bit harder, however, because they don't have a similar command on their shortcut menus.

Part

III

Ch

7

Regardless, you can rename the icons you see in Table 7.3 by changing the default value of the icon's class identifier in **HKCR\CLSID**. To rename Recycle Bin, change the default value of **HKCR\CLSID\{645FF040-5081-101B-9F08-00AA002F954E}** to the name that you want Windows 2000 to display on the desktop and in Windows Explorer. To rename Control Panel's icon, change the default value of **HKCR\CLSID\{21EC2020-3AEA-1069-A2DD-08002B30309D}**.

N O T E The default value of each class identifier in **Desktop\NameSpace** and **MyComputer\NameSpace** also contains the name of the icon. Changing it doesn't change the name of the icon on the desktop or in My Computer, however. ■

Removing a Shell Folder

How you remove a shell folder from the desktop depends on the folder. If you're removing the Recycle Bin or My Documents folders, for example, delete the folder's class identifier subkey from **HKLM\Software\Microsoft\Windows\CurrentVersion\explorer\Desktop\NameSpace**. Easy enough. You don't see a subkey for Internet Explorer or Network Neighborhood in the desktop's namespace, but you can remove them from the desktop by setting the following **REG_DWORD** values under **HKCU\Software\Microsoft\Windows\CurrentVersion\ Policies\Explorer**:

Icon	Value	Enabled	Disabled
Internet Explorer	**NoInternetIcon**	0x00000000	0x00000001
Network Neighborhood	**NoNetHood**	0x00000000	0x00000001

▶ **See** Chapter 8, "Using Microsoft Tweak UI" **p. 133**, to learn an easier way to remove icons from the desktop.

▶ **See** Chapter 15, "Per-Computer Settings" **p. 303**, for more information about namespaces in Windows Explorer.

Customizing Icons

Icons come from program files (.exe and .dll), icon files (.ico and .bmp), and similar files. You specify an icon in an icon file by specifying the path and filename of the file. EXE, DLL, and RES files can contain any number of icons, however. You reference a particular icon in such files using the icon's index, starting from 0. The first icon is 0, the second is 1, and so on. You specify an icon in an EXE, DLL, or RES file by giving the path and filename of the file, followed by the index of the icon, like this: *path\filename,index*.

There is one more convention of which you should be aware. Windows 2000 allows a programmer to assign a fixed identifier to each icon. This identifier is usually called a *resource identifier*. The resource ID is any arbitrary integer value, such as 1037, that provides an easier way for the programmer to reference an exact icon without having to figure out the icon's index. The programmer can assign the integer value to a symbol and then use that symbol in the code. You can also specify an icon using its resource ID, assuming you know it, by writing a line like this: *path\filename,-resource*. The following list shows you an example of both methods for specifying the location of an icon:

Index	C:\Windows\System\Shell32.dll,9
Resource ID	`C:\Windows\System\Shell32.dll,-37`

Changing the Icons for Files

Changing the icons for files is similar to changing the icon for a shell folder. Instead of changing the default value entry of **HKCR\CLSID\clsid\DefaultIcon** to the location of the icon, change the default value of **HKCR\progid\DefaultIcon**. The trick is to find the program identifier associated with a file extension. Look up the file extension in **HKCR**. For example, the subkey for the .doc file extension is **HKCR\.doc**. The default value of each file extension's subkey is the name of the program identifier it's associated with. Thus, to change the icon displayed for a file using a particular extension, follow these steps:

1. Note the default value entry of **HKCR\\.*ext***, where *.ext* is the file extension. The default value entry is the program identifier that the extension is associated with.

2. Open **HKCR*progid*\DefaultIcon**, where *progid* is the program identifier you looked up in step 1.

3. Change the default value of **DefaultIcon** to indicate the location of the icon you want to use for files associated with that program.

If after changing the icon for a program identifier and refreshing the display you don't notice a change, you'll have to do a bit of tracking to find any overriding **DefaultIcon** subkeys. Check to see if a class identifier is associated with the program identifier (look in the program identifier's **CLSID** subkey), and look up that class under **HKCR\CLSID**. If you see a **DefaultIcon** subkey under the class identifier's subkey, it might be overriding the icon specified in the program identifier. Note also that some icons are specified via the **ShellIcons** key, as you'll learn in the next section.

Shell Folders

Windows 2000 retrieves the icon to use for shell folders from the **DefaultIcon** subkey of the class identifier in **HKCR\CLSID**. The default value entry of this subkey contains the icon specification you just learned about. Thus, to change the icon that Windows 2000 uses for a shell folder, follow these steps:

1. Remove a file called `ShellIconCache` from *SystemRoot*. (See the upcoming note to learn more about this file.)

2. Change the default value entry of **HKCR\CLSID\clsid\DefaultIcon** to the location of the icon. *clsid* is the class identifier of the object you're changing. See Table 7.3 for a list of possibilities.

3. Refresh the desktop and Windows Explorer so that you can see your changes. To refresh the desktop, click Refresh on the desktop's shortcut menu. To refresh Windows Explorer, click Refresh on the View menu.

N O T E   Windows 2000 caches icons in a file called ShellIconCache, which you find in **SystemRoot**. It does this so that it doesn't have to reload the icons from their original locations, which makes icons display on the desktop and in Windows Explorer much faster. You can adjust the size of this cache by changing the value called **Max Cached Icons** in **HKLM\Software\Microsoft\Windows\CurrentVersion\ explorer** to any number greater than 512, which is the default value. Create this **REG_DWORD** value if it doesn't exist. ■

Shell Icons

The icons you see on the Start menu don't come from **HKCR**, as do the icons for shell folders and files. They come from Shell32.dll. Ditto for the icons that Windows 2000 displays for different types of disk drives.

You can replace any shell icon by adding a string value entry to **HKLM\Software\ Microsoft\Windows\CurrentVersion\explorer\Shell Icons**. If you don't see this subkey, add it. The name of the value entry is the index of the icon in Shell32. The value is the location of the icon: a path if you're using an .ico file, or a path and index if you're using a .dll, .exe, or .res file. Windows 2000 substitutes your icon for each entry it finds in **Shell Icons**. Thus, to use icon 28 in Cool.dll instead of the default icon for My Computer, create a new value called **15** in **Shell Icons** and set its value to **C:\Windows\System\Cool.dll,28**. If you don't see the change you made after refreshing the desktop, follow these steps to force Windows 2000 to notice the new icon:

1. Restart the computer in Safe Mode.

2. Delete the ShellIconCache file from \Windows. You might have to show hidden files in Windows Explorer to see this file.

3. Change the icon in **Shell Icons** as described in the preceding paragraph.

4. Restart the computer normally.

Specifying certain icons in **Shell Icons** has no effect. Windows 2000 uses the icon specified in the **DefaultIcon** subkey of a class identifier instead of the icon listed in **Shell Icons**. Thus, adding entries for the Recycle Bin, Dial-Up Networking, Control Panel, and Printers icons to **Shell Icons** doesn't do anything. To change these icons, change their **DefaultIcon** subkey as described in the earlier section "Shell Folders." Windows 2000 defines the icons for various **DefaultIcon** keys, too, so changing that icon in **Shell Icons** doesn't change what you see in Windows Explorer.

TIP Windows 2000 contains many files that have icons. The easiest way to view the icons in a file is to download an icon viewer from your favorite shareware site. My personal favorite is IconRipper, which you can download from http://www.hotfiles.com.

Folder Icons

Windows Explorer takes special notice any time it finds a hidden file called `Desktop.ini` within a system folder. The attribute of the folder in conjunction with this file indicates that the folder is special and usually points to an object that handles the folder's contents.

You can use this file to indicate an icon for any folder, as well as a tip that Windows Explorer displays when you hover over it with the mouse pointer. Create a `Desktop.ini` file and place it in the folder, setting the hidden attribute using the Attrib command or the General tab of the *file* Properties dialog box. You should also turn on the folder's system attribute, which you can only do by typing **attrib +s** *foldername* at the MS-DOS command prompt. The file should look similar to the following example of a `Desktop.ini` file. Set *IconFile* to the path of the .ico file or to the path of an .exe, .dll, or .res file and the icon's index. You can also set *InfoTip* to any text you want Windows Explorer to display in a pop-up window when you hover the mouse pointer over the folder.

```
[.ShellClassInfo]
IconFile=C:\Windows\Winupd.ico
InfoTip=This is the tip Windows displays when you hover over the folder.
```

Documenting Changes to the Registry

Keeping track of each change you make is difficult. You can keep a separate log file, but you're not likely to keep it updated, and the information isn't handy when you really need it.

The best way to document each change you make is to add a bogus value containing a description of the change you made. You might include the date you made the change, too, so you can relate changes you make to changes in the operating system's behavior. The best name to use for this bogus value entry is a combination of the changed value entry's name and the word "Note." Thus, if you change a value called **maxMTU**, add a new string value called **maxMTUNote** and set its value to a brief description of the change you made and the date you made it.

When you name the notes this way and put them within the subkey containing the changed value, they appear next to the original value. For instance, to continue the example, the two values **maxMTU** and **maxMTUNote** would appear next to each other in the subkey that contains them both.

Drive Letters

Windows Explorer examines an undocumented and seldom-used branch of **HKLM** called **Software\Microsoft\Windows\CurrentVersion\explorer\DriveIcons** to find drive icons. It looks for a subkey matching each possible drive letter and another subkey under those called **DefaultIcon**. The default value of **DefaultIcon** should be the specification of an icon. You

Part
III

Ch
7

may recall that you can specify the path and filename of an .ico or other image file. You can also use the path and filename of a .dll, .exe, or .res file in combination with an index number, or the path and filename of a .dll, .exe, or .res file in combination with a resource ID.

If you want to display a custom icon for drive D, for example, add **D\DefaultIcon** to **DriveIcons** and change the default value of **DefaultIcon** to the location of the icon. If you want to display a custom icon for drive X, add **X\DefaultIcon** to **DriveIcons**, and change the default value entry of **DefaultIcon**.

Disk Icons

Adding values **5** through **12** to **Shell Icons** affects every drive of that type. Specifying a new icon for removable drives by adding a value entry of **7** to **Shell Icons** changes the icon for every removable drive on the computer, for example.

You can use a different icon for each disk individually, however, including individual hard disks, floppy disks, and network volumes. Have you ever noticed that when you insert a certain CD-ROM into the drive, Windows 98 automatically starts it and changes the icon that it displays in Windows Explorer? This works because the disk has an Autorun.inf file in its root folder. This file contains a line that looks like icon=*location*, which causes Windows 2000 to display the icon specified by *location* in Windows Explorer as long as that disk is mounted. *location* can be the path to an .ico file, or it can be the path to a .dll, .exe, or .res file and an index.

The first trick to make this work for devices other than CD-ROMs is to enable Autorun.inf for those devices. Open **HKCU\Software\Microsoft\Windows\CurrentVersion\ Policies\Explorer**. You see a value entry called **NoDriveTypeAutoRun**. This value entry indicates the drives for which Autorun.inf is disabled. It's a four-byte binary value entry, and each bit corresponds to a different type of drive, as described in Table 7.4. Setting the bit corresponding to a drive type to 1 disables Autorun.inf for that type. Setting the bit to 0 enables Autorun.inf. The default value for this entry is 95 00 00 00, or 1001 0101 binary, which means that hard drives, CD-ROMs, and RAM drives are enabled although other drive types are not. Change this value to 91 00 00 00, or 1001 0001 binary, if you want to include removable disks such as floppy disks and ZIP disks in the list of drives for which Autorun.inf is enabled.

Table 7.4   The NoDriveTypeAutoRun Value Entry

Bit	Drive Type
0	Unknown Drives
2	Removable Drives
3	Hard Drives
4	Remote Drives
5	CD-ROM Drives
6	RAM Drives

Now that you've enabled `Autorun.inf` for the appropriate devices, you're ready to change the icon that Windows Explorer displays for each disk. Create an `Autorun.inf` file and place it in the root folder of each disk. The `Autorun.inf` file should look similar to the following sample Autorun.inf file. Replace everything to the right of `icon=` with the location of the icon, whether it's an .ico file or an indexed icon within an .exe, .dll, or .res file. Remember that you can create a unique `Autorun.inf` file for each disk. Every one of your floppy disks can use a distinct icon, for example, and you can store the icon file on the disk itself.

```
[autorun]
icon=c:\windows\system32\cool.dll,8
```

N O T E Changing a drive's icon by creating an `Autorun.inf` file will not work in all drive types in all computers. It depends largely on the hardware and the device driver provided by the manufacturer. Experiment with this file to see what you can customize. Note that you might have to press F5 in Windows Explorer to see the disk's new icon. ▪

Mastering Shortcut Menus

Figure 7.2 shows a typical shortcut menu, which you open by right-clicking a file or folder. Windows Explorer builds a shortcut menu from a variety of sources, all of which are under **HKCR** in the following order:

- ***class*\shell**   You see these at the top of the shortcut menu, as shown in the figure.
- ***class*\shellex\ContextMenuHandlers**   Each subkey under this key defines an object that adds commands to the shortcut menu. The name of the subkey is the class identifier of the object, and its default value entry is its name; or the subkey is the name of the object, and the default value entry contains its class identifier.
- ***\shell**   This key adds commands that are common to all types of files. You see these just below the class's own commands and just above the first divider.
- ***\shellex\ContextMenuHandlers**   Each subkey under this key defines an object that adds commands to every file's shortcut menu. See ***class*\shellex\ContextMenuHandlers**, earlier in this list.
- **\AllFilesystemObjects\shellex\ContextMenuHandlers**   Each subkey under this defines an object that adds commands to every file system object's shortcut menu. In most cases, this just adds the Send To command.
- **Shell32.dll**   Windows 2000 adds a number of commands that are built-in to the operating system. These are also known as *canonical verbs*, which means they're officially supported commands defined by the operating system. Windows Explorer places these at the bottom of each file's shortcut menu, including commands such as Cut, Copy, and so on.

FIGURE 7.2
Windows 2000 defines menu items such as Properties that you see below the first divider.

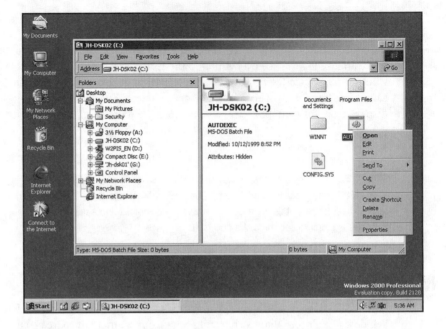

When you right-click a file for which Windows Explorer doesn't find an associated program, you see the Open With command. This is also the default command, so if you double-click a file with no association, you also see the Open With dialog box. The commands for files with no associations come from **HKCR\unknown\shell**. **unknown\shell** typically contains a single subkey, a verb, for the Open With command, but you can add additional commands to it, just as you can for any other file or class. You can add a command to **unknown\shell** that opens an unassociated file in Microsoft Notepad, for instance.

N O T E   The easiest way to find a subkey for a file type or object is to search for its name. To find the class identifier for the Recycle Bin in the Registry, for instance, search the Registry for the string "Recycle Bin." To quickly find a file type, note the description that Windows Explorer displays for it in a file's property sheet, and search for that string. ■

Windows Explorer handles the shortcut menu for objects similarly, except that it looks in **HKCR\CLSID*clsid*\shell** for commands instead, as well as in **HKCR\CLSID*clsid*\shellex\ ContextMenuHandlers**, which you learned about earlier in this section. One addition, however, is that it looks in **HKCR\CLSID*clsid*\shellfolder** for an **attributes** value entry that enables or disables built-in or canonical verbs defined in Shell32.dll. You'll learn more about **attributes** a bit later in this chapter.

The organization of each **shell** subkey is the same. The default value entry of the **shell** subkey contains the name of the verb that defines the default command on the shortcut menu.

You see a subkey for each verb, each of which has a **command** subkey whose default value entry contains the command line to execute. The default value entry for the verb optionally contains the text that Windows Explorer will display on the shortcut menu for the command. For example, the O̲pen command on a text file's shortcut menu is due to the values shown in Figure 7.3. What you don't see in the figure is that the default value entry of **shell** can contain the name of the default verb, and the default value entry of **open** can contain the text that Windows Explorer displays on the shortcut menu.

FIGURE 7.3
This figure shows two commands: O̲pen and Print.

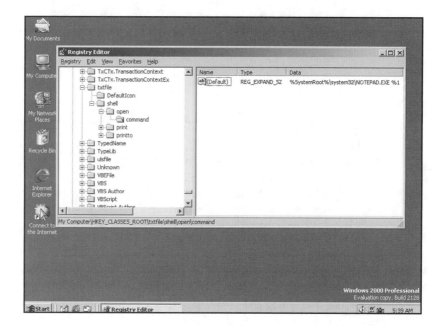

Adding Commands

Adding commands to a shortcut menu requires you to duplicate the structure under the class's **shell** key, which you learned about in the preceding section. This structure looks like ***verb*\command**. ***verb*** is the name of the verb, and the default value of ***command*** contains the command line you want to execute when the user chooses that verb. Thus, to add a command to a .txt file's shortcut menu that opens it in Microsoft Wordpad, follow steps similar to these (see Listing 7.1 for an outline of the subkeys and value entries added using these steps):

1. Look up the program identifier associated with a .txt file by looking at the default value entry of **.txt** under **HKCR**.

2. Open **HKCR*progid*\shell**, where ***progid*** is the program identifier you looked up in step 1. If you don't see the **shell** subkey, add it.

3. Add a subkey under **shell** called **wordpad**. Change the default value entry of **wordpad** to "Open in Wordpad" so that you'll see this text on the shortcut menu.

4. Add a subkey under **shell\wordpad** called **command**, and set its default value entry to **"C:\Program Files\Accessories\Wordpad.exe "%1""**, which causes Windows 2000 to open the target file in WordPad when you choose this command from the shortcut menu.

Listing 7.1   Adding a Command to a Text File's Shortcut Menu

```
HKEY_CLASSES_ROOT
    txtfile
        shell
            wordpad
                default = "Open in Wordpad"
                command
                    default = "C:\Program Files\Accessories\ Wordpad.exe "%1"
```

The command line for commands vary. In cases in which you want to open the file in a specific program, you can sometimes get away with providing just the path and filename of the program. You can use long or short (8.3 characters) filenames. Windows 2000 automatically passes the name of the target file as a command-line argument to the program. In other cases, you must explicitly specify the location of the filename by using the "%1" placeholder, which Windows 2000 substitutes with the target filename when it launches the command line. This becomes particularly important when the command line contains switches and you must include the filename in a specific place within it: **"myprog /p /k "%1" /s"**, for example. If you think the program might have trouble with long filenames that include spaces, be sure to put **"%1"** in quotes, as shown previously in Listing 7.1. This ensures that the program won't assume that everything up to the first space is the filename and that everything after the first space is additional filenames or garbage.

N O T E   Put **"%1"** in the command line at the exact location where you want Windows 2000 to expand the path and name of the target file when it launches the command line. ■

Useful Things to Add to a Context Menu

The following are some useful commands to add to a folder or file's shortcut menu:

- To open a command prompt with a particular folder as the current working directory, add a new verb to the **Directory** and **Drive** classes, whose command line is **%SystemRoot%\System32\cmd.com /k cd "%1"**. Then, right-click any folder or disk, and choose the new command you added to the shortcut menu.

- To open Windows Explorer with a particular folder at the root, add the following command to the **Folder** class: **explorer.exe /e,/root,/idlist,%I**. Then, right-click any folder and choose the new command you added to the shortcut menu.

- To open a Control Panel icon by typing its filename in the **Run** dialog box, rename the **cplopenkey** subkey of the **cplfile** file type to **open**. Then, type the filename, perhaps `Powercfg.cpl`, of the Control Panel icon in the Run dialog box.

- To open Tweak UI from My Computer, add the following command line to **{20D04FE0-3AEA-1069-A2D8-08002B30309D}**: **C:\WINDOWS\rundll32.exe shell32.dll,Control_RunDLL Tweakui.cpl**. Then, right-click My Computer, and choose the new command you added to the shortcut menu. You can add any other Control Panel application to My Computer's shortcut menu by replacing `Tweakui.cpl` with the application's filename.

Changing the Default Command

The default command of any shortcut menu is the command that Windows Explorer executes whenever you double-click the file. You'll also notice that the default command is bolded in the shortcut menu. Here's how to change the default for any shortcut menu:

1. Locate the class's **shell** subkey under **HKCR**. For instance, text files are in **HKC\txtfile\shell**.

2. Note the names of the verbs under **shell**, **open**, and **print** for text files, choosing the one you want to be the default command on the shortcut menu.

3. Change the default value entry of the **shell** key so that it contains the name of the verb representing the default command. Set it to **print** if you want the default command for text files to be printing them.

Here's a real-world example for changing the default command of a shortcut menu. When you open a folder on the desktop, Windows 2000 opens it in a single-pane window instead of a double-pane window. If you change the default command of **HKCR\folder** from **open** to **explore**, Windows 2000 will open it in a double-pane Explorer window instead of a single-pane window.

TIP Changing the default value of **folder\shell** to **explore** also changes the default command for the My Computer icon's shortcut menu. After making this change, double-click the My Computer icon on the desktop to open it in the double-pane Explorer window rather than the single-pane window.

Changing the Menu's Appearance

You can change the text that Windows Explorer displays on any shortcut menu command that comes from a **shell** key. It doesn't matter whether the key comes from a program identifier, defined as **HKCR*progid***, or from an object, defined as **HKCR\CLSID*clsid***. However, you can't change the text that a context menu handler, defined in a **ContextMenuHandler** subkey of a class, puts on a shortcut menu. Nor can you change the text that Windows 98 displays for the built-in commands you see at the bottom of a shortcut menu.

To change the text you see on a shortcut menu, find the class' **shell** key in the Registry. As you'll recall, each command is a verb in **shell**. Change the default value of each verb to the text you want to see on the shortcut menu. To change the text you see for the Open command of a text file's shortcut menu to Edit, for instance, change the default value entry of **txtfile\shell\open** to **&Edit** under **HKCR**. Windows Explorer maintains the capitalization you use in the default entry, and you can indicate a hotkey by putting an ampersand (&) in front of the letter. Here are a few examples of what various default value entries look like on a shortcut menu:

In the Registry	On the Shortcut Menu
open	open
&Open	Open
open in Wordpad	open in Wordpad
open in &Wordpad	open in Wordpad

Things get a bit more complicated if the default value entry for a verb is empty. Windows Explorer gets the name from one of two places if a name is not explicitly defined in the Registry:

- **Shell32.dll**   Windows 2000 retrieves the string to display on the shortcut menu from Shell32.dll. It does this for the canonical verbs Find, Open, Open With, and Print.

- **Subkey name**   Windows 2000 uses the name of the verb as the text it displays on the shortcut menu. For instance, if the **HCKR\txtfile\shell\edit** subkey's default value entry is empty, Windows 98 puts edit on the shortcut menu.

Removing Commands

To remove a command from a shortcut menu, identify where in the Registry the command is defined. Then remove the command as described in the following list:

- **shell**   If the command comes from a **shell** key, remove the command's verb. This is true for *, **unknown**, and any other place where you see a **shell** subkey.

- **shellex\ContextMenuHandler**   If the command comes from a **ContextMenuHandler** subkey of a file type or object, remove the handler's subkey. This might remove multiple commands from the shortcut menu, however, depending on how many commands it adds.

- **Shell32.dll**   If the command is on an object's shortcut menu and is one of the canonical verbs defined by Shell32.dll, change the object's **attributes** value. You'll learn more about this value following this list.

Many objects have an **attributes** value in **HKCR\CLSID**_clsid_**\ShellFolder**, where _clsid_ is the class identifier of the object. This value indicates the canonical verbs, or built-in commands, which Windows 2000 displays on the object's shortcut menu. **attributes** is a 4-byte binary value, with each bit representing a flag that enables or disables a specific command. Table 7.5 describes the bits currently used by Windows 2000. Setting a particular bit to 0 disables the command, and setting it to 1 enables the command. Remember that you count bits right to left in a binary value, so bit 0 is the first bit on the right, bit 1 is the second bit on the right, and so on. Because the Registry shows **attributes** as hexadecimal values, you must convert them to binary to figure out which commands are enabled. Work with this value in binary until you're ready to change **attributes**, and then convert it to hexadecimal.

Here's a real-world example. The **attributes** value for the Internet Explorer icon is 72000000 in hexadecimal, which is 11100100000000000000000000000000 in binary. Counting from right to left, bits 25, 28, 29, and 30 are 1s. Thus, Windows 2000 displays the Cut, Rename, Delete, and Properties commands on Internet Explorer's shortcut menu. You can remove the Cut command from the shortcut menu by turning off bit 25, which leaves you with a hexadecimal value of 70000000.

Table 7.5	Bits in the attributes Value
Bit Number	**Command**
30	Properties
29	Delete
28	Rename
25	Cut
24	Copy
16	Paste
5	Open and Explore for the Recycle Bin

TIP Many times, you'll need to convert hexadecimal to binary and vice versa as you edit the Registry. Use the Windows Calculator in Scientific mode to do so quickly.

Adding New Templates

Click New on a folder's shortcut menu to display a menu of new documents you can create in the folder, as shown in Figure 7.4. This is a quick way to create a new document. Then open the document to edit its contents.

HKCR*ext*\ShellNew, where .*ext* is a file extension such as .doc or .txt, defines a template for the New menu. You can put only one template on the New menu for each file extension. You add one of three value entries to this subkey to add the extension to the New menu:

- **NullFile**   Make sure this string value entry is empty, causing Windows 2000 to create an empty file in the folder when the user chooses this file type.

FIGURE 7.4
The Folder and
Shortcut items are
hard-coded by the
operating system;
you can't change
or remove them.

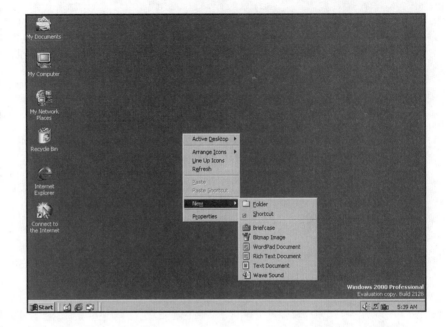

- **FileName**   Copy a template file with the same file extension to \Windows\ShellNew,
  and then set this value to the name of the file, excluding the path. When the user
  chooses this file type from the New menu, Windows 2000 creates a new file using
  the template in \Windows\ShellNew.

- **Data**   This is a binary value whose contents Windows 2000 uses to create the new file
  when the user chooses it from the New menu. Windows 2000 just copies the bytes
  from this value entry directly into the file.

▶ **See** Chapter 8, "Using Microsoft Tweak UI" **p. 133**, to learn a much easier way to add
templates to Windows 2000.

Customizing the Start Menu

The following sections describe various ways you can customize the Start menu. You'll learn

- How to disable any submenu on the Start menu
- How to restore a sorted Start menu
- How to customize a submenu's icon
- How to add shell folders as cascading menus

Disabling Commands

Each of the policies you see in Table 7.6 is under **HKCU\Software\Microsoft\Windows\CurrentVersion\Policies\Explorer**. If you don't find this subkey, create it. Then add the **REG_DWORD** value corresponding to the submenu or command you want to disable, as shown in the table. To disable the menu command, set the policy value to 1; to enable the menu command, set the policy value to 0.

Table 7.6   Start Menu Policies

Value	Description
NoFavoritesMenu	Enables or disables the Favorites menu
NoFind	Enables or disables the Find menu
NoRecentDocsMenu	Enables or disables the Documents menu
NoRun	Enables or disables the Run command
NoLogOff	Enables or disables the Log Off command

Restoring the Sort Order

With the introduction of Internet Explorer 4.0 into Windows 95 and the evolution of Internet Explorer 5 with Windows 200, the Start and Favorites menus are customizable. The user can sort the menu using drag and drop or even edit both menus in place by right-clicking the objects on it.

Windows 2000 stores the sort order of the Start menu in **HKCU\Software\Microsoft\Windows\CurrentVersion\Explorer\MenuOrder**. You find two subkeys here: **Favorites** and **Start Menu**. Within each, you find a value called **Order** that indicates the sort order of all the items on the menu. You can't really change the sort order by editing the **MenuOrder**, because editing it is almost impossible. You can use the following two tricks to make working with the Start menu's sort order easier, however:

- Export the entire **MenuOrder** branch to a REG file that you can later import to restore the sort order of the Start menu if it goes awry.
- Remove the **Favorites** and **Start Menu** subkeys of **MenuOrder** to restore the sort order for both menus to their Windows 2000 defaults.

Each level within this branch contains a **Menu** subkey that describes how the folders and shortcuts are sorted.

The Customizing Commands Icon

The earlier section "Shell folders" showed you how to customize the icons that Windows 2000 displays in various locations. These icons include the images you see on the Start menu. Specifically, you add a string value entry to **HKLM\Software\Microsoft\Windows\CurrentVersion\explorer\Shell Icons** that corresponds to the command you want to

Part

III

Ch

7

change, as described in Table 7.7. If you want to change the icon that the Start menu displays for the Settings command, for example, create a string value entry called **21** to this key. Assign to the default value entry of the new key the location of the icon you want to use. The location can be the path and filename of an .ico file, or it can be the path and filename of an .exe, .dll, or .res file combined with the index of the icon. Here are more specific instructions for changing an icon on the Start menu to make sure Windows 2000 updates your changes:

1. Restart the Computer in Safe Mode.
2. Delete the ShellIconCache file from \Windows. You might have to show hidden files in Windows Explorer to see this file.
3. Add the value entry corresponding to one of the value entries in Table 7.7, and set its default value entry to the location of the icon.
4. Restart the computer normally.

Table 7.7 Customizing Icons on the Start Menu

Value Name	Command
19	Programs
20	Documents
21	Settings
22	Find
23	Help
24	Run
25	Suspend
26	Eject PC
27	Shut Down

Adding Shell Folders

Some of the objects you saw earlier in Table 7.2 make great additions to the Start menu. In particular, the Control Panel, Network and Dial-Up Connections, Printers, Recycle Bin, and Scheduled Tasks folders work well on the Start menu (but the others don't). When you add them, Windows 2000 displays their contents as cascading menus instead of opening a separate folder to display their contents. Figure 7.5 shows you an example of what Control Panel looks like when you add it to the Start menu as a cascading menu.

To add one of the objects from Table 7.2 to the Start menu, create a new folder anywhere within the Start Menu folder and name it *name.clsid*. *name* is the name of the folder as shown in the table, and *clsid* is the class identifier of the folder as shown in the table. By the way, make sure you include the brackets in the class identifier. The following list shows you the names to use for the five folders just mentioned:

Control Panel	{21EC2020-3AEA-1069-A2DD-08002B30309D}
Networking...	{992CFFA0-F557-101A-88EC-00DD010CCC48}
Printers	{2227A280-3AEA-1069-A2DE-08002B30309D}
Recycle Bin	{645FF040-5081-101B-9F08-00AA002F954E}
Scheduled Tasks	{D6277990-4C6A-11CF-8D87-00AA0060F5BF}

FIGURE 7.5
Control Panel is much easier to access if you add it to the Start menu as a cascading menu.

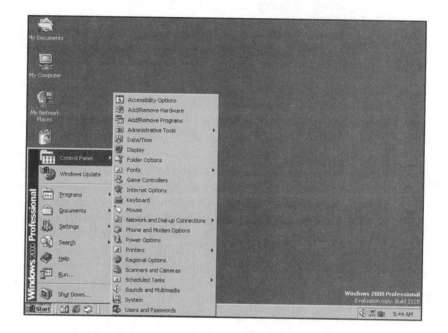

Personalizing Internet Explorer 5

Internet Explorer 5 provides a number of methods you can use to customize it. The Internet Explorer Administration Kit (IEAK) enables you to completely customize Internet Explorer. You can even change the text that appears on the browser's title bar. You can't change most of the settings via the Registry; you can only change them by creating INS files via the administration kit. *Microsoft Windows 2000 Resource Kit,* published by Microsoft Press, includes a copy of the Internet Explorer Administration Kit.

The remainder of this section describes three ways you can customize Internet Explorer 5 via the Registry. You can extend its shortcut menus, for one. You can also change the bitmap displayed on the background of toolbars and you can change the default protocol that the browser uses when you type a URL with the protocol.

Part
III

Ch
7

Extending the Shortcut Menus

Internet Explorer 5 displays a shortcut menu when you right-click anywhere within a Web page. You can add items to this shortcut menu, each of which are linked to scripts you create and place in an HTML file. You can customize the shortcut menu to open a frame in a new window, for example, or you can customize it to resize the font in a block of text.

To add a command to Internet Explorer 5's shortcut menu, create a new subkey under **HKCU\Software\Microsoft\Internet Explorer\MenuExt**. If you don't see **MenuExt**, add it. Internet Explorer uses this name for the command's text on the shortcut menu. You can put an ampersand (&) in front of any character to indicate it as a hotkey. Then, set the default value to the path and filename of the HTML file containing the script that executes the command. If you want to add a command called Test to the shortcut menu that launches an HTML file called Test.htm in C:\Windows, you would add a subkey called **&Test** to **MenuExt** and set its default value entry to C:\Windows\Test.htm.

When you click the command in the shortcut menu, Internet Explorer opens the HTML file and executes any inline scripts it finds there. The scripting property external.menuArguments contains the window object on which you executed the command. Thus, if you right-click a Web page and choose Test, external.menuArguments contains the window object on which you right-clicked. With access to the window object, you can pretty much do anything you want to the current Web page, including changing its contents, format, and so on. With all that said, the following listing is an example of an HTML file that changes the font size of a text selection so that you can read it easier. To try it out, type the listing in an HTML file, add a subkey to **MenuExt**, and set its default value entry to the path and filename of the HTML file. Then, open a Web page in Internet Explorer, select some text, right-click the selected text, and choose the new command you added.

```
<HTML>
<SCRIPT LANGUAGE="JavaScript" defer>
var objWin = external.menuArguments;
var objDoc = objWin.document;
var objSel = objDoc.selection;
var objRange = objSel.createRange();
objRange.execCommand( "FontSize", 0, "+2" );
</SCRIPT>
</HTML>
```

You can add an additional value, called **Contexts,** to the command's subkey that controls which context menus display the command. Add this 1-byte binary value to the command's subkey and set its value according to the masks described in the following table. If you wanted to limit the previous example so that it only appears on the shortcut menu displayed for text selections, add the binary value called **Contexts** to the new subkey under **MenuExt** and set its value to **0x10**. Note that you might have to restart Internet Explorer 5 to see your changes to this subkey.

Value	Menu
0x01	Default Menu
0x02	Image Menu
0x04	Control Menu
0x08	Table Menu
0x10	Text Selection Menu
0x11	Anchor Menu
0x12	Unknown Menu

N O T E This section assumes some familiarity with how to write scripts for Web pages, whether they are in VBScript or JavaScript. If you don't know how to write scripts, check out Macmillan Publishing's *Special Edition Using HTML* or one of Macmillan's other books on the topic. You can also find more information about extending Internet Explorer 5's shortcut menus at Microsoft's Web site: `http://www.microsoft.com/ie/ie40/powertoys/Contextm.htm`. ▪

Changing the Toolbar's Background

The background you see on Internet Explorer's toolbar is nothing more than a bitmap. To change the background, create a new string value entry called **BackBitmap** under **HKCU\Software\Microsoft\Internet Explorer\Toolbar**. Change the value to the path of the bitmap you want to display on the background of Internet Explorer's toolbar. If the bitmap doesn't fill the entire toolbar, Internet Explorer tiles it horizontally and vertically.

Changing the Default Protocol

If you type a URL in Internet Explorer's toolbar or in the Run dialog box, Internet Explorer automatically prefixes it with the appropriate protocol. If you type `www.microsoft.com`, for example, Internet Explorer changes it to `http://www.microsoft.com`. If you type `ftp.microsoft.com`, Internet Explorer changes it to `ftp://ftp.microsoft.com`. Notice that it chooses the protocol based on how the URL begins. But what happens when you type `rampages.onramp.net/~jerry`? By default, Internet Explorer is going to assume it's a Web page and add `http://` to the beginning of it. If this isn't the behavior you want, you can specify a different prefix by changing the default value entry of **HKLM\Software\Microsoft\Windows\CurrentVersion\URL\DefaultPrefix** to the protocol you want Internet Explorer to use by default—for example, `ftp://`.

Part

III

Ch

7

Clearing History Lists

Windows 2000 keeps various history lists, also called MRU or most recently used lists. It keeps histories of the documents you've opened recently, programs you've run, file specifications you've searched for, and computers you've searched for on the network. You might consider this a personal security risk if you're concerned about other people knowing what you've been up to recently. You can clear all these history lists by removing the keys listed in Table 7.8 from **HKCU\Software\Microsoft\Windows\CurrentVersion\explorer**.

Table 7.8   History Lists

Location	Location in Registry
Documents menu	**RecentDocs**
Run dialog	**RunMru**
Search Assistant	**Doc Find Spec MRU**
Search Assistant	**FindComputerMRU**

After removing these subkeys, you have to erase the contents of **\Windows\Recent** to finish clearing the contents of the Documents menu. If user profiles are enabled on the computer, erase the contents of *UserProfile*\Recent, where *UserProfile* is your logon name.

Clearing Automatically

You can clear these history lists automatically by creating an INF file to remove them. Right-click the INF file and choose Install. Listing 7.2 shows the INF file, which you might want to call Cleanup.inf or something similar.

Listing 7.2   An INF File to Clear the MRU Lists

```
[version]
signature=$Chicago$

[DefaultInstall]
DelReg=DelRegKey

[DelRegKey]
HKCU,"Software\Microsoft\Windows\CurrentVersion\Explorer\Doc Find Spec MRU",
HKCU,Software\Microsoft\Windows\CurrentVersion\Explorer\FindComputerMRU,
HKCU,Software\Microsoft\Windows\CurrentVersion\Explorer\RecentDocs,
HKCU,Software\Microsoft\Windows\CurrentVersion\Explorer\RunMRU
```

To automatically launch the INF file and simultaneously erase the contents of
\Windows\Recent, create a BAT file that looks like the following called Cleanup.bat.

```
@Echo Off
C:\Windows\rundll.exe setupx.dll,InstallHinfSection
➥DefaultInstall 132 Cleanup.inf
Echo Y | Erase C:\Windows\Recent
```

N O T E   The quotation marks around the first key in Listing 7.2 are a must. That's because the key name
contains spaces, which would confuse Windows 2000 if you didn't use the quotes. ■

Clearing When Windows 98 Starts

Launching the BAT file every time you want to clean up the MRU lists isn't convenient, particularly if you want to do it every time you start Windows 2000. You can add the .bat file to
your StartUp folder. Alternatively, add the .bat file to **HKLM\Software\Microsoft\Windows\
CurrentVersion\Run**. You'll learn more about this key in the following section.

Running Programs at Startup

Windows 2000 launches any shortcuts it finds in the StartUp folder after the user logs on to
the computer. These are obvious. What's not obvious is why certain programs run automatically even though they don't appear in the StartUp group. Programs that start automatically
before a user logs on to the computer do so because of entries in the **Run** and **RunOnce** subkeys under **HKLM\Software\Microsoft\Windows\CurrentVersion**. Windows 2000 launches
the command line specified in every value entry it finds there. It does so every time the operating system starts. **RunOnce** is a special case containing value entries for commands that
Windows 2000 will launch once and then remove. The name of each value entry isn't important, but it should be descriptive.

HKCU\Software\Microsoft\Windows\CurrentVersion also contains **Run** and **RunOnce**
subkeys. Windows 2000 launches the commands in these subkeys *after* the user logs on to
the computer. Again, the name of each value entry doesn't matter, but its value contains the
command line to execute. Windows 2000 executes commands in **Run** every time the operating system starts and executes commands in **RunOnce** a single time before removing them
from the Registry.

Logging On to the Network Automatically

Windows 2000 requires a username and password if you configure it to connect to the network. It also asks for a username and password even if you don't connect to a network.
Change the following value entries under **HKLM\Software\Microsoft\Windows\
CurrentVersion\Winlogon** so that you can log on to Windows 2000 automatically
without retyping your credentials:

Part
III

Ch
7

Value	Description
DefaultUserName	Set this string value entry to the username you use to log on to Windows.
DefaultPassword	Set this string value entry to the password you use to log on to Windows.
AutoAdminLogon	Set this string value entry to 1 to enable automatic logon, or set it to 0 to disable automatic logon.

CAUTION

Don't use this customization if you're logging on to a network on which security is a concern. This customization enables anyone to walk up to your computer and access the network without providing credentials.

CHAPTER 8

Using Microsoft Tweak UI

Getting Tweaked

Microsoft Tweak UI is a free, unsupported program that was part of Microsoft Power Toys, a defunct collection of must-have utilities for power users and administrators. Since the first versions of this grass roots effort at making customization easy, it has been a phenomenon that removed barriers preventing users from customizing their computers. No longer did they have to pop open Registry Editor and risk breaking their configurations just to tweak a few settings, such as whether the operating system annoyed them with the words "Click here to begin" bouncing around their task bars. To this day, Tweak UI is one of the most popular downloads at most online software libraries, barely surpassed by Microsoft Internet Explorer 5 at ZDNet Software Library (http://hotfiles.zdnet.com).

A small band of renegade Microsoft programmers created Tweak UI and the company turned the program loose on the public. The program was originally designed for Microsoft Windows 95, but the company updated it for Microsoft Windows 98 and Microsoft Internet Explorer 4. Heck, they even included the program on Windows 98's CD-ROM. Inexplicably, they dropped the program from Microsoft Windows 98 Second Edition's CD-ROM. Some journalists believe that Microsoft did this to appease hardware vendors who didn't like the idea of shipping an unsupported utility with their PCs. Still, users could find the missing program at online software libraries and even at Microsoft's own Web site.

Microsoft is updating Tweak UI for Microsoft Windows 2000. At this writing, Tweak UI is still in development and isn't available on the Windows 2000 CD-ROM or the resource kit's CD-ROM. You'll eventually find the program at many online software libraries, including http://hotfiles.zdnet.com and Microsoft's own download center, http://www. microsoft.com/downloads/search.asp.

> **N O T E** Although Microsoft insists that Tweak UI is an unsupported program, Microsoft Knowledge Base has many articles about it. Although the program doesn't work for everyone in every configuration, Tweak UI is problem free. ■

Installing Tweak UI

Unzip the files you downloaded into a folder. Then, click Install on the Tweakui.inf file's shortcut menu. This INF (Setup Information) file copies the program's files to the computer and adds various values to the Registry. It then displays online help with an overview of how to use Tweak UI. Close the help document to finish installing the program.

Tweakui.inf describes values that Windows 2000 writes to the Registry. These include values that help the operating system remove the program when users choose to do so in the Add/Remove Programs dialog box. It also includes values that enable the program to clear various history lists, such as the list of recent documents. Tweakui.inf copies these files to your computer:

- Tweakui.inf is the actual INF file that you installed earlier. Not only does this file describe how to install Tweak UI, it also describes how to remove the program.

- Tweakui.cpl is the Control Panel applet, which is actually a special DLL (Dynamic Link Library) file renamed using the .cpl file extension. Tweakui.inf copies this file to *SystemRoot\System32*.

- Tweakui.hlp and Tweakui.cnt are help files that contain brief instructions for using the program, as well as a handful of tips and tricks that are unrelated to the program. Check this help file for limitations and troubleshooting help.

N O T E   In the beta version of *Microsoft Windows 2000 Resource Kit*, I received an error that read, "Setup cannot copy the file TWEAKUI.CNT." If you see this error, which isn't likely, just ignore it and click Cancel; then, click Yes to confirm that you want to continue installing the program without this file. ▦

▶ **See** Chapter 10, "Scripting Customizations," **p. 179** for more information about INF files, how they work, and how to write them.

Checking for Newer Versions

The current version of Tweak UI is 1.27, but Microsoft updates it occasionally. To find out which version you're using, click Properties on Tweakui.cpl, which you find in *Systemroot\System32*. On the Version tab, note the file version at the very top. It'll look something like 1.27.0.0. The first number is the major version number and the second number is the minor version number.

Check in Microsoft's download center and the various software libraries to see if a more recent version is available. If so, download and install the program. With most programs, I suggest freshening up with the latest version only when the major version number changes, but Tweak UI's major version number never seems to change, and a small change in the minor version number usually indicates fairly big changes in the program.

Tweaking Your Settings

In Control Panel, double-click the Tweak UI icon, and you see a small window with 11 tabs. Each tab contains a different grouping of settings:

- **Mouse**   Contains settings to adjust the mouse's sensitivity, configure the mouse wheel, and enable a feature that enables you to point at windows to active them.

- **General**   Includes a list of check boxes that you use to enable or disable various special effects, such as smooth scrolling, the funky new shadow under the mouse pointer, and fading menus.

- **Explorer** Hasn't changed much since the early days. Changing the icon that Windows 2000 displays over shortcut icons and preventing the operating system from prefixing "Shortcut to" to the names of new shortcuts are examples.

- **IE** This setting isn't really that useful anymore. Most of these same settings are available in the Advanced tab of the Taskbar and Start Menu Properties dialog box, which you open by clicking Properties on the taskbar's shortcut menu.

- **Cmd** New and unique for Windows 2000, but it should have been around for Microsoft Windows NT 4.0. It contains two settings that enable you to turn on filename and directory completion.

- **Desktop** Contains a list of special icons that you can add to or remove from the desktop. You can also create them as files and folders, meaning that you can put them anywhere you want.

- **Control Panel** Has a list of Control Panel applets and enables you to hide each one of them. Great for removing clutter but doesn't actually disable the applet at all.

- **New** Contains the list of templates you see when you click New on a folder's shortcut menu. You can enable, disable, and remove any existing template. You can also create new templates.

- **Add/Remove** Has a list of all the programs that you can remove using the Add/Remove Programs dialog box. The purpose of this list is to repair broken entries or remove dead entries, preventing you from doing the same task in Registry Editor.

- **Repair** Enables you to fix various aspects of the operating system, including desktop icons and the ever troublesome Fonts folder.

- **Paranoia** Enables you to clean out various history lists each time you log on to the computer. These include document and search histories; no wonder it's called Paranoia.

Using Tweak UI is easy. Change settings on each tab. Click Apply to save your changes without actually leaving the program, or click OK to save them and quit. Some changes won't take effect until you log off and back on to the computer again. Tweak UI is good enough to notify you when this is the case. Other settings you see right away. Still more of the settings are per-computer, meaning they apply to everyone using the computer. None of these settings require you to restart the computer for them to take effect, however.

If your changes get unwieldy, you'll be glad that Tweak UI offers an easy way to restore the factory settings. On the Mouse and Explorer tabs, click Restore Factory Settings to restore the settings on those tabs to their originals.

TIP Most users overlook the Tips button on the Mouse tab. Don't. It opens Tweak UI's help file, which contains more than how-to information about using the program. It also has a handful of tips for doing things better in Windows 2000.

Customizing the Mouse

On Tweak UI's Mouse tab, shown in Figure 8.1, you can change Windows 2000's mouse settings. You find most of the values on this tab in the Registry in **HKCU\Control Panel\Desktop**; thus, unless noted otherwise, any subkeys you learn about in this section start there.

FIGURE 8.1
On the Mouse tab, configure the mouse in ways not possible via the Mouse icon in Control Panel.

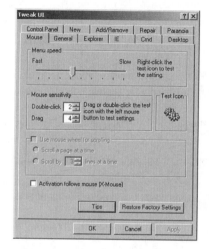

The Menu Speed area controls the span of time before a menu automatically follows the mouse pointer. Drag the slider to the left to make menus follow faster, or drag it to the right to make them follow slower. Right-click Test Icon to test this setting. Tweak UI writes this value to **MenuShowDelay**, a **REG_SZ** value containing a delay time in milliseconds (400ms is the default).

The Mouse Sensitivity area has two spin boxes. First, Double-click determines how close together two mouse clicks must be before Windows 98 knows you double-clicked the mouse. Drag determines how far the mouse pointer must move with the button held down, before Windows 98 recognizes that you're dragging something. Both values are in pixels, but Tweak UI stores the first in the Registry as half-pixels. Tweak UI stores these values in the following **REG_SZ** value entries:

- **HKCU\Control Panel\Desktop\DragWidth**
- **HKCU\Control Panel\Desktop\DragHeight**
- **HKCU\Control Panel\Mouse\DoubleClickWidth**
- **HKCY\Control Panel\Mouse\DoubleClickHeight**

Wheel mice, new fangled mice with a wheel between both buttons, are my favorite recent invention. They allow me to quickly scroll through long documents and Web pages without clicking on a single scrollbar. You can disable the wheel, if you like, by clearing the Use Mouse Wheel for Scrolling check box (Tweak UI disables this check box if you don't have a wheel mouse). If you've selected the check box, click Scroll a Page at a Time to cause the wheel to move forward and backward in whole pages, or click Scroll by *N* Lines at a Time to cause the wheel to move forward and backward *N* lines each time you feel the wheel click. Tweak UI stores these settings in the same spot, a **REG_SZ** value called **WheelScrollLines**. A **-1** indicates to scroll a page at a time, a **0** indicates that the feature is disabled, and any positive number indicates the number of lines to scroll at a time.

Activation Follows Mouse (X-Mouse) prevents you from having to click a background window to activate it, because each window automatically receives focus as you point to it. Windows 2000 reads this value from **UserPreferenceMask**, a binary value whose bits indicate a variety of user preferences and special effects. Note that this feature doesn't raise the window to the top, it just makes the window active, a small difference from X-Mouse.

▶ **See** Chapter 7, "Customizing Windows 2000," **p. 107**, to learn how to customize computers using the settings in **HKCU\Control Panel\Desktop**.

▶ **See** Chapter 14, "Per-User Settings," **p. 281**, for more information about **HKCU\Control Panel**.

Enabling Special Effects

Tweak UI's General tab, shown in Figure 8.2, contains a list of special effects that you can enable or disable by clicking the check box next to each. Each setting is self-explanatory. To enable a special effect, select the check box next to it; otherwise, clear the check box to disable it:

Window animation	Mouse hot tracking effects
Smooth scrolling	Fading menus
Beep on errors	Fading menu selections
Menu animation	ToolTip animation
Combo box animation	ToolTip fade
List box animation	Cursor shadow
Keyboard cues	Show Windows version on desktop

All these settings are in **HKCU\Control Panel**, albeit in different places:

■ **Desktop\PaintDesktopVersion**

■ **Desktop\UserPreferencesMask**

■ **Desktop\SmoothScroll**

■ **Desktop\WindowMetrics\MinAnimate**

■ **Sound\Beep**

FIGURE 8.2
Many of the same settings are available on the Effects tab Display Properties dialog box.

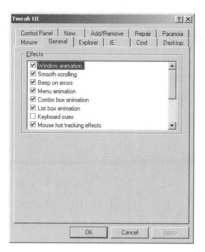

N O T E Conspicuously missing from the Tweak UI's General tab is the list of shell folders and the capability to relocate them. I suppose Microsoft feels that providing this feature conflicts with the administrator's ability to manage the network, considering that they make much of features such as Group Policies and IntelliMirror. Still, in Chapter 7, "Customizing Windows 2000," you learn how to relocate these shell folders manually. ▪

Customizing Shortcuts

Windows 2000 lays a small square icon over the bottom-left corner of each shortcut. This icon is an *overlay*. When you create a shortcut to a Microsoft Word document, for example, Windows 2000 combines the document's original icon with the overlay so that you can readily identify the icon as a shortcut to the document rather than the document itself.

You can choose which icon Windows 2000 uses for that overlay or even choose not to use an overlay at all. On Tweak UI's Explorer tab, shown in Figure 8.3, click either the Arrow, Light Arrow, None, or Custom radio buttons. If you click None, you won't be able to distinguish between shortcuts to documents and documents unless you click Properties on the icon's shortcut menu. If you click Custom, Tweak UI displays the Change Icon dialog box, allowing you to browse Tweakui.cpl, Shell32.dll, or any other file for a suitable icon. Well and good, but you won't find many icons on your computer that are suitable overlays.

When you customize the shortcut overlay, Tweak UI changes the following values in the Registry (these are per-computer settings that affect all users):

■ **HKLM\SOFTWARE\Microsoft\Windows\CurrentVersion\Explorer\Shell Icons**

■ **HKLM\SOFTWARE\Microsoft\Windows\CurrentVersion\Explorer\Shell Icons\ ShellIconOverlayIdentifier**

FIGURE 8.3
The sample icons
show what an icon
looks like with and
without the overlay.

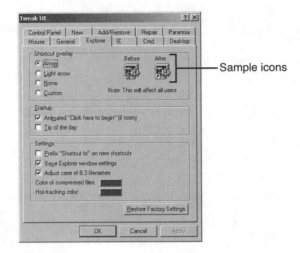

Sample icons

Aside from choosing a shortcut overlay, you can prevent Windows 2000 from prefixing the words "Shortcut to" to each shortcut's filename. Clear the Prefix "Shortcut to" on New Shortcuts check box. You don't need to worry about duplicate filenames, by the way, because shortcuts use the .lnk file extension, and the original document keeps its own file extension.

> **CAUTION**
>
> Windows 95 was known to misbehave when you disabled the shortcut overlay. Although I haven't confirmed this problem in Windows 98, revert this setting to its original value if you start experiencing bizarre problems after changing it.

Customizing Startup

Each time you start Windows 2000, it displays the Getting Started with Windows 2000 dialog box unless you cleared the Show This Screen at Startup check box. The first thing I did after installing Windows 2000 is get rid of that annoying dialog box, but from time to time I need to bring it back. The easiest way to do that is using Tweak UI. On Tweak UI's Explorer tab, which you saw in Figure 8.3, click to select Tip of the Day. This setting is a **REG_DWORD** value in **HKCU\Software\Microsoft\Windows\CurrentVersion\Explorer\Tips**.

Tweak UI still has the Animated "Click here to begin" on the Explorer tab. I haven't a clue why, since Microsoft abandoned that annoying animation with the first release of Windows 98. I suppose it's still available for users who are still struggling with Windows 95, because the program is backward compatible with earlier versions of 32-bit Windows. Just for laughs, Tweak UI stores this setting in a **REG_DWORD** value called **NoStartBanner** in **HKCU\Software\Microsoft\Windows\CurrentVersion\Policies\Explorer**.

Saving Windows Explorer Settings

Microsoft Windows Explorer saves its settings each time you close it and restores them when you open it. Settings it saves include the window's size and position. Thus, Windows Explorer restores its window to its previous size and position when you open it. Aside from restoring the size and position of Windows Explorer's window, when you start Windows 2000, the operating system restores any Windows Explorer windows that you left open when you shut down the operating system.

Things get a bit more complicated when you open multiple Windows Explorer windows. Windows Explorer always saves the last window's settings and uses those for the first window you open. Thus, no matter how many windows you open, no matter their sizes and positions, Windows Explorer only saves the size and position of the last window you close. Thus, if you go to great pains to get your Windows Explorer window just right and don't make sure that window is the last one you close, you'll lose all your hard work. Annoying.

To prevent Windows Explorer from saving the size and position of its window, on Tweak UI's Explorer tab clear the Save Explorer Window Settings check box. This setting prevents Windows 2000 from restoring Windows Explorer windows that you left open when you shut down the operating system, too. Tweak UI stashes this setting in **NoSaveSettings**, a **REG_DWORD** value, in **HKCU\Software\Microsoft\Windows\CurrentVersion\ Policies\Explorer**.

 TIP

Ensure that your Windows Explorer window always looks the way you want. Arrange your Windows Explorer window; then, clear the Save Explorer window settings on Tweak UI's Explorer tab. This ensures that Windows Explorer doesn't screw up your settings if you close numerous windows in the wrong order. A better option is to use a shareware program called EzDesk, which gives you complete control over your desktop's layout. You can download EzDesk from http://members.aol.com/EzDesk95/index.html.

Changing How Filenames Look

Tweak UI provides a handful of settings that control how files look in Windows Explorer:

- On the Explorer tab, select the Adjust Case of 8.3 Filenames option to convert filenames containing uppercase to title case.

- On the Explorer tab, click the button next to Color of Compressed Files to change the color that Windows Explorer uses to display the names of compressed files.

- On the Explorer tab, click the button next to Hot-Tracking Color to change the color that Windows Explorer uses to display filenames when you point at them. This only applies when you're using the single-click user interface, by the way, which you enable by double-clicking Folder Options in Control Panel; then, on the General tab, click Single-Click to Open an Item (Point to Select).

Configuring Internet Explorer 5

Tweak UI's IE tab, shown in Figure 8.4, contains a variety of settings that control the look and feel of Internet Explorer 5, the Web browser that comes with Windows 2000. Those settings are self-explanatory:

- Active Desktop enabled
- Add new documents to Documents on Start Menu
- Allow changes to Active Desktop
- Allow Logoff
- Clear document, run, typed-URL history on exit
- Detect accidental double-clicks
- IE4 enabled
- Show Documents on Start Menu
- Show Favorites on Start Menu

FIGURE 8.4
Most of these settings are actually policies that you can also configure using local and group policies.

What's not self-explanatory is where these settings are in the Registry. All the values are actually policies that Windows 2000 reads from **HKCU\Software\Microsoft\Windows\CurrentVersion\Policies\Explorer** (you won't see these settings in the Registry until after you change them in Tweak UI):

Settings	Location
Active Desktop enabled	**NoActiveDesktop**
Add new documents to Documents on Start Menu	**NoRecentDocsHistory**

Allow changes to Active Desktop	**NoActiveDesktopChanges**
Allow Logoff	**NoLogoff**
Clear document, run, typed-URL history on exit	**ClearRecentDocsOnExit**
IE4 enabled	**ClassicShell**
Show Documents on Start Menu	**NoRecentDocsMenu**
Show Favorites on Start Menu	**NoFavoritesMenu**

The one exception is Detect Accidental Double-Clicks, which you find in **UseDoubleClickTimer** under **HKEY_CURRENT_USER\Software\Microsoft\ Windows\CurrentVersion\Explorer\Advanced**.

Enabling Filename Completion

By default, you must copy or paste directory and filenames at the MS-DOS command prompt. Tweak UI's Cmd tab has two settings that enable directory and filename completion at the MS-DOS command prompt. Figure 8.5 shows the Cmd tab with both options enabled. Here's how to enable them:

1. In the Filename Completion list, click the key combination that you want to use to complete filenames automatically.

2. In the Directory Completion list, click the key combination that you want to use to complete directory names automatically.

At the MS-DOS command prompt, start typing a directory name; each time you press the key combination you configured in step 1—my favorite is Tab—Windows 2000 displays the next directory name that matches the characters you typed. Do the same for filenames. If you don't type any characters at all before pressing the key combination you configured in step 1, Windows 2000 iterates through each directory. The same thing goes for files.

Placing Shell Icons on the Desktop

A typical desktop includes the My Computer, Recycle Bin, My Network Places, My Documents, and Internet Explorer icons—and possibly more. Although there is little you can do to remove the My Computer icon from the desktop because Windows 2000 puts it there automatically, the operating system allows you to control the remaining icons.

FIGURE 8.5
Both lists offer many choices, but the most logical choice for this feature's key combination is Tab.

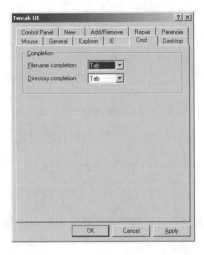

Tweak UI is the simplest method for adding or removing shell icons, special purpose icons that aren't actual folders or files on the disk, to or from the desktop. The Desktop tab, shown in Figure 8.6, contains a list of icons you can put on the desktop. Putting some of these icons on the desktop makes absolutely no sense—ActiveX Cache Folder, for example. The following icons *are* useful on the desktop, however:

- Control Panel
  {21EC2020-3AEA-1069-A2DD-08002B30309D}
- Internet Explorer
  {FBF23B42-E3F0-101B-8488-00AA003E56F8}
- My Documents
  {450D8FBA-AD25-11D0-98A8-0800361B1103}
- My Network Places
  {208D2C60-3AEA-1069-A2D7-08002B30309D}
- Network and Dial-Up Connections
  {7007ACC7-3202-11D1-AAD2-00805FC1270E}
- Printers
  {2227A280-3AEA-1069-A2DE-08002B30309D}
- Recycle Bin
  {645FF040-5081-101B-9F08-00AA002F954E}

CAUTION

As of this writing, putting many of these icons on the desktop causes Windows 2000 to create program errors repeatedly. The only way to stop the endless stream of program errors, which brings the computer to its knees, is to remove the icon from the desktop. One such example is the Microsoft FTP Folder icon.

FIGURE 8.6

Placing icons such as the Control Panel icon on the desktop provides instant access to frequently used folders.

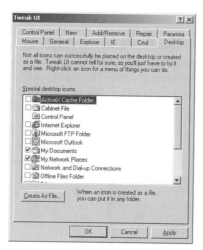

As described in the following sections, you can work with shell icons in two different ways: as a file or folder on the disk or as an object in the desktop's name space.

Shell Icons as Files or Folders on the Disk   To add a shell icon to any folder on the computer, in the Special Desktop Icons list, click the icon and then click Create As File. Select the folder in which you want to create the icon and click Save. Tweak UI creates files for some icons and folders for others. In particular, it creates the Control Panel and Printers icons as folders. To remove a shell icon you create this way, delete it in Windows Explorer.

Shell Icons as Objects in the Desktop's Name Space   To add a shell icon to the desktop as an object, in the Special Desktop Icons list, select the check box next to it. Clear a check box to remove the icon from the desktop. When you add an icon to the desktop's name space, Tweak UI doesn't create a file; it adds the icon's class identifier to **HKLM\Software\ Microsoft\Windows\CurrentVersion\Explorer\Desktop\NameSpace** instead. If you don't see a check box beside an icon's name, you can't add that icon to the desktop's name space; you must add the icon as a file or folder.

CAUTION

When you try to remove the My Network Places icon using Tweak UI, you see a message that reads, `Removing the Network Neighborhood from the desktop has additional conse-quences which are not obvious.` In a nutshell, after removing the My Network Places icon from the desktop, you won't be able to use UNC paths *Server**Resource* to access resources on the network. You'll have to map directly to those resources instead. This also prevents Direct Cable Connection from properly displaying the contents of the host computer.

Specific Drive Letters

Tweak UI allows you to easily disable specific drive letters in My Computer. Although this does prevent drives from showing up in My Computer or Windows Explorer, it doesn't prevent those same drives from showing up in the Save As and Open dialog boxes; thus, don't look at this as a way to prevent users from copying files to a floppy disk. If that's your requirement, disable the disk in the BIOS.

On Tweak UI's My Computer tab, shown in Figure 8.7, clear each drive's check box that you want to hide. To show a drive that's hidden in My Computer, select the drive's check box.

FIGURE 8.7
This dialog box helps reduce clutter in My Computer or Windows Explorer, but it's not a security measure.

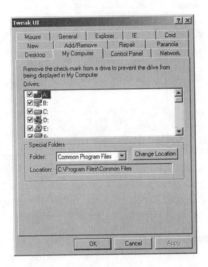

How Tweak UI stores these settings in the Registry deserves a brief explanation. Windows 98 uses each bit of a 32-bit value to indicate whether a drive is enabled or disabled. The first bit corresponds to drive A, the second to B, and so on. Thus, in the binary value 1010, drives B and D are disabled because the second and fourth bits are 1. Note that Tweak UI stores this **REG_DWORD** value as a binary value, so when you look at it in the Registry, you must reverse the order of the bytes. If you see 06 00 00 00 in the Registry, reverse the order of the bytes to 00 00 00 06; then examine each bit to determine which drives are disabled. The name of the value is **NoDrives** in **HKCU\Software\Microsoft\Windows\CurrentVersion\ Policies\Explorer**.

Relocating Shell Folders

On the My Computer tab, you can change the location of shell folders, which are folders with a special purpose. In the Folder list, click the name of the folder that you want to relocate; then, click Change Location and select the folder you want to use for that shell folder. Tweak UI enables you to change the location of any shell folder defined in the **Software\ Microsoft\Windows\CurrentVersion\Explorer\Shell Folders** branch of either

HKEY_LOCAL_MACHINE or **HKEY_CURRENT_USER**. Here are some typical examples of the folders in this list:

Name	Default Location
Common Program Files	C:\Program Files\Common
Desktop	C:\Windows\Desktop
Document Templates	C:\Windows\ShellNew
Favorites	C:\Windows\Favorites
My Documents	C:\My Documents
Program Files	C:\Program Files
Programs	C:\Windows\Start Menu\Programs
Recent Documents	C:\Windows\Recent
Send To	C:\Windows\SendTo
Start Menu	C:\Windows\Start Menu
Startup	C:\Windows\Start Menu\Programs\Startup

N O T E Changing the location of a shell folder using Tweak UI doesn't actually move the current shell folder. It just points Windows 98 to a different folder for that purpose. You must move the contents of the original folder to the new one if you want to keep it. ■

▶ **See** Chapter 9, "Tracking Down Registry Settings," **p. 155**, to learn more about how Windows 98 stores the location of shell folders.

Hiding Control Panel Icons

Tweak UI enables you to reduce the clutter in Control Panel by hiding icons that you don't use frequently. On Tweak UI's Control Panel tab, shown in Figure 8.8, clear each check box next to any applets you don't want to see in Control Panel. Select check boxes next to applets you do want to see. Note that Tweak UI displays each applet's filename and title.

Don't rely on hiding an applet as a security measure. Just because its icon isn't visible in Control Panel doesn't mean that users can't still use it. Tweak UI merely adds a **REG_SZ** value to **HKCU\Control Panel\don't load** for each icon you choose not to display. Control Panel uses these values to determine whether to display each applet's icon. The name of each value is the filename of the applet and its value is either **yes** or **no**, indicating whether Control Panel displays it or not.

TIP An alternative way to disable a specific applet is to remove its file from *SystemRoot*\System32. Not only does this prevent Control Panel from displaying its icon, but also it prevents users from running the applet at all.

FIGURE 8.8
Tweak UI shows you
the filename and title
of each icon.

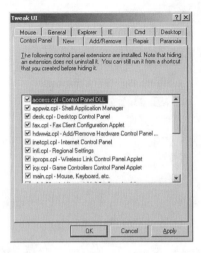

Logging on Automatically

If you aren't logging on to a network, or you're logging onto a network in which security isn't much of a concern, avoid typing your credentials every time you start Windows 2000.

> **CAUTION**
>
> Tweak UI doesn't encrypt your password when you use this feature. It's stored in the Registry as plain text that anyone can read.

On Tweak UI's Network tab, shown in Figure 8.9, select Log on Automatically at System Startup. In the User Name text box, type the name you use to log on to Windows 2000 and, in Password, type your password. Tweak UI stores these in **HKLM\Software\Microsoft\ Windows\currentVersion\WinLogon**:

- **AutoAdminLogon** contains a logical value that enables or disables this feature.
- **DefaultPassword** contains the readable text password that you typed in the Network tab.
- **DefaultUserName** contains the username you provided.

FIGURE 8.9
Even though Tweak UI
doesn't display your
password, it stores
your password in the
Registry as plain text.

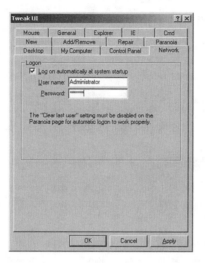

Adding to the New Menu

Click New on any folder's shortcut menu, and you see a list of file types that you can create
from a template. Rename the file and open it. Windows 2000 populates this menu from the
Registry. It looks in **HKEY_CLASSES_ROOT** for any file extension subkey that contains a
subkey called **ShellNew**. It adds each subkey it finds to the New menu. Some **ShellNew** subkeys refer to an additional template file, stored in *UserProfile*\Templates that Windows 2000
uses to create the new file.

Tweak UI enables you to define additional templates that you'll see on the New menu. In
every case, you create a template from a file that you create and drag it onto Tweak UI's
New tab, shown in Figure 8.10. Tweak UI copies the file to *UserProfile*\Templates and adds
the **ShellNew** subkey to the file's extension subkey.

FIGURE 8.10
Temporarily hide
templates or remove
them from the menu.

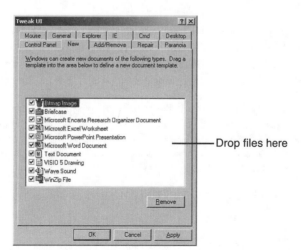

Drop files here

There are two ways to remove a type from the New menu:

- Clear a file type's check box, and Tweak UI merely hides the file's **ShellNew** subkey so that it no longer appears on the menu. Tweak UI hides the subkey by affixing a dash to the end of its name, like this: **ShellNew-**. You can restore it by reselecting the check box.

- Click a file type and click <u>R</u>emove. This permanently removes the file type from |the <u>N</u>ew menu and removes the file extension subkey's **ShellNew** subkey.

Editing the Add/Remove List

In Control Panel, double-click the Add/Remove Programs icon to display the Add/Remove Programs dialog box. Use this dialog box to remove programs from your computer or to change their optional components.

If you manually remove a program from your computer, that program might still have an entry in the Add/Remove Programs dialog box. On the flip side, if an application has an uninstall program but did not register it; it doesn't show up in this dialog box. Either way, you can edit the list you see in the Add/Remove Programs dialog box so that it more accurately reflects the programs on your computer. Just remember that editing this list doesn't actually change the programs on your computer; in other words, removing a program from this list doesn't remove the program, just its uninstall information.

On Tweak UI's Add/Remove tab, shown in Figure 8.11, do one of the following:

- Click the program whose install information you want to remove, and then click <u>R</u>emove.

- Click <u>N</u>ew. Type the program's name in <u>D</u>escription, and type the command that removes the program from the computer in <u>C</u>ommand.

- Click the program whose install information you want to change and then click <u>E</u>dit. Type the program's name in <u>D</u>escription, and type the command that removes the program from the computer in <u>C</u>ommand.

Windows 2000 organizes uninstall information in **HKLM\Software\Microsoft\Windows\ CurrentVersion\Uninstall**. You find one subkey for each application and each application's subkey has two **REG_SZ** values. **DisplayName** is the name of the program and **UninstallString** is the command that removes the program from the computer.

 TIP Removing an item from the list of programs in the Add/Remove programs dialog box is a decent way to keep users from removing programs when you don't want them to. Although you can edit this list at users' computers using Tweak UI, you're better off distributing an INF (as described in Chapter 10, "Scripting Customizations") or editing users' Registries remotely (as described in Chapter 4, "Editing with Regedt32").

FIGURE 8.11
Removing an item from this list doesn't remove the program from the computer.

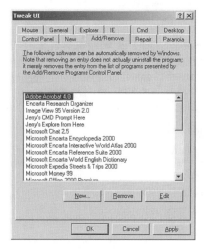

Repairing Windows 2000

Tweak UI's Repair tab, shown in Figure 8.12, provides the capability to fix a variety of common problems, particularly those problems that afflict people who tinker with the Registry. In the list, click the item you want to repair, and then click Repair Now. The following options are self-explanatory:

- Rebuild Icons
- Repair Font Folder
- Repair Regedit
- Repair Temporary Internet Files

FIGURE 8.12
In the middle of the dialog box, Tweak UI provides a brief description of the repair it's going to make.

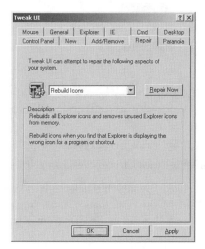

Keeping Your Activities Private

If you're uncomfortable with the fact that other people using your computer can come along and see everything you've been doing, you need to check out Tweak UI's Paranoia tab, shown in Figure 8.13. It provides a good measure of privacy by clearing Windows 98's MRU (Most Recently Used) lists each time the operating system starts. The options you see in the Covering Your Tracks list are self-explanatory:

- Clear Document history at logon
- Clear Find Computer history at logon
- Clear Find Files history at logon
- Clear Internet Explorer history at logon
- Clear Network Connection history at logon
- Clear Run history at logon
- Clear Telnet history at logon

FIGURE 8.13

Tweak UI helps keep your activities private.

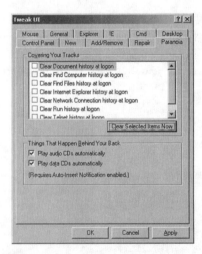

TweakUI implements these settings through the following three Registry keys:

- **HKLM\Software\Microsoft\Windows\CurrentVersion\Winlogon\DontDisplayLastUserName**
- **HKLM\Software\Microsoft\Windows\CurrentVersion\Applets\TweakUI\1**
- **HKLM\Software\Microsoft\Windows\CurrentVersion\Explorer\RecentDocs**

This tab also keeps you from embarrassing yourself thanks to Windows 98's AutoPlay feature. If you've ever had a game CD-ROM start automatically, blaring loud music to the entire office, you know what I'm talking about. Prevent audio CDs from starting automatically upon insertion by deselecting Play Audio CDs Automatically. Prevent CD-ROMs from starting automatically by deselecting Play Data CDs Automatically. Windows 98 retrieves these settings from **HKCR\AudioCD\Shell\(default)** and **HKCU\Software\Microsoft\Windows\ CurrentVersion\Policies\Explorer\NoDriveTypeAutorun**. ●

Tracking Down Registry Settings

Finding Changes in the Registry

No easier method exists for locating changes in the Registry than to compare two registration (REG) files. Export the Registry before and after performing steps that change the Registry; then, compare both REG files using a file-comparison utility. The utility highlights differences between each file, enabling you to figure out which subkeys are inserted or deleted; and which values are inserted, deleted, or changed. This method is quicker than most Registry tracking tools, and the results are often easier to read. I tracked one particular setting by exporting the Registry to a file called `Before.reg`. Then, on the Start Menu Options tab of the Taskbar Properties dialog box, I selected the Scroll the Programs check box. After changing this setting, I exported the Registry to a file called `After.reg` and compared it to `Before.reg`. The result? Microsoft Windows 2000 puts this setting in **StartMenuScrollprograms**.

Recall from Chapter 3, "Editing with Regedit," that REG files are nothing more than text files that look similar to configuration (INI) files, so they're ideally suited to comparison. The fully qualified name of each subkey is on a line by itself, enclosed in brackets: **[*name*]**. Fully qualified names begin with a root key, so **regfile\shell** is not a fully qualified name, but **HKCR\ regfile\shell** is one. Each of its entries appear below each subkey. Each entry looks like ***name=value***, except for each subkey's default value, which looks like **@=*value***. For more information about the format of REG files, see Chapter 10, "Scripting Customizations," which shows how to interpret different types of Registry values, too.

Registry Editor supports two file formats for REG files. Version 4 uses ANSI character encoding and begins with `REGEDIT4`. Version 5 uses Unicode character encoding and begins with `Windows Registry Editor 5.00`. Version 5 is unique to Windows 2000. The difference between ANSI and Unicode character encoding is that ANSI represents each character with one byte while Unicode represents each character with two bytes. By default, Registry Editor saves REG files as version 5, Unicode. Unfortunately, few file-comparison utilities understand Unicode; so make sure you always create version 4 REG files if you want to compare them. For more information about the differences between ANSI and Unicode character encoding, see Chapter1, "Understanding Registries." In the meantime, here are the steps you use to export the Registry to a version 4, ANSI REG file:

1. On the Registry menu, click Export Registry File.
2. In the File Name box, type the REG file's name.
3. In the Save As Type list, click Win9x/NT4 Registration Files (REGEDIT4) to save the REG file as a version 4, ANSI REG file.
4. Click All to export the entire Registry.
5. Click Save and be patient for a few minutes while Registry Editor creates the REG file.

Registry Editor's command-line options are a convenient way to export the Registry at the MS-DOS command prompt, within batch files, or from a desktop shortcut. The only problem with creating REG files using Registry Editor's command-line options is that it only creates Unicode text files, so you can't use file-comparison utilities that only understand ANSI text files. Nevertheless, `Fc.exe` and a few others do support Unicode. If in doubt, give it a go; file-comparison utilities that don't support Unicode usually display each character on a line by itself. To export the Registry using Registry Editor's command-line options, type the following command at an MS-DOS command prompt or in the Run dialog box:

```
regedit /e filename.reg
```

The following sections describe a handful of file-comparison utilities you can use to compare REG files. All do a good job but aren't equally suited to the task. My preference is Microsoft WinDiff. It's easy to use, comes with *Microsoft Windows 2000 Resource Kit* (MS Press, 2000), and is fast enough to make short work of the process. The other file-comparison utilities you learn about in this chapter do the job, too. As a last resort, use your word processor's comparison feature, but expect to wait a long, long time while the word processor crunches the thousands of lines found in a typical REG file. Regardless of which utility you choose, the process of comparing REG files is the same:

1. Export the entire Registry, including both **HKEY_LOCAL_MACHINE** and **HKEY_USERS**, to a REG file. Name this file `Before.reg` or something similar. If you're using WinDiff or another file-comparison utility that doesn't support Unicode, make sure you create version 4, ANSI text files.

2. Perform the steps necessary to change the Registry. If you want to see how a program stores options in the Registry, change those options. If you want to see what values a setup program changes, install the application.

3. Export the entire Registry to another REG file. Name this file `After.reg` or something similar. Make sure you export to the same type of file that you did in step 1, however.

4. Compare both REG files, `Before.reg` and `After.reg`, using a file-comparison utility. The utility will indicate the differences between both. If you exported to version 5, Unicode REG files, a file-comparison utility that doesn't support Unicode will display each character on a line by itself.

 TIP

If the change you're seeking is in a specific part of the Registry, don't export the entire thing; just export that specific branch, but make sure you export the same branch in both REG files. To export a specific branch, select the branch's top-most subkey before clicking Export Registry File on the Registry menu. Click Selected Branch instead of All.

▶ **See** Chapter 1, "Understanding Registries" **p. 7**, for a description of ANSI and Unicode character encoding.

▶ **See** Chapter 3, "Editing with Regedit" **p. 39**, to learn how to create a REG file using Registry Editor's command-line options.

▶ **See** Chapter 10, "Scripting Customizations" **p. 179**, to learn how to build REG files. Understanding how to create REG files helps you understand the results of a comparison.

Snapshot Shareware

Vincent Chiu's RegView and Vita RegSnap are two shareware utilities that automate the process of finding changes in the Registry. You don't have to export the Registry to REG files, and you don't have to compare REG files using a file-comparison utility. Both RegView and RegSnap compare snapshots so quickly that they leave your head spinning.

Download RegView, shown in the following figure, from `http://www.xnet.com/~vchiu`. On the Tools menu, clicking Record Current Registry makes a snapshot of the Registry, and clicking Compare to Last Recorded Registry compares the current Registry to the last snapshot. Note that you can only keep one snapshot with RegView, but it's a full-fledged Registry editor in its own right, sporting features such as *Search and Delete* and *Search and Replace*. RegView's bigger and more expensive brother, RegView Pro, provides many more capabilities and allows you to maintain multiple Registry snapshots.

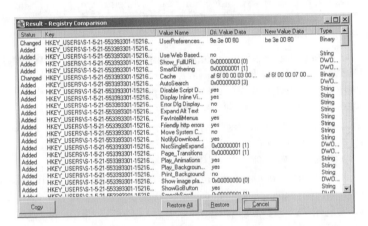

Download RegSnap from `http://www.webdon.com`. RegSnap is a bit clunky compared to RegView, but it has similar features. In the toolbar, click New Snapshot to take a new snapshot of the Registry. Click Compare to compare two different snapshots of the Registry. What RegSnap has over RegView is that you save each snapshot as a separate file and can compare any two files; thus, you're not limited to comparing the current Registry to the previous snapshot. Still, RegSnap is not as intuitive to use as RegView.

WinDiff

WinDiff is the classic file-comparison utility with which most programmers are already familiar. That's because it comes with the software development kit (SDK) that they use to write Windows-based programs. *Microsoft Windows 2000 Resource Kit* provides WinDiff, too, as does Windows 2000 Resource Kit Support Tools, which is on the Windows 2000 CD-ROM in Support\Reskit. Install the resource kit or support tools; then, at the MS-DOS command prompt or in the Run dialog box, type **windiff**. `Windiff.exe` is in *SystemDrive*\Program Files\Resource Kit. Along with a plethora of other utilities, WinDiff is available in the Tools Management Console. To start the console from the Start menu, point to Programs, point to Resource Kit, and then click Tools Management Console. It's under File Tools. Now that you know how to run WinDiff, here's how to use it to compare two REG files:

1. On the File menu, click Compare Files to choose the files you want to compare.
2. Select the first file and click Open.
3. Select the second file and click Open. WinDiff displays a single line at the top of the window that indicates whether the files are different.
4. On the View menu, click Expand to show which lines are inserted, deleted, or changed in the second file. Alternatively, click Expand on the toolbar or double-click the initial line that shows whether the two files are different.

Part
III

Ch
9

Figure 9.1 shows what WinDiff looks like after comparing two REG files. WinDiff combines both files, highlighting differences between each one. Press F8 to view the next difference, and press F7 to view the previous difference. WinDiff indicates differences with a red or yellow background, and lines with a white background are common to both files. A red background means that the line is present in the first file but not in the second. A yellow background means that the line is in the second file but not in the first. Thus, a red background indicates lines that are missing from the second file, and a yellow background indicates lines that are new in the second file. You also see arrows (< >) beside each changed line that point left or right. They are easier to remember than the colors. An arrow pointing to the left means that the line is missing from the second file, and an arrow pointing to the right means that the line is new in the second file. When using WinDiff, refer to the following table to jog your memory about what each color and arrow means:

Color	Arrow	Meaning
Red	<!	Line deleted from second file
Yellow	!>	Line inserted in the second file

The bars you see along the left edge of WinDiff's window are a pictorial representation of the files' differences. You see two columns. The first represents the first file, and the second represents the second file. Click anywhere in the picture to display that portion of the files in WinDiff. You also see red and yellow bands within each column. These bands indicate differences between the two files. A great way to move directly to each difference is to click one of these bands. The two blue vertical lines on either side of the columns show what portion of the files WinDiff is displaying in the window.

FIGURE 9.1
You can't see the colors in this figure, but the darker band is red, and the lighter band is yellow.

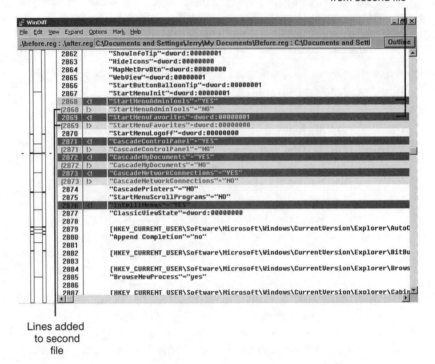

Lines removed from second file

Lines added to second file

N O T E WinDiff represents changed lines by showing them deleted from the first file and added to the second. Thus, alternating red and yellow bands indicate changes rather than additions or deletions. Also, note the line numbers. When WinDiff detects a changed line, it shows the line as it appears in the first file with a line number like 2868. It shows the line as it appears in the second file with a line number like (2868. ■

▶ **See** Chapter 1, "Understanding Registries" **p. 7**, to learn how to install Windows 2000 Resource Kit Support Tools and to use the Microsoft Windows 2000 Resource Kit.

FC (File Compare)

If you install Windows 2000 from a network share or from an OEM CD-ROM, you might not have access to WinDiff. Don't worry if you don't, because every Windows 2000 user still has FC (`Fc.exe`), an MS-DOS program that you find in *SystemRoot*\System32. FC supports Unicode, so you can create REG files from the MS-DOS command prompt and don't have to remember to export to version 4, ANSI REG files. The following list describes FC's command-line options:

FC	[/A] [/B] [/C] [/L] [LB*n*] [/N] [/T] [/U] [/W] [/*nnnn*] [*filename1*] [*filename2*]
/A	Displays the first and last lines of the differences that FC finds
/B	Performs a binary comparison and must be the only command-line option given
/C	Disregards the case of letters
/L	Compares files as ANSI text files
/LB*n*	Sets the maximum number of consecutive lines that can be different without FC stopping
/N	Displays line numbers during ANSI comparisons; helps pinpoint the location of changes within a REG file
/T	Does not expand tabs to spaces
/U	Compares files as Unicode text files
/W	Compresses whitespace, tabs and spaces, during the comparison
/*nnnn*	Sets the number of consecutive lines that must match after a mismatch
filename1	Path and filename of the older file
filename2	Path and filename of the newer file

To use FC effectively, you must specify the /N and /U command-line options. The /N command-line option displays the line number of each difference that FC finds. In addition, because Registry Editor exports to version 5, Unicode REG files by default, use the /U command-line option for the output to make sense—unless, of course, you export the Registry to version 4, ANSI REG files. For example, to compare Before.reg and After.reg, both of which are in C:\Registry, type this command at the MS-DOS command prompt:

```
fc /n /u c:\Registry\before.reg c:\Registry\after.reg
```

Listing 9.1 shows FC's output. It displays differences in groups of consecutive lines, with each group starting with the name of the first file, followed by the name of the second file, and ending with a handful of asterisks (*). Because FC isn't smart enough to display the subkey that owns each value, the line numbers are your only way to see them in their original contexts. For example, to see which subkey owns **CascadeMyDocuments**, look at line 5472 in After.reg. Look at line 5475 of After.reg to see which subkey owns **StartMenuScrollPrograms**. This makes FC a less-than-ideal way to compare REG files but, without WinDiff, it's the best thing going.

Part
III

Ch
9

Listing 9.1   Output of FC

```
Comparing files Before.reg and AFTER.REG
***** Before.reg
 5470:   "StartMenuLogoff"=dword:00000000
 5471:   "CascadeControlPanel"="NO"
 5472:   "CascadeMyDocuments"="YES"
***** AFTER.REG
 5470:   "StartMenuLogoff"=dword:00000000
 5471:   "CascadeControlPanel"="YES"
 5472:   "CascadeMyDocuments"="YES"
*****

***** Before.reg
 5473:   "CascadeNetworkConnections"="YES"
 5474:   "CascadePrinters"="YES"
 5475:   "StartMenuScrollPrograms"="NO"
***** AFTER.REG
 5473:   "CascadeNetworkConnections"="YES"
 5474:   "CascadePrinters"="NO"
 5475:   "StartMenuScrollPrograms"="NO"
*****
```

 TIP   ZDNet Software Library, `http://www.hotfiles.com`, maintains numerous file-comparison utilities. The most popular and possibly the most powerful is PrestoSoft ExamDiff, a freeware utility.

Norton File Compare

Symantec Norton Utilities for Windows 95/98 contains one of the better file-comparison utilities, Norton File Compare. The problem is that this program isn't part of Norton Utilities for Windows NT 4.0 (Symantec hasn't announced Norton Utilities for Windows 2000). No problem—copy the following files from *SystemDrive*\Program Files\Norton Utilities, or whichever directory contains the utilities, to any computer running Windows 2000 (make sure you don't delete your license agreement in the process):

- Ncompare.exe
- Ncompare.hlp
- Nuabout.dll
- Numisc.dll
- Nusplash.dll
- S32krnll.dll
- S32util.dll
- s32guil.dllg
- Trkeng.dll

Listing 9.2 is a Setup Information (INF) file you can use to automatically install and uninstall Norton File Compare. Aside from enabling you to remove Norton File Compare after installing it, this INF file also adds a shortcut for it to the Start menu. For more information about creating INF files, see Chapter 10, "Scripting Customizations." Using any text editor, such as Notepad, type Listing 9.2 and save it to Ncompare.inf in the same directory as the other eight files. To install Norton File Compare, click Install on the INF file's shortcut menu. To start Norton File Compare, on the Start menu point to Programs, point to Norton File Compare, and then click Norton File Compare. Use Control Panel's Add/Remove Programs icon to uninstall the program.

Part III

Ch 9

Listing 9.2 An INF File to Install Norton File Compare

```
[Version]
Signature=$CHICAGO$

[DefaultInstall]
AddReg=Uninstall.Reg
CopyFiles=Product.Files,INF.File
UpdateInis=Add.Inis

[DefaultUninstall]
DelReg=Uninstall.Reg
DelFiles=Product.Files,INF.File,Help.File
UpdateInis=Del.Inis

[Uninstall.Reg]
HKLM,%Uninstall%%Product%,"DisplayName",,"%Product%"
HKLM,%Uninstall%%Product%,UninstallString,,"Rundll32.exe
setupapi.dll,InstallHinfSection DefaultUninstall 132
%17%\Ncompare.inf"

[Add.Inis]
setup.ini,progman.groups,,"group1=""%Product%"""
setup.ini,group1,,"""%Product%""","""""""%24%\Program
Files\%Product%\Ncompare.exe """""""

[Del.Inis]
setup.ini,progman.groups,,"group1=""%Product%"""
setup.ini,group1,,"""%Product%"""

[INF.File]
Ncompare.inf

[Product.Files]
Ncompare.exe
Ncompare.hlp
Nuabout.dll
Numisc.dll
Nusplash.dll
S32krnll.dll
```

continues

Listing 9.2　Continued

```
S32utill.dll
Trkeng.dll

[Help.File]
Ncompare.gid

[DestinationDirs]
INF.File=17
Product.Files=24,"Program Files\%Product%"
Help.File=24,"Program Files\%Product%"

[SourceDisksNames]
1=%Diskname%

[SourceDisksFiles]
Ncompare.inf=1
Ncompare.exe=1
Ncompare.hlp=1
Nuabout.dll=1
Numisc.dll=1
Nusplash.dll=1
S32krnll.dll=1
S32utill.dll=1
Trkeng.dll=1

[Strings]
Product="Norton File Compare"
Diskname="Norton File Compare, Setup Disk #1"
Uninstall="Software\Microsoft\Windows\CurrentVersion\Uninstall\"
```

After starting Norton File Compare, it prompts for the left and right files. These correspond to the first and second files. On the File menu, select new files by clicking Open Left Pane and Open Right Pane. After scanning both files for changes, Norton File Compare displays them, one in each pane, as shown in Figure 9.2. When you scroll up and down, it synchronizes the files in both panes. This makes it possible to compare both side-by-side as you move up and down. Note how it recognizes that you're comparing REG files and formats the output properly. It shows Registry keys and subkeys using the appropriate hierarchy and displays the correct icons for each value's type. It doesn't change the format of each text line, however, leaving each as it appears in the REG file.

Norton File Compare indicates unchanged text with black characters and changed text with red characters. If these colors are difficult to see, you can change them: On the Options menu, click Settings and then click the Display tab. You scroll up and down to look for differences or use the Search feature to locate individual differences:

1. On the Options menu, click Search.

2. Click Non Matching Block and then click Search Down or Search Up. Norton File Compare brings each block of differences to the top of the window.

FIGURE 9.2
Norton File Compare shows you the path and filename above each pane. It also indicates which file is newer.

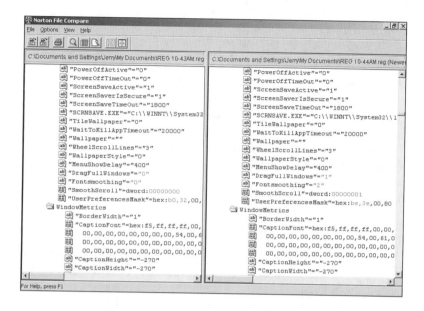

If you only want to see changes, collapse the display so you only see the lines that are different between each file. On the <u>V</u>iew menu, click Show <u>D</u>ifferences Only. You won't see changed lines in their original contexts, but this is the best way to locate changes in the Registry.

Word Processors

Short of using WinDiff and the others, you *can* use a word processor's Compare feature to find differences between REG files. Popular word processors, including Microsoft Word and Corel WordPerfect, have this feature. Using a word processor to compare REG files is not the best life has to offer, however, because doing so is much slower than using a program designed for that purpose. Still, using a word processor might be your only choice if you don't have access to WinDiff or something similar.

Revision tracking, as most word processors call the feature, works differently in dissimilar programs. In most cases, you open the second REG file first and compare it to the first. Opening the files in this order ensures that the word processor correctly interprets the order of events. In other words, you want to know the current value of an entry in the second, newer REG file in comparison to that same entry in the older file. To compare REG files using Microsoft Word, for example, follow these steps:

1. Open the second REG file. On the <u>F</u>ile menu, click <u>O</u>pen. In the Files of <u>T</u>ype list, click All files so that you can see REG files, not just documents. Select the second REG file and click <u>O</u>pen.

2. Compare to the first REG file. On the Tools menu, point to Track Changes and then click Compare Documents. Select the first REG file and click Open. Be patient, because this process takes a while.

Word doesn't actually open the last file. It highlights the differences between the open REG file and the REG file to which you chose to compare it. By default, Word formats deleted lines using strikethrough and inserted lines using underline, as shown in Figure 9.3. You can change how Word formats inserted, deleted, and changed lines, however: On the Tools menu, click Options; then, click the Track Changes tab and configure how you want Word to display changes.

FIGURE 9.3
Differences aren't as easy to discern in Microsoft Word as they are in a utility such as WinDiff.

Deleted line

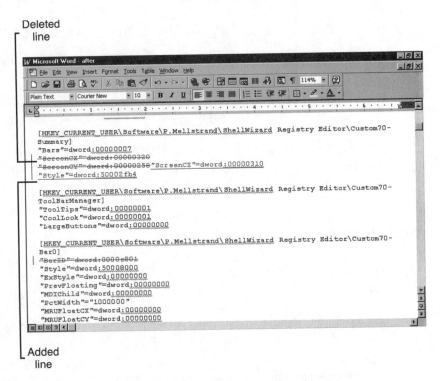

Added line

TIP If you must use your word processor to compare REG files, make sure you disable its spelling and grammar checkers. If you leave these features enabled, your computer's hard disk will thrash about madly while the word processor finds spelling and grammar errors on every line of the file. Consult your word processor's documentation to learn how to disable spell and grammar checking. In Microsoft Word, on the Tools menu, click Options and, on the Options dialog box, click the Spelling & Grammar tab; then, clear the Check Spelling As You Type and Check Grammar As You Type check boxes.

Some Changes Just Don't Matter

After comparing a few REG files, you'll notice some changes repeatedly. They don't mean anything. They're just normal changes that occur over time and have little to do with the changes for which you're searching. If you compare REG files that you created before and after restarting the computer, for instance, you'll find several changes to **HKLM\System**. These changes just reflect the results of Plug and Play's configuring the hardware as you start the operating system. In the course of normal operation, too, various values change in the Registry. A variety of MRU lists change as you run programs, open documents, or search for files. Windows Explorer saves different settings that indicate the position, size, and appearance of each Explorer window. Ignore all these incidental changes and focus on finding the important ones.

Auditing the Registry to Detect Changes

Comparing before and after snapshots of the Registry is only one way to track down how programs use it; another is *auditing,* which enables you to track users' activities. You choose the types of events you want to monitor, as well as the objects on which they occur, and Windows 2000 records those events in the security log. A typical use for auditing is to track when users log on and off their computers. Another is to monitor particular directories or files so that you know precisely when users access them. You have the choice of auditing successful, failed, or both types of accesses. In this case, you're going to audit portions of the Registry for both types of accesses so that you know how programs are using it.

Auditing Registry access is only viable when you know the general vicinity that a program targets. For example, audit **HKCU\Software\Microsoft\Windows\CurrentVersion** to discover values that Windows Explorer uses when it sets advanced options. If you audit too much of the Registry, Windows 2000 grinds to a halt, because the operating system can access the Registry thousands of times per second, and each access generates an entry in the security log. Enabling an audit of the entire Registry for all access types turns a two-minute operation into an unbearably long task that lasts over an hour. Aside from focusing on a particular part of the Registry, you can further limit the impact of auditing it by watching specific types of access, such as *delete* and *write,* instead of all types of access. More on preventing coffee breaks later.

▶ **See** Chapter 6, "Administering Registries" **p. 95**, for a description of how to use auditing for a more commendable purpose: security. You'll also find more details about policies than you find in this chapter.

Setting the Audit Policy

Auditing the Registry is a two-step process, just as it was in Windows NT 4.0 (to Windows 98 users, this is all new information). First, enable auditing; then, choose the objects you want to audit. Both require administrator rights. To enable auditing, set the local audit policy in Local Security Policy:

1. In Control Panel, double-click the Administrative Tools icon and then double-click Local Security Policies. This opens `Secpol.msc` in Microsoft Management Console.

2. Click Audit Policies, which is Local Policies.

3. In the details pane, click Audit Object Access; then, on the Action menu, click Security. You see the Local Security Policy Setting dialog box.

4. Select the Success and Failure check boxes, as shown in Figure 9.4. Note that you can choose to audit only successful or only failed attempts but, in this case, auditing both is more useful.

FIGURE 9.4
If the effective and local policy settings differ, give Windows 2000 time to update or try logging off and on.

N O T E Windows 2000 might ignore certain local policy settings. The operating system processes the local group policy object (GPO), followed by site, domain, and OU (organization unit) GPOs. Thus, a domain-based policy might override a site-based policy, which might override a local policy. If Local Security Policy shows an effective policy setting that differs from the local policy, a network policy is overriding the local policy. Contact your administrator for support. ■

Auditing a Subkey

The new Registry editor (Regedit.exe) doesn't support auditing, but the older Registry editor (Regedt32.exe) does. The following instructions show you how to audit a subkey using Regedt32 after setting the local audit policy, and recommend options that give you the best results when tracking down how programs use the Registry:

1. In Regedt32's key pane, click the subkey you want to audit. If the subkey you want to audit isn't in the current window, change to the appropriate window by clicking its title in the Window menu.

2. On the Security menu, click Permissions to display the Permissions dialog box; then, click Advanced.

3. On the Auditing tab of the Access Control Settings dialog box, click Add to add an auditing entry.

4. In the Select User, Computer, or Group dialog box, click the user, computer, or group whose access you want to audit. If you want to look in another account database, click its name in the Look In list. Click OK to continue. For our purposes, add Everyone. For more information about more appropriate choices if you want to audit the Registry for security purposes, see Chapter 4, "Editing with Regedt32."

5. In the Auditing Entry dialog box, select the Success and Failure check boxes next to each event that you want to audit. You get the best results by watching for successful and failed queries and successful writes, as shown in Figure 9.5. The remaining check boxes don't help much when you're just trying to figure out how a program uses the Registry. The following list describes each check box:

Query Value	Attempts to read a value
Set Value	Attempts to set a value
Create Subkey	Attempts to create subkeys
Enumerate Subkeys	Attempts to identify all the subkeys of a particular key
Notify	Attempts to notify events from a particular Registry subkey
Create Link	Attempts to create symbolic links to a particular subkey
Delete	Attempts to delete an object
Write DAC	Attempts to write a subkey's ACL
Read Control	Attempts to read a subkey's ACL

6. To enable auditing for the entire branch, including all the key's subkeys, click This Key and Subkeys in the Apply Onto list. If you're monitoring a particular value and you know its exact location, don't monitor the entire branch because that's an incredible waste. If, on the other hand, you're scouting out how a program uses the Registry and only know the general vicinity, your best bet is to watch the branch.

Viewing the Results

Each time an event that you're auditing occurs, Windows 2000 adds an entry to the security log. You view these events in Event Viewer:

1. In Control Panel, double-click the Administrative Tools icon and then the Event Viewer icon.

2. In the tree pane, click Security Log. In the details pane, click the event you want to view; then, on the Action menu, click Properties.

FIGURE 9.5
The Registry Key
Auditing dialog box is
similar to other audit-
ing dialog boxes in
Windows 2000.

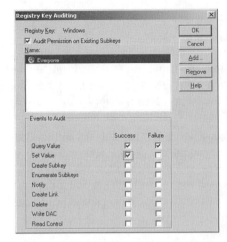

Monitoring the Registry for Changes

Up to this point, you've learned how to compare snapshots that you take at different times and audit access to the Registry. Watching in real time how programs use the Registry might be a better way to learn what you want to know, however. Registry Monitor is a program that helps you do just that. A small program, it downloads from **http://www.sysinternals.com** in just minutes.

Figure 9.6 shows Registry Monitor. Registry Monitor divides its window into rows and adds a new line to the list every time a program accesses the Registry. The window contains six columns. The first contains line numbers. The second and third contain the name of the process accessing the Registry and the type of request the process is making. Table 9.1 describes each of the different requests, which correspond to the different API (application programming interface) functions available to programs for accessing the Registry, you'll see in this column. The remaining columns contain the fully qualified name of the subkey, the result (success or failure), and any other data as described in Table 9.1.

Table 9.1   Registry Monitor Request Types

Type	Data in Other Column
CloseKey	Unused
CreateKey	Handle to the newly created subkey
CreateKeyEx	Handle to the newly created subkey
DeleteKey	Unused
DeleteValue	Unused
EnumKey	Name of the next enumerated subkey

Type	Data in Other Column
EnumKeyEx	Name of the next enumerated subkey
EnumValue	Unused
FlushKey	Unused
OpenKey	Handle to the opened subkey
OpenKeyEx	Handle to the opened subkey
QueryValue	Value queried from the entry
QueryValueEx	Value queried from the entry
SetValue	Value stored in the entry
SetValueEx	Value stored in the entry

FIGURE 9.6
Although Registry
Monitor tracks every
access to the Registry,
it doesn't affect your
computer's perfor-
mance.

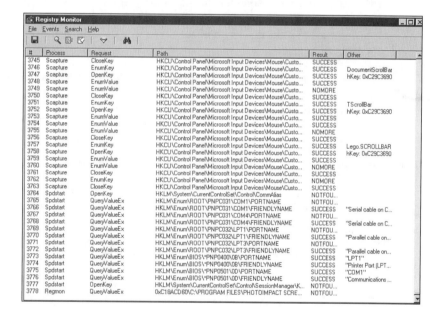

N O T E Most times, Registry Monitor displays the name of each subkey you see in the window. If a program opened a subkey before you started Registry Monitor, though, Registry Monitor won't be able to look up the subkey's name and thus can't display it in the window. In those cases, Registry Monitor displays the subkey's handle instead of its name. The best you can do is take an educated guess at which subkey the handle represents.

Filtering Information   Without filtering, Registry Monitor wouldn't be suitable for tracking down specific Registry changes. In one example, Registry Monitor recorded over 12,000 accesses to the Registry within minutes. Pinpointing small changes is almost impossible in this case. The program does allow you to filter the information it displays, though, so you can focus on access by a particular process or specific types of access by any program. On the Events menu, click Filter; you'll see the Regmon Filter dialog box. Type the name of the process you want to watch in the Process box. You can also choose the types of access you want to observe: **Log Reads**, **Log Writes**, **Log Success**, and **Log Errors**. Note that an asterisk (*) is a wildcard, which matches everything.

Make sure you use the application's process name when filtering in Registry Monitor, not the application's name or file name. The best way to discover the application's process name is to observe the names that Registry Monitor displays in the second column. Note that some processes have names like Run32dll, indicating that the process is a dynamic link library (DLL) running within Run32dll's (Run32dll.exe) address space. Run32dll is a program that loads and executes functions within DLLs. You won't see the name of the DLL file, just Run32dll.

TIP   You can watch for hits to a specific subkey by filtering on it. In the Regmon Filter dialog box's Path Include box, type the fully qualified name of the branch you want to watch. Be sure to format the path just as you'd see it in Registry Monitor's window. That is, use the abbreviated root keys, such as **HKLM** and **HKCU**.

Comparing Two Computers' Registries

Microsoft Compreg (Compreg.exe) is on the *Microsoft Windows 2000 Resource Kit* CD-ROM but not in Windows 2000 Resource Kit Support Tools. It's an MS-DOS program that compares two different subkeys, whether they're on the same computer or not. That is, you can compare two subkeys on the same computer, or you can compare the same subkey on two different computers. The program's output looks like Listing 9.3.

Listing 9.3   Sample Output from Compreg

```
1 \ShellNew
1 \ShellEx
2 \Wordpad.Document.1
2 \Word.Document.6
2 \WordDocument
2 \ShellEx
2 \Word.Document.8
1 ! REG_SZ,[Paint.Picture]
2 ! REG_SZ,[Word.Document.8]
1 !Content Type REG_SZ,[image/bmp]
2 !Content Type REG_SZ,[application/msword]
End of search : 9 differences found.
```

After installing the resource kit, type **compreg** at the MS-DOS command prompt and include any of the following command-line options:

compreg	<1> <2> [-v] [-r] [-e] [-d] [-q] [-n] [-h] [-?]
1	Path of the first subkey
2	Path of the second subkey
-v	Shows differences and matches
-r	Visits subkeys that exist only in 1 or 2
-e	Sets errorlevel to the previous error code
-d	Limits output to just subkey names, not values
-q	Limits output to the number of differences
-n	Disables the use of color in the output
-h	Displays help
-?	Displays command-line options

Some aspects of Compreg's command-line options bear more explanation. In particular, 1 and 2 specify the Registry subkeys you're comparing. The notation is *Name**Subkey*. *Name*, if provided, can be the name of any computer on the network. *Subkey* is a subkey within that computer's Registry. If you don't provide a computer name, Compreg assumes the subkey is in the local Registry. *Subkey* is usually a fully qualified name starting from one of the root keys. You must use one of the abbreviations shown in Table 9.2, though, not the conventional abbreviations you learned about in Chapter 1, "Understanding Registries." If you specify just a computer name for 2, Compreg compares the subkey specified by 1 to the same subkey on the machine specified by 2. To speed you along, the following list shows several examples:

```
compreg lm\software cu\software

compreg us\.default us\jerry

compreg lm\software \\Other

compreg \\Workstation\lm \\Other\lm

compreg \\Workstation\lm\software \\Server
```

N O T E   If the paths you specify to Compreg contain spaces, make sure you enclose the entire path in quotation marks. ■

Table 9.2   Root Key Abbreviations for Compreg

Abbreviation	Subtree
lm	**HKEY_LOCAL_MACHINE**
cu	**HKEY_CURRENT_USER**
cr	**HKEY_CLASSES_ROOT**
us	**HKEY_USERS**

If you don't have *Microsoft Windows 2000 Resource Kit*, you do have Windows 2000 Resource Kit Support Tools on the Windows 2000 CD-ROM in Support\Reskit. The support tools provide Microsoft Reg (Reg.exe), a general-purpose Registry utility that supplants other Registry utilities. Reg's compare command does the same thing as Compreg. Here are its command-line options:

reg compare *src*	[*computer*] [*dest*] [*computer*] [-oM|-oD|-oMD] [-q] [-e]
src	Fully qualified name of the source subkey or value (the first subkey)
dest	Fully qualified name of the destination subkey or value (the second subkey)
//computer	Name of the remote computer (uses local computer if omitted)
-oM	Don't output matches
-oD	Don't output differences
-oMD	Don't output matches or differences
-q	Display only the number of differences
-e	Set the error level to the error code that Reg returned the last time it ran (default is to set the error level to the number of differences)

Tracking Remote Registries

Tracking a remote computer's Registry isn't too useful for individual users, but doing so might be useful for administrators. You use all the same tools, but you connect to the computer via the network.

In Registry Editor, click <u>C</u>onnect Network Registry on the <u>R</u>egistry menu; then, in <u>C</u>omputer name box, type the name of the remote computer. You'll see both the local and the remote computers. "Finding Changes in the Registry," earlier in this chapter, described how to export the Registry.

To audit a subkey on a remote computer, enable auditing via local or network policy, first. Open Regedt32 and click <u>S</u>elect computer on the <u>R</u>egistry menu. In the <u>C</u>omputer box, type the name of the remote computer. "Auditing a Subkey," earlier in this chapter, described how to audit a subkey or even an entire branch.

Tracking the Registry with ConfigSafe

ConfigSafe's publisher, imagine LAN, designed this program to help OEMs (original equipment manufacturers) better support customers. The OEMs record a computer's configuration before shipping it; then, when customers call the helpdesk, support technicians use ConfigSafe to determine changes in the computer's configuration.

ConfigSafe is just as valuable to you. Use it to take occasional *snapshots* of your computer's configuration; then, you can see what changed on your computer from time to time, snapshot to snapshot. For example, if you installed a program that changed your Autoexec.bat without asking, you can see exactly what the program changed. If a program fouled up the Registry, you can use ConfigSafe to see exactly how it did so. ConfigSafe is also a good program to use for tracking the Registry when you're hunting down that next Registry hack.

Part III
Ch 9

The fastest way to start using ConfigSafe is to download an evaluation copy. Follow the instructions you see on `http://www.configsafe.com`. You can also order ConfigSafe from imagine LAN:

> imagine LAN, Inc.
> 76 Northeastern Blvd., Suite 34B
> Nashua, NH 03062-3174
> (603) 889-3883

When you first install ConfigSafe, it takes an initial snapshot of the computer's configuration. After the first snapshot, you don't really have to do much. Just sit back and let ConfigSafe do its job. By default, ConfigSafe takes a new snapshot once a week. This is frequent enough to protect your configuration from most problems. As you see from the list of items it records in each snapshot, ConfigSafe covers all the bases:

- **Configuration files**   Protocol.ini, System.ini, Win.ini, Autoexec.bat, Config.sys, and Msdos.sys
- **System information**   processor, coprocessor, memory, and Windows version
- **Drive information**   free space on each drive
- **Directory information**   files in C:\Dos, if any, and in *SystemRoot* and all its subdirectories
- **Registry information**   all values for all subkeys in the Registry

Even though ConfigSafe tracks a large variety of configuration data, I limit this discussion to how you use the program to track Registry changes. ConfigSafe's help describes the program's remaining features.

N O T E   At this writing, imagine LAN is preparing a newer version of ConfigSafe that works better with Windows 2000. Check the company's Web site for more information.

Viewing Changes

To run ConfigSafe, on the Start menu, point to Programs, point to ConfigSafe, and then click ConfigSafe. By default, it monitors **HKEY_LOCAL_MACHINE** and **HKEY_USERS**, both of which include every subkey and value in the Registry. You don't need to add any other subkeys to the list. On the toolbar, click Registry Information to see subkeys that ConfigSafe is tracking and the changes to each value. You'll see a window similar to Figure 9.7. See "Sniffing Out Hacks" later in this chapter to learn how to use this view to track down changes in the Registry. (My only beef with this program is that it doesn't use a tabbed interface as similar programs do).

FIGURE 9.7
Snapshots help you determine what has changed in the Registry.

Compare these two snapshots.

Subkeys included in snapshot

Changes to selected Registry subkey

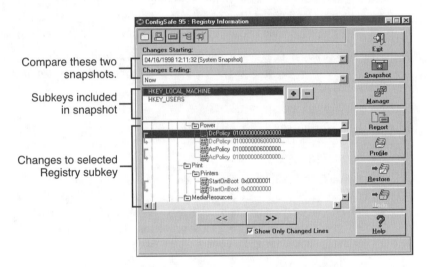

You have to tell ConfigSafe which snapshots to compare. Any two snapshots will do, and you can compare the computer's current configuration to any other snapshot. For example, you can compare a snapshot you took two weeks ago to the current configuration, represented as **Now** in the list of snapshots. You can also compare a snapshot you took four weeks ago to a snapshot you took two weeks ago. In the **Changes Starting** list, click the beginning snapshot and, in the **Changes Ending** list, click the ending snapshot. Ideally, you'd choose snapshots on either side of an action that changed the Registry.

N O T E   Typically, you'll want to compare the most recent snapshot to the current configuration. Doing this allows you to determine recent changes to your configuration. Other times, you'll want to compare two different snapshots that occur before and after a specific configuration change, such as installing a new program, allowing you to sort out how it changed the Registry. ■

To see changes to a particular branch, select a root key from the list. ConfigSafe will go away again, possibly for a very long time. Look under the list of root keys to see the actual subkeys and values that have changed. You see a plus sign by each new item and a minus sign beside each deleted item. ConfigSafe displays changed entries with a green arrow pointing from the entry's previous value to the entry's new value. The following table describes these conventions:

Type	Color	Icon
Add	Blue	+
Delete	Red	−
Change	Green	↵

Taking New Snapshots

Create a new snapshot anytime by clicking Snapshot. Type a name in the Create Configuration Snapshot dialog box.

Maybe changing ConfigSafe's snapshot schedule is what you really wanted to do. By default, ConfigSafe takes a configuration snapshot every week. If you take a manual snapshot every morning, change the schedule so that the program does so automatically. A monthly snapshot may be more suitable for users who don't use their computers much. A daily snapshot is more appropriate for someone like me, who toys with his configuration regularly. Follow these steps to change the schedule:

1. Click Manage to display the Manage Configuration Snapshots dialog box.
2. Select the Enable Scheduled Snapshot check box.
3. Click Daily, Weekly, Monthly, or At Windows Startup.

N O T E   If ConfigSafe misses a snapshot because either you didn't start the computer that day or because you temporarily disabled the program, it will take the snapshot immediately the next chance it gets. ▨

Sniffing Out Hacks

ConfigSafe can track down Registry settings that a program changes. Compare a snapshot after the program makes its changes to a snapshot you take beforehand. The process is very similar to how you take and compare snapshots using Registry Editor. Here's how:

1. Create a new profile so that you can easily clean up your mess when you're finished. Profiles are collections of snapshots that have unique names. Click Profile, name the profile.

2. Take a snapshot of the configuration by clicking Snapshot, typing a name.

3. Perform actions that change the Registry. Run a program, perhaps. You might have to set various options, move the window, and so on. The steps depend on what you're trying to discover.

4. Run ConfigSafe again and compare the previous snapshot to the current configuration.

N O T E   This chapter has shown you how to track Registry changes using ConfigSafe. You must understand that ConfigSafe is more than that. As its name implies, it's a good way to stash your configuration for safekeeping. You can restore any portion of your configuration if needed. Few problems can sneak by ConfigSafe, meaning that as long as it's protecting your computer, you can fix any problem. ▨

Scripting Customizations

Updating Values with REG Files

Registration Entries (REG) files are the classic method for updating subkeys and values in the Registry. In Chapter 3, "Editing with Regedit," you learned that they're easy to create, easy to read and understand, and easy to import by double-clicking the file or by clicking Merge on the file's shortcut menu. Even though REG files are the easiest way to update the registry, they're not as powerful as batch files, scripts, and Setup Information (INF) files—but more on those later.

Regedit supports two file formats for REG files: version 4 and version 5. The first line of a REG file, the header, determines its format. Files that begin with REGEDIT4 are version 4, and the file format is consistent in all recent versions of Microsoft Windows, including Windows 98, Windows NT Workstation 4.0, and Windows 2000. Files that begin with Windows Registry Editor Version 5.00 are version 5. Version 5 is unique to Windows 2000, and you can't use it in earlier versions of Windows. Versions 4 and 5 have important differences that affect how you use them:

- Version 4 files use ANSI character encoding, but version 5 files use Unicode. This means that each character in version 4 files is a single byte, whereas each character in version 5 files is two bytes. Thus, the letter *A* is 0x41 in version 4 files but is 0x0041 in version 5 files. The best way to understand the difference between each file is to examine each in a binary editor. (Chapter 1, "Understanding Registries," has a figure that shows each in a binary editor.)

- Version 4 encodes **REG_EXPAND_SZ** and **REG_MULTI_SZ** values using ANSI character encoding, but version 5 encodes them using Unicode. A **REG_EXPAND_SZ** value that looks like **hex(2):48,49,00** in a version 4 file will look like **hex(2):48,00,49,00,00,00** in a version 5 file. Even if you convert a Unicode REG file to ANSI, the hexadecimal **REG_EXPAND_SZ** and **REG_MULTI_SZ** values are still Unicode; thus, you can't convert Unicode REG files to ANSI and expect them to work properly in any version of Windows. Nevertheless, you can use version 4 in all recent versions of Windows.

> **CAUTION**
>
> To edit a REG file, click Edit on the file's shortcut menu. Don't double-click the file because doing so merges it into the Registry.

Listing 10.1 shows a typical REG file. It makes several changes to the registry, most of which you learned about in Chapter 7, "Customizing Windows 2000." The first line always contains the header REGEDIT4 or Windows Registry Editor Version 5.00, depending on its version. The second line must always be blank because Regedit won't import a file that doesn't begin with a proper header followed a blank line. The remainder of Listing 10.1 changes various values, adding them if they don't already exist. The file contains three sections, with each subkey in its own section. The fully qualified name of the subkey is between brackets: **[name]**.

Remember that a fully qualified name includes the subkey's entire name, beginning with the root key. **HKCR\txtfile\shell** is a fully qualified name; **txtfile\shell** is not. In this file, the three sections are for the following subkeys:

HKCU\Control Panel\Desktop
HKCU\Control Panel\Mouse
HKCU\Control Panel\Sound

In Listing 10.1, under each subkey, you see a list of corresponding values. Except for default values, the name appears in quotation marks. An at sign (@) is the default value within a sub-key. Obviously, each section contains only one default value. The name is on the left side of the equal sign, as shown, and the data you're assigning to it is on the right side. Table 10.1 shows how different types of data look in each file format, version 4 and 5. The string **hex:** prefixes **REG_BINARY** values. The string **dword:** prefixes **REG_DWORD** values, **hex(2):** prefixes **REG_EXPAND_SZ** values, and **hex(7):** prefixes **REG_MULTI_SZ** values. Quotation marks enclose string data.

Listing 10.1   Sample REG File

```
Windows Registry Editor Version 5.00

[HKEY_CURRENT_USER\Control Panel\Desktop]
@="yes"
"DragFullWindows"="1"
"FontSmoothing"="2"
"MenuShowDelay"="400"
"UserPreferencesMask"=hex:be,3e,00,80

[HKEY_CURRENT_USER\Control Panel\Mouse]
"ActiveWindowTracking"=dword:00000001

[HKEY_CURRENT_USER\Control Panel\Sound]
"Beep"="yes"
"ExtendedSounds"="yes"
```

Part
III

Ch
10

Table 10.1   Sample Formatting

Data Type	Version 4	Version 5
REG_BINARY	hex:00,00,00,01	hex:00,00,00,01
REG_DWORD	dword:00000001	dword:00000001
REG_EXPAND_SZ	hex(2):48,49,00	hex(2):48,00,49,00,00
REG_MULTI_SZ 31,00,4C,69,6E, 65,20,32,00,00	hex(7):4C,69,6E,65,20, 6E,00,65,00,20,00,31, 00,00,00,4C,00,69,00, 6E,00,65,00,20,00,32, 00,00,00,00,00	hex(7):4C,00,69,00,
REG_SZ	"A string"	"A string"

▶ **See** Chapter 1, "Understanding Registries," to learn more about ANSI and Unicode character encoding. You learn the differences between both encoding schemes and where you find them in the Registry.

▶ **See** Chapter 3, "Editing with Regedit," to learn how you create REG files by exporting subkeys. This is the easiest way to create a subkey from which you can inspect and learn about REG files.

Creating REG Files

Creating a REG file by hand is easy enough. Make sure that you save the file with the `.reg` extension and use the appropriate character encoding, ANSI or Unicode, depending on the version you're creating. Here's how:

1. Open Microsoft Notepad and create the file's header by doing one of the following:

   - To create a version 4 REG file, put `REGEDIT4` at the top of the file, and follow it with a blank line.

   - To create a version 5 REG file, put `Windows Registry Editor Version 5.00` at the top of the file, and follow it with a blank line.

2. For each subkey that you want to add or change, create a section below the header.

   Put each subkey's name in square brackets: **[name]**. Make sure that you use the subkey's fully qualified name, starting from the root key, and don't use abbreviations such as **HKCR**.

3. For each value that you want to add or change, add a line below the subkey's section.

   Each line looks like **"name"=value**, where **name** is the name of the value that you're adding or changing. If you're changing the default value, use the at sign for the value's name, without quotes. Pay attention to the different formats you use for the different data types. If in doubt, look again at Table 10.1.

4. Save your changes.

   Click Save As on Notepad's File menu (see the Save As dialog box in Figure 10.1). In the Save as Type list, you must click All Files in order to save a text file with the REG file extension. Also, do one of the following:

   - To save a version 4 REG file, click ANSI in the Encoding list.

   - To save a version 5 REG file, click Unicode in the Encoding list.

N O T E   REG files don't have separate syntaxes for adding and changing values. If you specify subkeys or values that don't exist, Regedit creates them. If you specify values that do exist, Regedit merely changes them to the new values. Note, too, that REG files can't remove subkeys or values. ■

FIGURE 10.1
Don't encode version 4 files as Unicode and vice versa; otherwise, Windows 2000 won't import them correctly.

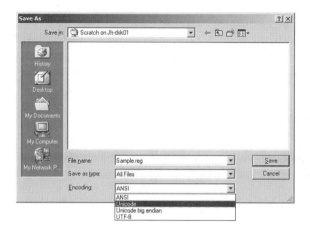

Exporting to REG Files

Creating REG files by hand seems easy enough, but I don't recommend it. Human error finds too many ways to creep into the files—especially if you're a poor typist. Thus, use Regedit to export a subkey to a REG file. You can refine the REG file later but, by allowing Regedit to create the file, you have much less work to do. Although Chapter 3 shows you how to create a REG file, I repeat the instructions here:

1. On the Registry menu, click Export Registry File.

2. In the File Name box, type the REG file's name.

3. In the Save as Type list, click one of the following:

    • To create a version 4 file, click Win9x/NT4 Registration Files (REGEDIT4).

    • To create a version 5 file, click Registration Files.

4. In the Export range area, do one of the following:

    • Click All.

    • Click Selected branch.

5. Click Save to create the REG file.

Be aware of the following issues when you use this method to create a REG file:

■ **Trimming**—When you export a subkey using Regedit, you're exporting all its descendent subkeys and values. Thus, you need to open the REG file (click Edit on its shortcut menu) and remove any subkeys and values that you don't want.

■ **Editing**—You can change any values in the REG file. If you're not satisfied with the settings you exported using Regedit, alter them before distributing the file. Make sure you use the formats shown earlier in Table 10.1.

Part
III

Ch
10

TIP An interesting aspect of REG files is the order in which Regedit writes values under each subkey. Although you might expect the program to write values in alphabetical order by name, it doesn't. Regedit writes values in the order of creation. For instance, export **HKCU\Control Panel\Desktop** to a REG file and, within each section, you can see the older values toward the top and the younger values toward the bottom.

CAUTION

If you're working with versions of Windows other than Windows 2000, always create version 4 REG files. Otherwise, down-level versions of Regedit can't read them.

▶ **See** Chapter 3, "Editing with Regedit," to learn how to export all or part of the registry to a REG file. You also learn how to choose between the two different file formats.

▶ **See** Chapter 7, "Customizing Windows 2000," for more information about preventing Regedit from importing REG files when you double-click them.

Using Alternative Representation

Recall that, in a REG file, **hex:** prefixes **REG_BINARY** data, **hex(2):** prefixes **REG_EXPAND_SZ** data, and **hex(7):** prefixes **REG_MULTI_SZ** data. That might make you wonder what **hex(1)**, **hex(3)**, and the others prefix. Merge Listing 10.2 into the Registry. What do you think it's going to do? Did you expect the results shown in Figure 10.2?

Listing 10.2   Advanced Data Types

```
Windows Registry Editor Version 5.00

[HKEY_CURRENT_USER\Test]
"Test0"=hex(0):00,00,00,00
"Test1"=hex(1):48,00,49,00
"Test2"=hex(2):48,00,49,00
"Test3"=hex(3):12,34,56,78
"Test4"=hex(4):12,34,56,78
"Test5"=hex(5):12,34,56,78
"Test6"=hex(6):48,00,49,00,00,00,00,00
"Test7"=hex(7):48,00,49,00,00,00,00,00
"Test8"=hex(8):48,00,49,00,00,00,00,00
"Test9"=hex(9):48,00,49,00,00,00,00,00
```

You can specify any type of value using the format hex(*type*):*data*. The number *type* indicates the value type. You specify *data* in hexadecimal notation; thus, look again at Chapter 1 to recall how to represent different data types in hexadecimal notation. The numbers 0 through 9 are Windows 2000's internal representation for different data types and are the same values that programmers use to specify value types in software. Therefore, when you write a line that's like `"MyValue"=hex(4):78,56,34,12`, Regedit creates a new value named **MyValue**, sets its type to **REG_DWORD**, and stuffs the number 0x12345678 in it. The following list shows the type corresponding to different numbers:

hex(0)	**REG_NONE**
hex(1)	**REG_SZ**
hex(2)	**REG_EXPAND_SZ**
hex(3)	**REG_BINARY**
hex(4)	**REG_DWORD**
	REG_DWORD_LITTLE_ENDIAN
hex(5)	**REG_DWORD_BIG_ENDIAN**
hex(6)	**REG_LINK**
hex(7)	**REG_MULTI_SZ**
hex(8)	**REG_RESOURCE_LIST**
hex(9)	**REG_FULL_RESOURCE_DESCRIPTOR**
hex(10)	**REG_RESOURCE_REQUIREMENTS_LIST**

FIGURE 10.2

These values come from the REG file in Listing 10.2.

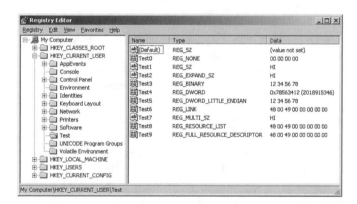

Most of these are familiar. You've seen **REG_SZ**, **REG_EXPAND_SZ**, **REG_BINARY**, and **REG_DWORD** many times. **REG_DWORD_LITTLE_ENDIAN** is the same as **REG_DWORD** because Intel-based architectures store double-word values in little-endian order (little bytes first or reverse-byte order). Windows 2000 stores **REG_DWORD_BIG_ENDIAN** values in big-endian order (big bytes first or forward-byte order). **REG_LINK** and the other data types are of little interest to users, but you learn about all the Registry data types in Chapter 1. Listing 10.3 is the same as Listing 10.1, shown earlier in this chapter, except that it uses this new notation for each value.

Part

III

Ch

10

Listing 10.3   Sample REG File

```
Windows Registry Editor Version 5.00

[HKEY_CURRENT_USER\Control Panel\Desktop]
@= hex(1):79,00,65,00,73,00,00,00
"DragFullWindows"=hex(1):31,00,00,00
"FontSmoothing"=hex(1):32,00,00,00
"MenuShowDelay"=hex(1):34,00,30,00,30,00,00,00
"UserPreferencesMask"=hex(3):BE,3E,00,80

[HKEY_CURRENT_USER\Control Panel\Mouse]
"ActiveWindowTracking"=hex(4):01,00,00,00

[HKEY_CURRENT_USER\Control Panel\Sound]
"Beep"=hex(1):79,00,65,00,73,00,00,00
"ExtendedSounds"=hex(1):79,00,65,00,73,00,00,00
```

▶ **See** Chapter 1, "Understanding Registries," to learn about the data types that the registry supports. This chapter also describes the little-endian and big-endian addressing schemes in more detail.

Gulliver's Travels

A **REG_DWORD** value is a four-byte, 32-bit integer number. Take 52,059, for example, which is 0x0000CB5B in hexadecimal notation. Within memory, Intel-based computers store **REG_DWORD** values in reverse-byte order *(little-endian)*; so they store 0x0000CB5B as 5B CB 00 00. Even though Intel-based computers store numbers in little-endian order, programs correctly display them because the processor restores the order of the number's bytes as it reads them from memory.

The only time you care about little-endian order is when you try to write a **REG_DWORD** value in hexadecimal notation. You might have to do this in a REG file, for example, or in an INF file. Just to make sure you get it, the following table contains a few examples. The first two columns show the decimal and hexadecimal equivalents of a value, and the third column shows the little-endian order of the bytes as they would appear in memory.

Decimal	Hexadecimal	Little-Endian
1	0x00000001	01,00,00,00
331	0x0000014B	4B 01 00 00
4096	0x00001000	00 10 00 00
5001	0x00001389	89 13 00 00
7779863	0x0076B617	17 B6 76 00
53896313	0x03366479	79 64 36 03
2147483649	0x80000001	01 00 00 80

Just remember that little-endian is an addressing scheme in which the bytes with lowest significance are stored first in memory (little end first). Big-endian (big end first) is an addressing scheme in which the bytes with the most significance are stored first. Intel-based computers use little-endian addressing.

Encoding Special Characters

Some string values contain special characters. Common practice is to put quotes in commands so programs can open long filenames that contain spaces—`'Wordpad.exe "%1"'` is one example. I've also seen string values that contain returns and linefeeds. Regedit makes special provisions for these special characters in REG files: *escaping*. When you prefix a special character with a backslash, Regedit replaces the backslash and following character with the actual character that the combination represents. It does this as it merges REG files into the registry. The string `\n` represents a newline character, for example, which is an ASCII 10. Table 10.2 describes special characters that Regedit supports and examples, and here's what escaping looks like in a REG file:

```
"MyValue"="Everyone voted but none could be \"quoted\""
```

Table 10.2   Escape Characters

Esc	Expanded	Escaped in the REG File	Expanded in the Registry
\\	\	"\\\\Server\\Drive"	\\Server\Drive
\"	"	"This is \"quoted\""	This is "quoted"
\n	Newline	"First\nSecond"	First *newline* Second
\r	Return	"First\rSecond"	First *return* Second

Editing the Registry Within Batch Files

Microsoft Windows 2000 Resource Kit (Microsoft Press, 1999) provides the ultimate MS-DOS–based registry program: Microsoft Registry Console Tool. The name is a bit awkward and, because its filename is `Reg.exe`, I call it *Reg* throughout the rest of this chapter. The resource kit's younger cousin, Windows 2000 Resource Kit Support Tools, also includes Reg. You find it on the Windows 2000 CD-ROM in `Support\Reskit`. For more information about the full resource kit and the support tools, see Chapter 1.

Regedt32-in-a-box, my pet name for Reg, does almost as much from the MS-DOS command prompt as Regedt32 does with its cheesy graphical user interface. It's perfect for logon scripts because Windows 2000 still uses batch files for that purpose. Use it to add, change, delete, search, back up, restore, and perform other operations in the Registry. And with the appropriate administrative rights, perform those same operations on remote computers, making Reg ideally suited for remote administration in batch files. `Regchg.exe`, `Regdel.exe`, `Regread.exe`, and other MS-DOS–based programs are in earlier resource kits, and they might be in the final release of *Microsoft Windows 2000 Resource Kit*, but Reg replaces all of them with a single program, one that has a familiar command-line interface:

Syntax:

```
REG COMMAND options [\\computer]
```

Options:

COMMAND	ADD, COMPARE, COPY, DELETE, EXPORT, IMPORT, LOAD, QUERY, RESTORE, SAVE, UNLOAD (the sections following this describe each command in detail)
options	Options for *COMMAND*
\\computer	Name of a remote computer (uses local computer if omitted)

> **N O T E** As of this writing, the Resource Kit's setup program doesn't update the computer's path to include its installation directory. To run Reg without typing its full path, add to the computer's path the directory in which you installed the resource kit. In Control Panel, double-click the System icon, and then click Environment Variables on the Advanced tab to update the path. ■

To use Reg, type a command at the MS-DOS command prompt. Issuing these commands one at a time isn't the most effective way to use this program, however. A better way is to use it in batch files and logon scripts. Listing 10.4 shows a sample batch file that uses Reg to manipulate the registry. Note that this batch file is a viable logon script, too. It simply clears out the various history lists that Windows 2000 keeps and sets a couple of registry-based policies. (See, you *can* set policies without Group Policy.) If you choose to use Reg in a logon script, make sure that it's accessible to all network users. The easiest way to do that is by copying Reg.exe to an accessible network share—perhaps the Netlogon share on a Microsoft network.

Listing 10.4   Sample Logon Script

```
@Echo Off
If Not Exist H:\ Net Use H: /Home
If Exist H:\Logon.bat H:\Logon.bat

Set HKZV=HKCU\Software\Microsoft\Windows\CurrentVersion

REM Clear various history lists
Reg Delete %HKZV%\Explorer\RecentDocs /f
Reg Delete %HKZV%\Explorer\OpenSaveMRU /f
Reg Delete %HKZV%\Explorer\RunMRU /f

REM Limit Internet Explorer integration; beats using Group Policy
Reg Delete %HKZV%\Policies\Explorer /f
Reg Add %HKZV%\Policies\Explorer /v Classicshell /t REG_DWORD /d 1
Reg Add %HKZV%\Policies\Explorer /v NoActiveDesktop /t REG_DWORD /d 1
Reg Add %HKZV%\Policies\Explorer /v NoInternetIcon /t REG_DWORD /d 1
```

Reg provides shortcuts. You don't have to type the complete name of each root key; just use the now-ubiquitous abbreviations: **HKCR**, **HKCC**, **HKCU**, **HKLM**, and **HKU**. If you give a subkey without a root key, such as **software\txtfile**, Reg assumes that the subkey is under

HKLM. Note that Reg has historically had a few limitations (*quirks* is too generous) that limited its usefulness. These are now fixed in the version of Reg that comes with *Microsoft Windows 2000 Resource Kit*:

- Reg's add command couldn't replace a value. You had to test whether ERRORLEVEL had failed and, if it had, use the update command. This is fixed.

- Reg's query command didn't query **HKCR** correctly. You had to query **HKLM\Software\Classes** or **HKCU\Software\Classes** instead. This is fixed.

- Reg's commands aren't as fussy about subkey and value names that contain spaces. In many cases, enclosing the entire subkey in double quotation marks (") or individual names in single quotation marks (') solved the problem. In other cases, that solution simply didn't work. This is fixed.

- Reg better handles situations where a key has a subkey and a value with the same name. For example, if **HKLM\My** had a subkey named **Example** and a value named **Example**, Reg was likely to get ill if you used a command such as reg delete my\ example. In most cases, Reg saw the value but not the subkey. This is fixed.

Reg Problems

The previous versions of Reg were very temperamental in Windows 2000, if not downright unreliable. For instance, Reg's copy, export, and import commands just didn't work. Worse, most times, its delete, restore, and find commands crashed, and Dr. Watson logged the failure. The fatal twist of the dagger was that many of the commands didn't work properly with remote computers, reporting various errors such as The parameter is incorrect.

Reg had a sense of humor, too. Its save command did a great job of saving a subkey to a hive file, but its restore command failed to restore the hive file to the subkey (it crashed). Its import command was my personal favorite, though. It treated the -u command-line option as though it were the name of a remote computer and tried to connect to it. If you added the name of a remote computer to the command, the import command reported an error that said To many command-line parameters. In short, using the -u command-line option was impossible.

Incidentally, the To in the previous error message was not my doing. Reg was full of spelling and typographical errors. One of the better typos was the continual reference to HKRC, which should be HKCR.

Part
III

Ch
10

Adding Subkeys and Values

Use Reg's add command to add new subkeys and values. The following list describes this command:

Syntax:

```
REG ADD [\\computer\]subkey [/ve | /v value] [/t type] [/s separator]
➥[/d data] [/f]
```

Options:

`computer`	Name of a remote computer (uses local computer if `\\computer\` is omitted)
`subkey`	Fully qualified name of the subkey, beginning with the root key (you can use abbreviations: **HKLM**, **HKU**, and so on)
`/ve`	Changes the subkey's default value
`/v value`	Name of the new value to add in `subkey` (enclose in quotation marks if `value` contains whitespace)
`/t type`	Data type of the value (**REG_SZ** is the default and any type not in Table 10.3 is unavailable)
`/s separator`	Escape character that separates each string in a **REG_MULTI_SZ** value (the default is the number `0`, and you use it like this: `First\0Second`)
`/d data`	Data to assign to `value`
`/f`	Forces Reg to replace subkeys and values without confirmation

Table 10.3   Data Types for *Reg's Add* Command

Data Type	Usage
REG_BINARY	Binary data: FE06CD040214
REG_DWORD	Decimal numbers: 198
REG_DWORD_LITLE_ENDIAN	Decimal numbers: 1313
REG_DWORD_BIG_ENDIAN	Decimal numbers: 1313
REG_EXPAND_SZ	Expandable strings: `"Temp: %TEMP%"`
REG_MULTI_SZ	Multiple strings, with each string separated by the escape character specified by the `/s` command-line option: `"Line 1\0Line 2"`
REG_SZ	Simple strings: `"This is a string"`

Comparing Subkeys and Values

Reg's `compare` command replaces similar utilities in earlier resource kits. At this writing, `Comreg.exe` is no longer available in *Microsoft Windows 2000 Resource Kit*. Here is a summary of this command:

Syntax:

```
REG COMPARE [\\computer\]subkey [\\computer\]subkey [/ve | /v value]
➥[/s] [/oa | /od | /os | /on]
```

Options:

computer	Name of a remote computer (uses local computer if *computer*\ is omitted)
subkey	Fully qualified name of the subkey, beginning with the root key (you can use abbreviations: **HKLM**, **HKU**, and so on)
/ve	Compares the subkeys' default value
/v *value*	Name of the value to compare (enclose in quotation marks if *value* contains whitespace)
/s	Compares all the subkeys' descendent subkeys and values
/oa	Outputs all differences and matches
/od	Outputs differences only
/os	Outputs matches only
/on	Outputs nothing

Copying Values and Subkeys

Reg's copy command is a good way to copy subkeys or values from one computer to another. For example, repair a file association on numerous computers by copying **HKCR\type** from the source computer to each of the target computers. You can also copy subkeys from one location to another within the same computer's Registry, a handy trick for backing up specific portions of the Registry quickly. The following is a summary of this command:

Syntax:

```
REG COPY [\\computer\]subkey [\\computer\]subkey [/s] [/f]
```

Options:

computer	Name of a remote computer (uses local computer if *computer*\ is omitted)
subkey	Fully qualified name of the subkey, beginning with the root key (you can use abbreviations: **HKLM**, **HKU**, and so on)
/s	Copies all the subkeys' descendent subkeys and values
/f	Forces Reg to replace subkeys and values without confirmation

Deleting Subkeys and Values

Use Reg's delete command to remove subkeys or values from the Registry. Here's a summary of this command:

Syntax:

```
REG DELETE [\\computer\]subkey [/va | /ve | /v value] [/f]
```

Part

III

Ch

10

Options:

`computer`	Name of a remote computer (uses local computer if `\\computer\` is omitted)
`subkey`	Fully qualified name of the subkey, beginning with the root key (you can use abbreviations: **HKLM**, **HKU**, and so on)
`/va`	Deletes all values from `subkey`
`/ve`	Deletes the subkey's default value
`/v value`	Name of the value to delete from `subkey` (enclose in quotation marks if `value` contains whitespace)
`/f`	Forces Reg to delete subkeys and values without confirmation

Exporting Subkeys to REG Files

Reg's export command is the same as Regedit's Export Registry File command. Use it to create version 5 REG files, the default, or version 4 REG files using the `/nt4` command-line option. Here's a summary of this command:

Syntax:

```
REG EXPORT subkey filename [/nt4]
```

Options:

`subkey`	Fully qualified name of the subkey, beginning with the root key (you can use abbreviations: **HKLM**, **HKU**, and so on)
`filename`	Name of the REG file to create
`/nt4`	Create version 4, ANSI REG files

Importing REG Files

Reg's import command is the same as Regedit's Import Registry File command. Use it to import REG files that you create using the export command or Regedit. Here's a summary of this command:

Syntax:

```
REG IMPORT filename
```

Options:

`filename`	Name of the REG file to import

Saving Subkeys to Hive Files

Reg's save command is the same as Regedt32's Save Key command and is useful for performing quick backups. The location in which Reg saves hive files differs depending on the target computer and platform:

Local computer	Current directory
Remote computer running Windows NT or Windows 2000	*SystemRoot*\System32
Remote computer running Windows 95 or Windows 98	*SystemRoot*

The following is a summary of Reg's save command:

Syntax:

    REG SAVE [*computer*\]*subkey* *filename*

Options:

computer	Name of a remote computer (uses local computer if *computer*\ is omitted)
subkey	Fully qualified name of the subkey, beginning with the root key (you can use abbreviations: **HKLM**, **HKU**, and so on)
filename	Name of the hive file to create

Loading Hive Files Temporarily

Reg's load command is the same as Regedt32's Load Hive command. It loads a hive file into a temporary subkey you specify, which must already exist. This command's changes are not persistent, meaning that Windows 2000 unloads the hive file when you restart the computer. Here's a summary that describes how to use this command:

Part III

Ch 10

Syntax:

    REG LOAD [*computer*\]*subkey* *filename*

Options:

computer	Name of a remote computer (uses local computer if *computer*\ is omitted)
subkey	Fully qualified name of the subkey, beginning with the root key (you can use abbreviations: **HKLM**, **HKU**, and so on)
filename	Name of the hive file to load

Restoring Saved Hive Files

Reg's restore command is the same as Regedt32's Restore command. It loads a hive file into the subkey you specify, replacing any subkeys and values it finds there. Changes that the restore command makes are persistent, meaning that they remain after you restart the computer. Here's a brief description of the restore command:

Syntax:

```
REG RESTORE [\\computer\]subkey filename
```

Options:

computer	Name of a remote computer (uses local computer if \\computer\ is omitted)
subkey	Fully qualified name of the subkey, beginning with the root key (you can use abbreviations: **HKLM**, **HKU**, and so on)
filename	Name of the hive file to restore

Unloading Temporary Subkeys

Reg's unload command is the same as Regedt32's Unload Hive command. It removes the subkey you created when you loaded a hive using the load command or Regedt32's Load Hive command. Here's a summary of this command:

Syntax:

```
REG UNLOAD [\\computer\]subkey
```

Options:

computer	Name of a remote computer (uses local computer if \\computer\ is omitted)
subkey	Fully qualified name of the subkey, beginning with the root key (you can use abbreviations: **HKLM**, **HKU**, and so on)

N O T E You can't unload a hive that Windows 2000 loads, such as **HKLM\HARDWARE**. Additionally, you can't unload any hive when the operating system or a program is using a subkey or value in that hive. ■

Querying Values

Use Reg's query command to display a single value, all values within a subkey, or all values in a branch. If you don't give the name of a value, Reg queries all values in the subkey. The following is a summary of this command:

Syntax:

```
REG QUERY [\\computer\]subkey [/ve | /v value] [/s]
```

Options:

computer	Name of a remote computer (uses local computer if *computer*\\ is omitted)
subkey	Fully qualified name of the subkey, beginning with the root key (you can use abbreviations: **HKLM**, **HKU**, and so on)
/ve	Queries the default value
/v *value*	Name of the value in *subkey* to query (enclose in quotation marks if *value* contains whitespace)
/s	Queries all of *subkey*'s descendent subkeys and values

Repeating Commands for a List of Items

All recent versions of MS-DOS provide the for command to automate repetitive tasks. Use it in a batch file or at the MS-DOS command prompt. It repeats a command for each item in a list or each file matching a specification such as *.doc. You substitute items in the command using an arbitrary placeholder, such as %I. Using this capability, write commands such as the following, which repeats Reg's query command for each item in the parenthetical list:

```
For %I In (jh-dsk01, jh-dsk02, jh-prt01) Do Reg Query \\%I\HKCR\txtfile
```

I'll take it a bit at a time. The for command runs everything appearing after the word Do one time for each item in the list, (jh-dsk01, jh-dsk02, jh-prt01). Each time it repeats the command, it substitutes the actual list item for the placeholder, %I in this case. Thus, this for command runs the following commands:

```
Reg Query \\jh-dsk01\HKCR\txtfile

Reg Query \\jh-dsk02\HKCR\txtfile

Reg Query \\jh-prt01\HKCR\txtfile
```

Other forms of the for command provide more advanced capabilities. You can write a command such as For %I In (*.doc) Do Del "%1", and the for command will repeat Del "%1" once for each file with the .doc extension it finds in the current directory, substituting %1 with the file's actual name. Note the use of the quotation marks, which ensures that long filenames work properly. Using the command's /D command-line option, you can repeat commands for directory names, instead of filenames. Using the /R option, you can repeat commands for an entire directory tree. For example, For /R C:\ %I In (*.TMP) Do Del "%I" removes every file with the .tmp extension from every directory on drive C. The /L option iterates through a fixed range of numbers, much like a for loop in C++; and the /F option parses files and program output. The /F option is useful to administrators because it can take the output of something such as Net's view command and repeat a command for each line of its output.

Part

III

Ch

10

N O T E For more information about the different forms of the `for` command, type `for /?` at the MS-DOS command prompt. You also will find extensive information in Windows 2000 Help.

To parse files and commands using the `for` command's `/F` command-line option, make sure that you enable the MS-DOS command extensions. Enabled is the default setting. To learn about enabling and disabling the MS-DOS command extensions, at the MS-DOS command prompt, type `cmd /?`.

The MS-DOS command extensions aren't available in Windows 98; so don't use them in logon scripts if you must support Windows 98 computers on the network. ■

The following sections show examples that use the `for` command to automate repetitive tasks. I'm hoping that these examples fire up your imagination. Note that to use these commands in batch files, placeholders must have two percent signs (%%) instead of one. Percent signs are special characters in batch files, so you must use two of them to represent a single percent sign in the command. Just remember that you use a single percent sign at the MS-DOS command prompt or two percent signs in a batch file, like this:

```
Command Prompt    For %I In (*.*) Do Del %I
Batch File        For %%I In (*.*) Do Del %%I
```

List of Options in Text Files

The following repeats a command for every line in a text file, substituting the placeholder `%I` with each line:

```
For /F "tokens=*" %I In (Values.txt) Do Reg Add %I /f
```

This form of the `for` command is a timesaving way to script Registry changes. Create a text file similar to the one shown in Listing 10.5, name it `Values.txt`, and it'll add each value using Reg. This is frighteningly similar to importing REG files.

Note a few things about this command. First, `"tokens=*"` instructs the `for` command to substitute `%I` with all of each line. Normally, the `for` command breaks lines into tokens that it separates with space or tab characters; then it passes the first token to the command and throws away the rest. Normally, the command only sees the first part of each line up to the first tab or space character. Additionally, the quotation marks around `%I` are required because Reg doesn't handle names with spaces very well.

Listing 10.5   Sample *Values.txt*

```
"HKCU\Control Panel\Desktop" /v DragFullWindows /t REG_DWORD /d 1
"HKCU\Control Panel\Desktop" /v FontSmoothing /t REG_DWORD /d 2
"HKCU\Control Panel\Desktop" /v MenuShowDelay /t REG_DWORD /d 400
```

You can create variations of this command that separate each line into tokens. First, it might help if you think of tokens as fields and delimiters as characters that separate each field.

Identify the fields you want to put in the text file. You might want a subkey, a data type, and a value. Then, choose the delimiters you want to use to separate each field. They don't have to all be the same, but make sure the delimiters won't appear anywhere else in the file. That is, make sure the delimiters you choose won't be part of subkeys or values—semicolons (;) and pipes (|) are good choices; backslashes (\) aren't. Assuming you're using a comma as a delimiter, the lines in your text file might look like Listing 10.6.

Now it's time to write the `for` command. You specify the delimiters you're using with the `delims=` option which, if you're using a comma and semicolon as delimiters, looks like this: `delims=,;`. You specify the tokens (fields) you want to receive with the `tokens=` option. If you want the first three tokens on each line, it looks like `tokens=1,2,3`. If you want the fourth and fifth tokens, it looks like `tokens=4,5`. The `for` command creates consecutive placeholders for each token, starting with the placeholder you specify in the command. If the placeholder is `%I`, the first token replaces `%I`, the second replaces `%J`, and the third replaces `%K`. Add an asterisk (*) to the end, `tokens=4,5*`, and the `for` command creates another token that contains everything remaining on the line. You put all this together within quotation marks and add it to the `for` command:

```
For /F "delims=,; tokens=1,2,3,4" %I In (Values.txt) Do Reg Add "%I" /v "%J"
➥/t %K /d %L /f
```

Listing 10.6   Sample *Values.tx*

```
HKCU\Control Panel\Desktop,DragFullWindows,REG_SZ,1
HKCU\Control Panel\Desktop,FontSmoothing,REG_SZ,2
HKCU\Control Panel\Desktop,MenuShowDelay,REG_SZ,400
```

Commands on Multiple Computers

Net's `view` command lists the computers on the network. You can use this command's output with the `for` command to do something to each computer's registry, as long as you have administrative rights on each computer.

At the MS-DOS command prompt, type `net view`. You see output similar to Listing 10.7. The first three lines are useless, as is the last line. Moreover, any line that means anything begins with two backslashes (\\). Net separates the fields `server name` and `remark` with spaces. Use the `skip=` option to skip the first three lines of Net's output. With the `for` command's default delimiters—space and tab—it will parse the computer names correctly, but there isn't anything to do about the last line of the file. Armed with this information, you can write the following command, which removes **HKLM\Software\Name** from each computer's Registry:

```
For /F "skip=3" %%I In ('Net View') Do Reg Delete \\%I\HKLM\Software\Name /f
```

Listing 10.7   Output from Net's *View* Command

```
H:\>net view
Server Name                Remark

----------------------------------------------------------------------------
\\CC-PRT01                 Charlene's Portable
\\JH-DSK01                 Jerry's Desktop
\\JH-DSK02                 Windows 2000 Professional
\\JH-PRT01                 Jerry's Portable
\\PDC-2000                 Windows 2000 Server
\\PDC-CAMELOT              Primary Domain Controller
The command completed successfully.
```

If you're ready for some real power, combine the previous section's example with this section's example so that you can add a list of values to all the computers on the network. This one ought to get you a raise!

Create a batch file that accepts a computer name as a command-line option. Name the file Values.bat. When a batch file runs, it substitutes the first command-line option for %1, the second for %2, the third for %3, and so on. Thus, use %1 to represent the remote computer name. In that batch file, execute the following command (mind the percent signs—we're not at the command prompt, Toto), which adds values from the text file Values.txt to the each computer's registry:

```
For /F "tokens=*" %%I In (Values.txt) Do Reg Add "\\%1\%%I"
```

The batch file adds values to a single computer's registry. Use the for command to execute that batch file for each computer on the network:

```
For /F "skip=3" %%I In ('Net View') Do Values.bat %%I
```

Logs from Multiple Computers

One last example of using the for command. The following queries **HKLM\HARDWARE\ DESCRIPTION\System** in each network computer's registry and outputs the result to a text file that has the same name as the computer:

```
For /F "skip=3 delims=\ " %I In ('Net View') Do Reg Query
➥\\%I\HKLM\HARDWARE\DESCRIPTION\System >%I
```

In this case, delims=\ strips off the two backslashes, leaving only the computer's name. This is so the command can create a text file using the computer's name. The result is a text file for each network computer that contains a brief description of the computer's hardware, which includes the BIOS version, BIOS date, and video adapter. Oh! I'm getting drunk with power.

Writing Scripts for Windows Script Host

Microsoft Windows Script Host is to Windows 2000 what batch files were *supposed* to be to MS-DOS. Scripts are a powerful way to automate mundane and repetitive tasks. Although they are equally suited to the needs of administrators and power users, the reality is that users seldom have the skills necessary to write scripts; administrators do. Administrators use scripts to automate complex tasks such as connecting users to network resources, updating users' Registries, or managing an organization's workflow. As well, anyone can write scripts to update the Registry with the customizations you learn about in this book, and this chapter gives plenty of examples.

If you're the type who likes to put names to faces, you'll want to know what programs are behind Windows Script Host. When you run a script, Windows 2000 runs either `Cscript.exe` or `Wscript.exe` and passes the script to them as a command-line option. These two programs *are* Windows Script Host. `Jscript.dll` and `Vbscript.dll` are the JScript and VBScript scripting engines. Because the host is language-agnostic, it uses these engines to interpret scripts. `Scrrun.dll` provides the host's runtime library and `Scrobj.dll` is the host's object library. A few others play supporting roles but are unimportant.

Version 2.0 is the latest version of Windows Script Host and version 5.0 is the latest version of the scripting engines. These are the versions that come with Windows 2000. If your organization uses recent versions of Windows throughout, a homogeneous organization, you don't have to worry about installing or upgrading Windows Script Host. Additionally, installing Internet Explorer 5 updates any 32-bit version of Windows with the latest version of the host. To recap, the following combinations of products provide the latest version of the host:

- Windows 2000
- Windows 98 Second Edition
- Internet Explorer 5 with any 32-bit Windows

N O T E For more information about installing Windows Script Host in Windows 95 or upgrading to the most recent version, visit the scripting site at `http://msdn.microsoft.com/scripting.`

Teaching you everything you need to know about writing scripts is beyond the scope of this book (you knew it was coming). You must learn about keywords such as `if`, `then`, and `for`; how to write different kinds of statements; how to write and use functions and objects; and how to put it all together in a script that does something useful and actually works. Nevertheless, help is available from good sources, all of which are nearby. On the Windows 2000 CD-ROM, look in `Valuadd\Xtradocs\Script` for a handful of help files. These files describe how to use the host and contain handy references for the two scripting engines the come with the operating system. If you need more information, turn to the Web. Microsoft maintains `http://msdn.microsoft.com/scripting`, which contains a plethora of information about the scripting. Even though I can't teach you everything you need to know about writing scripts, I can show you how to write scripts that manipulate the Registry; thus, in the following sections, you learn how to add, remove, and change values. You also learn how to check for errors and report them to users.

Hardware Requirements

I realize this book is about Windows 2000 but, as an administrator, you'll have to write scripts for other versions of Windows, including Windows 98 and Windows NT 4.0. Thus, knowing the requirements is helpful.

The host and your scripts will run anywhere a suitable 32-bit Windows operating system will run; thus, if a computer runs Windows 98 well, the host will run well on that same computer. If a computer runs Windows NT 4.0 well, the host will run well. Examine the hardware requirements for each version of Windows in order to clarify the requirements for Windows Script Host.

Windows 98, Windows NT Workstation 4.0, and Windows 2000 have many common requirements. They all require a VGA or better resolution monitor. They all require a mouse or similar pointing device. None requires a CD-ROM drive but all are less cantankerous if it's available.

On the subject of processors and memory, I depart from the official Microsoft rhetoric. No recent version of Windows runs well on anything less than a Pentium or compatible processor. Windows 98 requires at least 32MB of memory but 64MB makes for a better experience. Windows NT Workstation 4.0 and Windows 2000 Professional are nothing short of doggish on computers that don't have at least 64MB of memory, but nothing less than 96MB excites me. Windows NT Server 4.0 and Windows 2000 Server just about double those requirements.

Creating Script Templates

Scripts are text files that have the file extensions in Table 10.4. The .js extension is for JScript, Microsoft's incarnation of JavaScript, and the .vbs extension is for VBScript. In addition, the table shows you a sample from each language. Note the JScript statement is alarmingly similar to a C++ statement. That's because the syntax of JScript is based loosely on C++, which is the reason I tend to favor JScript over VBScript. JScript statements end with a semicolon. VBScript statements don't. A third file, which has the .ws file extension, allows you to use statements from both languages in a single file.

Table 10.4   VBScript and JScript

Extension	Language	Sample Statement
.js	JScript	`WSHShell.RegDelete("HKCU\\MyKey\\");`
.vbs	VBScript	`WSHShell.RegDelete "HKCU\MyKey\"`

Scripts begin life as an empty file, unless you make a template from which to start. Listing 10.8 is a template for JScript. There isn't much to it. The first line is a comment (comments begin with two forward slashes) and the third line creates a Shell object. Anything you do to the Registry, you must do via the Shell object; it provides methods for manipulating the Registry.

Listing 10.8   JScript Template

```
// Template.js - JScript template

var WshShell = WScript.CreateObject( "WScript.Shell" );
```

Objects such as Shell provide methods, properties, and events. *Methods* are functions unique to that object, *properties* are the object's attributes, and events are tougher to explain. *Events* are things that happen to an object, such as a mouse click. You associate a function, or *event handler*, with an event so that the object calls the event handler any time the event occurs. Thankfully, you don't have to write event handlers to manipulate the Registry, so I'll skip right by that one for now. If you don't feel comfortable writing scripts and all this seems confusing, content yourself with copying and modifying the examples in this chapter. It'll do the trick.

Listing 10.9 is a VBScript template. The differences between this and Listing 10.8 are that comments begin with an apostrophe and you write statements a bit differently. To assign an object to a variable, for example, you use the set keyword. Note, too, that statements don't end with a semicolon. JScript and VBScript have significant differences, particularly regarding keywords and syntax, but for our purpose, both languages are similar.

Listing 10.9   VBScript Template

```
' Template.vbs - VBScript template

Set WshShell = WScript.CreateObject( "WScript.Shell" )
```

Windows Script Host runs both templates well. They don't do anything, but you can try them out. Open Notepad and type either Listing 10.8 or Listing 10.9. Don't forget to use the appropriate file extension: .js for Listing 10.8 and .vbs for Listing 10.9. To run the script, type its path and filename in the Run dialog box. As well, because Windows 2000 associates a script's Open command with Windows Script Host and makes it the default, you can run a script by double-clicking the file in Microsoft Windows Explorer. If you want more action when you try out your first script, add the following line to the end of the JScript template:

```
WshShell.Popup( "This is a basic JScript script!" );
```

N O T E   When writing JScript scripts, letter case is important. WSHShell is not the same thing as WshShell, in other words, and results in an error when you run the script. Letter case isn't as important in VBScript scripts. ■

Part

III

Ch

10

Running in MS-DOS and Windows

Windows 2000 includes two different hosts, Windows-based and MS-DOS–based. The Windows-based host is Wscript.exe. It handles scripts that you run from Windows Explorer, the Run dialog box, and other places. The MS-DOS–based host is Cscript.exe, and it handles scripts that you run from the MS-DOS command prompt. To run scripts in the MS-DOS–based host, you must provide the script as a command-line option to `Cscript.exe`: `cscript.exe sample.vbs`.

Both the MS-DOS–based and Windows-based hosts allow you to specify options that change their behaviors. The MS-DOS–based host accepts a number of command-line options. Note that each of these options begins with two forward slashes, not one. That's because you can pass options to the script itself, and you specify these options using a single forward slash. In general, the command line for `Cscript.exe` looks like this:

Syntax:

> **cscript** *filename* [*host_options*] [*script_options*]

Options:

`//?`	Displays help
`//i`	Allows Windows Script Host to display prompts and script errors
`//b`	Prevents Windows Script Host from displaying prompts and script errors
`//T:`*n*	Kills the script if it runs for longer than *n* seconds
`//Logo`	Displays an execution banner
`//Nologo`	Doesn't display an execution banner
`//H:CScript`	Registers `Cscript.exe` as the default script interpreter in the Registry
`//H:Wscript`	Registers `Wscript.exe` as the default script interpreter in the Registry
`//S`	Makes current options the default

The Windows-based host supports similar options. Click Properties on a script's shortcut menu, and you see the *Name* Properties dialog box shown in Figure 10.3. You recognize the options on the Script tab because they're similar to the command-line options for `Cscript.exe`. When you click OK to save your options, Windows 2000 creates a file with the .wsh extension, a WSH file, in the same directory as the script. This file looks like a Configuration Settings (INI) file. Think of WSH files as you do shortcuts, which contain options for running MS-DOS–based programs. Listing 10.10 shows a typical WSH file. You can run WSH files, and the operating system will find the script file because the script's path is in the [ScriptFile] section.

Listing 10.10   Sample WSH File

```
[ScriptFile]
Path=C:\Documents and Settings\Jerry\Desktop\Sample.js

[Options]
Timeout=10
DisplayLogo=1
BatchMode=0
```

FIGURE 10.3

A script's Properties dialog box allows users to set options similar to the MS-DOS–based host's.

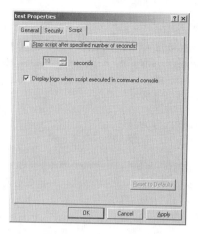

Formatting Subkey and Value Names

When writing scripts, format subkey and value names as you do anywhere else or, for that matter, as you see in this book. Use long or short names, **HKEY_LOCAL_MACHINE** or **HKLM**, and separate each portion of a subkey with a single backslash. Short names are **HKCR**, **HKCC**, **HKCU**, **HKLM**, and **HKU**, all which you know by now. You end subkey names with a backslash but not value names. **HKLM\Software\Microsoft** is the name of a subkey, but **HKCR\txtfile\flags** is the name of a value (a value named **flags** in **HKCR\txtfile**).

VBScript is straightforward with regard to how you write subkey and value names as strings, but JScript is not. JScript uses the backslash as an escape character (see Table 10.2.). Thus, within a string, JScript substitutes \ " with a quotation mark and \n with a newline character. Because the backslash is a significant character, you must escape the backslash in subkey and value names. This only applies to JScript, though. Thus, if you write a subkey named **HKLM\Software\Microsoft** as a string, you'd write **"HKLM\\Software\\Microsoft"** because \\ is an escape sequence that JScript replaces with a single backslash. To make all this clear, Table 10.5 shows how to write subkey and value names as strings in both languages.

Part

III

Ch

10

Table 10.5	Subkey and Value Names in Strings	
Description	**VBScript**	**JScript**
Subkey	**"HKLM\Sample\"**	**"HKLM\\Sample\\"**
Value	**"HKLM\Sample\Value"**	**"HKLM\\Sample\\Value"**

N O T E Table 10.5 describes how you write subkey and value names as strings, but you might wonder about default values. Simple. The Shell object's methods allow you to assign values to a subkey, which is the same as setting a subkey's default value. Use a subkey name anywhere you'd normally use a value name in order to access the subkey's default value. ▪

Adding and Changing Values

Use the Shell object's RegWrite method to add or change an entry. If the entry exists, it changes the entry's value; otherwise, it creates the entry before setting the entry's value. Here's the syntax for the RegWrite method:

JScript:

```
object.RegWrite(name, value [,type]);
```

VBScript:

```
object.RegWrite name, value [,type]
```

Parameters:

object	Shell object
name	Subkey to create
value	Default value of the subkey
type	**REG_SZ, REG_EXPAND_SZ, REG_DWORD**, or **REG_BINARY**; all else causes RegWrite to return E_INVALIDARG

The first parameter, *name*, and the last parameter, *type*, are always strings. The *type* parameter is optional and the default is **REG_SZ**. The *value* parameter's type depends on *type*. If *type* is **REG_SZ** or **REG_EXPAND_SZ**, use a string in the second parameter. If it's **REG_DWORD** or **REG_BINARY**, use a number in the second parameter.

Listing 10.11 is an example that adds and changes values. In fact, it enables many of the settings on the Effects tab of the Display Properties dialog box, which you open from Control Panel by double-clicking Display Properties. The fifth line causes Windows 2000 to display the entire contents of a window when you drag it. The sixth line has the operating system smooth fonts when it displays them, removing the jagged edges that result from font aliasing on low-resolution displays, and the last lines control how the operating system displays menus and screen tips, in this case causing them to fade in and out. For more information about these and other customizations, see Chapter 7.

Listing 10.11   Change Display Effects

```
// Change display effects

var WshShell = WScript.CreateObject( "WScript.Shell" );

WshShell.RegWrite( "HKCU\\Control Panel\\Desktop\\DragFullWindows", "1",
➥"REG_SZ" );
WshShell.RegWrite( "HKCU\\Control Panel\\Desktop\\Fontsmoothing", "2",
➥"REG_SZ" );
WshShell.RegWrite( "HKCU\\Control Panel\\Desktop\\SmoothScroll", 1,
➥"REG_DWORD" );
WshShell.RegWrite( "HKCU\\Control Panel\\Desktop\\WindowMetrics\\MinAnimate",
➥"1", "REG_SZ" );
```

N O T E The RegWrite method doesn't handle binary numbers very well. First, it only supports four-byte decimal numbers, which is really nothing more than a **REG_DWORD** value. You can get around this little problem by creating a small REG file and importing that REG file by starting it with the Shell object's Run method: WshShell.Run("Sample.reg");. ▪

Setting a Subkey's Default Value

The Shell object doesn't have a separate method for setting a subkey's default value. Instead, you pass the subkey's name, ending with a backslash, and the value to which you want to set its default value. Note, too, that the Shell object doesn't provide a method for creating new subkeys. The only way to create a new subkey is by setting its default value using the RegWrite method:

```
WshShell.RegWrite( "HKLM\\Software\\Sample\\", "Hello", "REG_SZ" );
```

Listing 10.12 is an example that changes a subkey's default value. By setting to explore the default value of **HKCR\Folder\shell**, double-clicking a folder opens it in a two-pane window rather than a single-pane window. Also, if the subkey doesn't already exist, the RegWrite method creates it. As an added bonus, this example shows you how to display messages using the Popup method.

Listing 10.12   Change the Default Command for Folders

```
// Change the Default Command for Folders

var WshShell = WScript.CreateObject( "WScript.Shell" );
WshShell.RegWrite( "HKCR\\Folder\\shell\\", "explore" );
WshShell.Popup( "Double-click My Computer to open Windows Explorer" );
```

CAUTION

The RegWrite method allows you to change the type of a subkey's default value. Ouch. You do so by passing a type other than **REG_SZ** as the third parameter. You should leave default values as strings, however, because you can't predict the results.

Removing Subkeys and Values

Use the Shell object's **RegDelete** method to remove subkeys and values. Be careful, though. Hacking the Registry into little bits is so easy that it gives Hitchcock chills, so give this method the respect it deserves. Here's how the **RegDelete** method looks:

JScript:

```
object.RegDelete(name);
```

Part

III

Ch

10

VBScript:

```
object.RegDelete name
```

Parameters:

object	Shell object
name	Subkey to create

The RegDelete method's only parameter is the name of the subkey or value you're removing. To remove a subkey, end the name with a backslash; to remove a value, don't end the name with a backslash. When you remove a subkey, the **RegDelete** method removes the entire branch, beginning with that subkey, so be careful. The **RegDelete** method would allow you to remove **HKLM\Software\Microsoft**, for example—catastrophic to the configuration.

Listing 10.13 is an example that removes a handful of subkeys. It clears out various history lists, which you learned about in Chapter 7. I wrote this particular script using VBScript for two reasons. First, it demonstrates a complete script using that language. Second, it takes advantage of VBScript's On Error statement to handle any errors, which are likely to occur because there is a good chance that one of the subkeys might not exist or might be in use by another process. Error handling keeps the script from blowing up when it runs.

I've done something new in Listing 10.13. Variables are buckets of data that have names and from which you can retrieve data by using the bucket's name. I've assigned a subkey to the variable EXPLORER and then used it in lieu of retyping the same subkey repeatedly. Note that I used all uppercase letters to make the variable stand out as a constant. Not only does this technique make code easier to write, it makes code easier to read. In VBScript, you concatenate two strings using the & operator: MYSTR & "Sample", STR1 & STR2, and "My" & "Code" are examples. In JScript, you concatenate two strings using the + operator (you see a JScript example in Listing 10.14).

Listing 10.13   Remove History Lists from the Registry

```
' Remove History Lists from the Registry, including RecentDocs,
' RunMRU, Map Network Drive MRU, and OpenSaveMRU

EXPLORER = "HKCU\Software\Microsoft\Windows\CurrentVersion\Explorer\"

Set WshShell = WScript.CreateObject( "WScript.Shell" )

On Error Resume Next

WshShell.RegDelete EXPLORER & "RecentDocs\"
WshShell.RegDelete EXPLORER & "OpenSaveMRU\"
WshShell.RegDelete EXPLORER & "RunMRU\"
WshShell.RegDelete EXPLORER & "Map Network Drive MRU\"
```

> **CAUTION**
>
> In the process of experimenting with these methods, I made more than a few typos, such as leaving out the last backslash, typing the subkey's name wrong, and forgetting to provide the value name. The results were costly, particularly in the latter case. Windows 2000 removed the entire branch instead of simply removing the value I wanted to nuke. So, back up the registry first.

Reading Values from the Registry

The `Shell` object's `RegRead` method allows you to read values from the Registry and assign them to variables. After putting a value in a variable, you can do a variety of things with it—write it to a new location in the Registry or display it to the user. The following examples show the syntax for the **RegRead** method:

JScript:

```
object.RegRead(name);
```

VBScript:

```
object.RegRead name
```

Parameters:

object	Shell object
name	Value to read

The only argument to **RegRead** is the name of the value you're reading. To read a subkey's default value, end the name with a backslash; otherwise, don't end the name with a backslash. A limitation is that trying to read a value that doesn't exist will stop a script. Worse, Windows Script Host doesn't provide a way to check whether a value exists before trying to read it. Go figure. If you're familiar with JScript, you can use the `try` and `catch` keywords to prevent Windows Script Host from displaying errors when you read values that don't exist.

Listing 10.14 is an example that toggles options on and off. These are the settings on the Start Menu Options tab of the Taskbar Properties dialog box. The **REG_DWORD** value **HKCU\Software\MyConfig** indicates which of two possible configurations is current. A 0 indicates the first and a 1 indicates the second. This script uses the `try` and `catch` keywords to prevent the host from displaying errors if **HKCU\Software\MyConfig** doesn't exist when the script reads its value. The code in the `try` statement attempts to read the value and the code in the `catch` statement sets the value to a default if an error occurred.

Part

III

Ch

10

Listing 10.14   Toggle *DragFullWindows* On and Off

```
// Toggle Options On and Off

var CONFIG = "HKCU\\Software\\MyConfig";
```

continues

Listing 10.14 Continued

```javascript
var WINDOWS = "HKCU\\Software\\Microsoft\\Windows\\";
var ADVOPTS = "CurrentVersion\\Explorer\\Advanced\\";

var CADCP = WINDOWS + ADVOPTS + "CascadeControlPanel";
var CADMD = WINDOWS + ADVOPTS + "CascadeMyDocuments";
var CADNC = WINDOWS + ADVOPTS + "CascadeNetworkConnections";
var CADP  = WINDOWS + ADVOPTS + "CascadePrinters";
var INTEL = WINDOWS + ADVOPTS + "IntelliMenus";
var SMADM = WINDOWS + ADVOPTS + "StartMenuAdminTools";
var SMCHV = WINDOWS + ADVOPTS + "StartMenuChevron";
var SMFAV = WINDOWS + ADVOPTS + "StartMenuFavorites";
var SMSCR = WINDOWS + ADVOPTS + "StartMenuScrollPrograms";

var WshShell = WScript.CreateObject( "WScript.Shell" );

try
{
  var numConfig = WshShell.RegRead( CONFIG );
}
catch(e)
{
  numConfig = 1;
}

if( numConfig == 1 )
{
  numConfig = 0;
  WshShell.RegWrite( CADCP, "YES" );
  WshShell.RegWrite( CADMD, "YES" );
  WshShell.RegWrite( CADNC, "YES" );
  WshShell.RegWrite( CADP, "YES" );
  WshShell.RegWrite( INTEL, "YES" );
  WshShell.RegWrite( SMADM, "YES" );
  WshShell.RegWrite( SMCHV, 1, "REG_DWORD" );
  WshShell.RegWrite( SMFAV, 1, "REG_DWORD" );
  WshShell.RegWrite( SMSCR, "YES" );
}
else
{WshShell.Popup( "Hello" );
  numConfig = 1;
  WshShell.RegWrite( CADCP, "NO" );
  WshShell.RegWrite( CADMD, "NO" );
  WshShell.RegWrite( CADNC, "NO" );
  WshShell.RegWrite( CADP, "NO" );
  WshShell.RegWrite( INTEL, "NO" );
  WshShell.RegWrite( SMADM, "NO" );
  WshShell.RegWrite( SMCHV, 0, "REG_DWORD" );
  WshShell.RegWrite( SMFAV, 0, "REG_DWORD" );
  WshShell.RegWrite( SMSCR, "NO" );
}

WshShell.RegWrite( CONFIG, numConfig, "REG_DWORD" )
```

Editing the Registry with INF Files

Setup information (INF) files are a generic way to install just about anything. Programmers use them to install device drivers and applications. For you, power user, programmer, or administrator, INF files are useful any time you need to copy files to a specific location on users' computers, delete files, change the registry, and update INI files. Here's some inspiration for you, in the form of things you can do with INF files:

- Install documents on users' computers
- Customize users' computers via the Registry
- Upgrade components on users' computers
- Copy and run installation packages
- Disable features by removing files

Few people know about INF files and fewer, still, use them. Regardless, INF files are the method I prefer to use any time I need to distribute Registry changes, particularly to large numbers of people. (Note that I use INF files extensively throughout this book.) INF files aren't completely intuitive and take some work. After you learn to write them, however, they're easy and, with the help of programs such as INF-Tool, which you learn about later, they're simple to create.

Listing 10.15 is a complete example of an INF file that changes the Registry by adding and removing values. The file looks similar to an INI or REG file. It contains a number of sections that look like [section] and within each section is any number of entries, which you can also call items or lines. This example also shows how to remove subkeys from the Registry. You learn how to build INF files in the sections that follow this but, for now, try out this INF file using these steps:

1. Open Notepad and type Listing 10.15.
2. Save your changes.

   Click Save As on Notepad's File menu. In the Save as Type list, click All Files in order to save a text file with the .inf file extension.

3. Click Install on the INF file's shortcut menu. Open Registry Editor to observe the changes.

Part III

Ch 10

Listing 10.15 Sample INF File

```
[Version]
Signature=$CHICAGO$

[DefaultInstall]
AddReg=My.Add.Reg
DelReg=My.Del.Reg

[My.Add.Reg]
HKCU,Control Panel\Desktop,SmoothScroll,1,01,00,00,00
HKCU,Control Panel\Desktop,ScreenSaveUsePassword,1,00,00,00,00

[My.Del.Reg]
HKCU,Software\Microsoft\Windows\CurrentVersion\Explorer\RecentDocs
HKCU,Software\Microsoft\Windows\CurrentVersion\Explorer\OpenSaveMRU
HKCU,Software\Microsoft\Windows\CurrentVersion\Explorer\RunMRU
HKCU,Software\Microsoft\Windows\CurrentVersion\Explorer\Map Network Drive MRU
```

N O T E INF files are complex. This chapter introduces you to a good number of concepts concerning these files, but there is much more to learn. Microsoft's developer site, http://msdn.microsoft.com, has extensive documentation on the subkey. Search using the keywords *inf* and *addreg*. ▓

An Alternative: INF-Tool

If you plan to produce more than a handful of INF files, Richard Fellner's INF-Tool is a must-have utility. I use it to produce the INF files available on my Web site. It allows you to ponder the programs orRregistry hacks you're installing and not the format of the INF file. An evaluation copy of INF-Tool is available at Richard's Web site, http://inner-smile.com. Registration enables all of this program's features and is only $39 US.

INF-Tool creates advanced INF files that go far beyond what most people can do on their own. You can install files into specific locations on users' computers. You can make any number of changes to the Registry, create shortcuts on the Start menu, or change INI files. Additionally, you can display messages before and after installation and allow users to uninstall your program or Registry hack. The part I like best is that you can create CAB and ZIP files as well as self-extracting distribution packages, just like the big kids. To tell you the truth, I find very little about INF-Tool that I don't like and strongly recommend this program to administrators who have to distribute anything to anybody and to programmers looking for a great way to create installation packages for the Internet.

Creating an Empty INF File

The only section that *must* appear in all INF files is [Version]. Some call it a header. It contains a single entry, signature, which identifies the file as a valid INF file. You'll frequently see additional entries in this section, all of which are optional or are not useful when installing programs or Registry hacks. The `Class` and `ClassGUID` entries define the class and GUID of devices in the Registry. The `LayoutFile` entry names a layout file, which describes each installation file's source and destination. You can specify the same information within the INF file, though. The only entry that might prove useful when changing the Registry is `Provider`, which identifies the party or person responsible for the file. For our purposes, changing the registry, this section always looks like the following:

```
[Version]
signature=$CHICAGO$
```

When users click Install on an INF file's shortcut menu, Windows 2000 looks for the `[DefaultInstall]` section. This section names other sections within the INF file that contain actual installation instructions. The operating system defines a specific set of names that you can use for entries in the `[DefaultInstall]` section and each name serves a particular purpose. The `AddReg` entry names other sections that add subkeys and values to the Registry, for example, and the `CopyFiles` entry names sections that copy files to the user's computer. For each entry that you want to use in the `[DefaultInstall]` section, you add its name and assign a list of sections to it. The format of this entry is *name=section[,section]*. As shown, you can assign more than one section to any entry. Look again at Listing 10.15. The `[DefaultInstall]` section contains two entries, `AddReg` and `DelReg`. The `AddReg` entry's list contains the name of a single section: `My.Add.Reg`. The `[My.Add.Reg]` section contains a list of values to add to the Registry. Likewise, the `DelReg` entry's list has a single section name, `My.Del.Reg`, and this section contains a list of values to remove from the Registry. The following list describes many but not all of the entry names you use in the `[DefaultInstall]` section:

AddReg	Add subkeys and values
CopyFiles	Copy files to the computer
DelReg	Remove subkeys and values
DelFiles	Remove files from the computer
Ini2Reg	Move entries from INI files to the Registry
RenFiles	Rename files on the computer
UpdateIniFields	Update fields in an INI file
UpdateInis	Change entries in an INI file

Part
III

Ch
10

N O T E The order in which you list the `AddReg` and `DelReg` entries within `[DefaultInstall]` has no bearing on how Windows 2000 processes the INF file. The operating system processes the `DelReg` sections first, followed by the `AddReg` sections. You can use this to completely remove a subkey, clearing out its contents, before replacing it with new contents. ■

Adding Subkeys and Values

Each [add-registry-section] section, where add-registry-section is the name of a section that contains subkeys and values to change in the Registry, must appear in an AddReg entry of the [DefaultInstall] section. Each line in an [add-registry-section] section can have up to five parameters. Use the first two to add a subkey; use all five to add or change a value. Each line within an [add-registry-section] section has a similar format, as shown in the following list:

Syntax:

HKEY, subkey, name, flags, value

Parameters:

HKEY	Long or short root key names: **HKCR**, **HKCU**, **HKLM**, and **HKU**
subkey	Subkey to create or subkey containing value to change
name	Name of the value to create or change; leave name blank to work with the subkey's default value
flags	Type of the value (see Table 10.6)
value	Data to put in the value; use the format most appropriate for flags

N O T E In the INF files of most device drivers, you see **HKR**. Not a short root key name, it's a subkey that Windows 2000 passes to the INF file and is the root of the device's configuration information in the registry.

The flags parameter, among other things, determines what type of value you're adding or changing. Table 10.6 shows the flags you can use. In general, the first two bytes of flags contain general information about the value and the second two bytes define the value's type. You can combine 0x00000002 through 0x00000020 with other flags, but you can't combine them together. If you're logic-challenged and you skipped Chapter 1, add them together: 0x00000008 + 0x00010000 is 0x00010008. If you don't include flags in an entry, the type defaults to **REG_SZ**.

Table 10.6   Flags for [add-registry-section]

Flag	Description
0x00000000	**REG_SZ** data
0x00000001	**REG_BINARY** data
0x00000002	Don't overwrite the subkey or value if it already exists
0x00000004	Delete the value from the Registry
0x00000008	Append a value to an existing value; works for **REG_MULTI_SZ** values only
0x00000010	Create the subkey and ignore the value
0x00000020	Set value only if it already exists

Flag	Description
0x00010000	**REG_MULTI_SZ** data
0x00010001	**REG_DWORD** data
0x00020000	**REG_EXPAND_SZ** data
0x00020000	**REG_NONE** data
0xFFFF0001	Mask data

How you write *value* depends on *flags*. If it's a **REG_SZ, REG_MULTI_SZ,** or **REG_EXPAND_SZ** value, write the string as always: "Between quotes, like this". If it's any other type of value, write it in hexadecimal notation, like this: **01,00,FF,CD**. When using hexadecimal notation, you must have at least two bytes, so there will be no less than one comma in the value. The digits' order depends on the value's type, too. If it's a **REG_DWORD** value, reverse the digits (*little-endian*). If it's a **REG_BINARY** value, keep the digits in order. For more information about how to represent different types of data in hexadecimal notation, see Chapter 1.

To make things just a bit clearer, the following list contains numerous examples and, following each example, is an explanation:

- HKCU,Sample,Value,0,"Hello"

  Adds Value to **HKCU\Sample**, sets its type to **REG_SZ**, and stores "Hello" in it.

- HKCU,Sample,Value,,"Hello World"

  Adds Value to **HKCU\Sample**, sets its type to **REG_SZ**, and stores "Hello World" in it.

- HKCU,Sample,Value,1,77,34,05,20

  Adds MyValue to **HKCU\MyKey**, sets its type to **REG_BINARY** and puts 77,34,05,20 in it.

- HKLM,Software,Example,0x10001,04,03,02,01

  Adds Example to **HKLM\Software**, sets its type to **REG_DWORD**, and puts 0x01020304 in it.

- HKLM,Software,txtfile\shell,,,"notepad"

  Sets the default value of **HKLM\Software\txtfile\shell** to "notepad."

- HKCU,Software\Sample

  Adds the subkey Sample to **HKCU\Software**.

Part

III

Ch

10

Deleting Subkeys and Values

The name of each section containing subkeys and values to delete from the Registry, *del-registry-section*, must appear in the [DefaultInstall] section's DelReg entry. Each line in a [*del-registry-section*] section can have up to three parameters. Use the first two to delete a subkey; use all three to delete a value. Here's what each line within a [*del-registry-section*] section looks like:

Syntax:

```
HKEY, subkey, name
```

Parameters:

HKEY	Long or short root key names: **HKCR, HKCU, HKLM,** and **HKU**
subkey	Subkey to delete or subkey containing value to delete
name	Name of the value to delete; leave *name* blank to delete a subkey

The following list contains a few examples that show you how to remove subkeys and values using the [*del-registry-section*] section of an INF file:

▪ HKCU,Software\Example

Remove **HKCU\Software\Example** from the Registry.

▪ HKLM\Software\Sample,Goner

Remove the value **Goner** from **HKLM\Software\Sample**.

Copying Files to the Computer

The name of each section containing files to copy to users' computers, *file-list-section*, must appear in the [DefaultInstall] section's CopyFiles entry. Each line in a [*file-list-section*] section can have up to four parameters, but one parameter is the norm. Here's what each line within a [*file-list-section*] section looks:

Syntax:

> *destination, source, temporary, flags*

Parameters:

destination	Name of destination file
source	Name of source file (don't use if source and destination filenames are the same)
temporary	Ignored
flags	Flags that control how the operating system copies files (see Table 10.7)

Table 10.7   Flags for [*file-list-section*]

Flag	Description
0x00000001	Display a warning if users try to skip copying the file after an error occurs
0x00000002	Don't allow users to skip copying the file
0x00000004	Ignore file versions and write over existing files in the destination
0x00000008	Pretend that the file is in use during the copy operation, forcing the operating system to copy the file when it restarts
0x00000010	Don't overwrite existing files in the destination directory

Flag	Description
0x00000020	Don't overwrite existing files in the destination directory if they're newer than the source file
0x00000040	Copy the source file to the destination directory only if it already exists

Listing 10.16 shows you an INF file that creates a new directory in *SystemRoot* called Scripts. It copies three script files, Desktop.js, Cleanup.js, and Backup.js, to the new directory. Notice that it has three additional sections about which you haven't learned:

▪ **[DestinationDirs]**—Without this section, Windows 2000 copies files to *WinDir*\System32. This section must appear exactly as shown in Listing 10.16 and has one item for each *[file-list-section]* section. The format is *file-list-section=LDID,subdirectory*. In the listing, you see My.Copy.JS=10,"Scripts". This means that the operating system should copy all the files in the [My.Copy.JS] section to *SystemRoot*\Scripts. The *logical disk identifier* (LDID) 10 represents *SystemRoot*. If you wanted put your scripts in *SystemDrive*\Script Files, you'd have an entry such as My.Copy.JS=30,"Script Files". The LDID 30 represents the root of the boot drive. Table 10.8 describes other ordinals that you can use in your INF files (many are undocumented).

▪ **[SourceDisksNames]**—This section identifies the name of each source disk. The format of each entry is *disk-number="description"[,[label],[,path]*. *disk-number* is a unique number that identifies the disk, the *description* parameter is a brief description of the disk, which Windows 2000 displays when asking users to insert the disk in a drive, the *label* parameter is the volume label of the disk, which the operating system uses to check that users insert the right disk, and the *path* parameter is the path to the source files. Because, presumably, you're distributing files from the network or a single disk, you'll have a single entry. In most cases, you can just use what you see in Listing 10.16. You must include this section in all your INF files if you want the operating system to copy any files.

▪ **[SourceDisksFiles]**—The files you see under this section are the same as those you see in each *[file-list-section]*. The format of each entry is *name=disk-number[,subdirectory][,size]*. *name* is the filename, the *disk-number* parameter is the disk number containing the file, the *subdirectory* parameter is the subdirectory that contains the file, and the *size* parameter is the uncompressed size of the file. All parameters but the first are optional. You assign to each filename the disk number containing that file and, if necessary, the subdirectory that contains it. Backup.js=1 means that Backup.js is on disk 1, for example, and Backup.js=1,Scripts means that the Backup.js is in the Scripts directory on disk 1. Again, although this seems like a futile exercise, you must associate each filename with a source disk if you want the operating system to copy your files.

Part

III

Ch

10

Listing 10.16   Copy Files to Users' Computers

```
[version]
Signature="$CHICAGO$"

[DefaultInstall]
CopyFiles=My.Copy.JS

[My.Copy.JS]
Desktop.js
Cleanup.js
Backup.js

[DestinationDirs]
My.Copy.JS=10,"Scripts"

[SourceDisksNames]
1="Scripts"

[SourceDisksFiles]
Desktop.js=1
Cleanup.js=1
Backup.js=1
```

Table 10.8   Logical Disk Identifiers

LDID	Description
-1	Absolute path
0	Null LDID
1	Source drive:\path
10	Windows directory
11	System32 directory
12	Drivers directory
17	Inf directory
18	Help directory
20	Fonts directory
21	Viewers directory
23	Color directory
24	Applications directory
25	Shared directory
30	Boot driver's root directory
50	System directory

51	Spool directory
52	Spool drivers directory
53	User profile directory
54	Directory containing `NTLDR` or `Osloader.exe`
16386	Programs directory (for current user)
16389	My Documents directory (for current user)
16390	Favorites directory (for current user)
16391	Startup directory (for current user)
16392	Recent directory (for current user)
16393	SendTo directory (for current user)
16400	Desktop directory (for current user)
16403	NetHood directory (for current user)
16404	Fonts directory
16405	Templates directory (for current user)
16406	Start Menu directory (for all users)
16407	Programs directory (for all users)
16408	Startup directory (for all users)
16409	Desktop directory (for all users)
16410	Application Data directory (for current user)
16411	PrintHood directory (for current user)
16412	Local Settings directory (for current user)
16415	Favorites directory (for all users)
16417	Cookies directory (for current user)
16419	Application Data directory (for all users)
16420	Windows directory
16421	System32 directory
16422	Program files directory
16423	My Pictures directory (for current user)
16424	User profile directory
16427	Common Files directory
16429	Templates directory (for all users)
16430	Documents directory (for all users)
16431	Administrative Tools directory (for all users)
16432	Administrative Tools directory (for current user)

Part
III

Ch
10

Deleting Files from the Computer

The name of each section containing files to delete from users' computers, *file-list-section*, must appear in the [DefaultInstall] section's DelFiles entry. Each line in a [*file-list-section*] section can have up to four parameters: Two are always empty, but one parameter is the norm. Note that you can assign the name of a single [*file-list-section*] section to a CopyFiles and a DelFiles entry. Here's what each line within the section looks like:

Syntax:

    destination,,,flags

Parameters:

destination	Name of destination file
flags	Flags that control how the operating system copies files (see Table 10.9)

Table 10.9   Flags for *[file-list-section]*

Flag	Description
0x00000001	If the file is in use, delete the file when Windows 2000 restarts.
0x00010000	If the file is in use, delete the file when Windows 2000 restarts. (Use this flag instead of 0x00000001 when using the file list to copy *and* delete files.)

Renaming Files on the Computer

The name of each section containing files to rename, *file-list-section*, must appear in the [DefaultInstall] section's RenFiles entry. Each line in a [*file-list-section*] section must have two parameters. You can't use a single [*file-list-section*] to copy *and* rename files. Here's what each line within the section looks like:

Syntax:

    new-name,old-name

Parameters:

new-name	New name of the file
old-name	Old filename, which must be in a [SourceDisksFiles] section

Making INF Files Easier to Read

Each INF file can have a [Strings] section, which you typically see at the bottom of the INF file. This section makes INF files easier to read and easier to translate because entries in different sections become much shorter and all the file's localizable text accumulates in one place. The [Strings] section has one or more entries. Each entry gives a name to a string and you can use that string anywhere in the file by enclosing its name in percent signs (%): *%string-name%*.

Listing 10.17 combines all this section's examples into one and uses a [Strings] section to make it a bit more readable. Notice that, instead of using flags such as 0x00010001 and 0x00000001, this INF file's [Strings] section assigns those flags to meaningful names and each entry in the [*add-registry-section*] uses the name. Much easier to read. This INF file assigns subkeys to names, too, and the [*add-registry-section*] and [*del-registry-section*] sections both use them, making those sections much easier to read at a glance.

Listing 10.17 Sample INF File

```
[Version]
Signature=$CHICAGO$
Provider=%Provider%

[DefaultInstall]
AddReg=My.Add.Reg
DelReg=My.Del.Reg
CopyFiles=My.Copy.JS

[My.Add.Reg]
HKCU,%R_Desktop%,%R_SmoothScroll% ,%REG_BINARY%,01,00,00,00
HKCU,%R_Desktop%,%R_ScreenSavePassword% ,%REG_DWORD%,00,00,00,00

[My.Del.Reg]
HKCU,%R_Explorer%,%R_RecentDocs%
HKCU,%R_Explorer%,%R_OpenSaveMRU%
HKCU,%R_Explorer%,%R_RunMRU%
HKCU,%R_Explorer%,%R_MapNetworkMRU%

[My.Copy.JS]
Desktop.js
Cleanup.js
Backup.js

[DestinationDirs]
My.Copy.JS=10,%Where%

[SourceDisksNames]
1=%Diskname%

[SourceDisksFiles]
Desktop.js=1
Cleanup.js=1
Backup.js=1
```

Part
III

Ch
10

continues

Listing 10.17   Continued

```
[Strings]
Provider="Jerry Honeycutt"
Diskname="Scripts from Jerry Honeycutt"
Where="Scripts"

REG_SZ="0"
REG_BINARY="1"
REG_DWORD="0x10001"

R_Desktop="Control Panel\Desktop"
R_SmoothScroll="SmoothScroll"
R_ScreenSavePassword="ScreenSaveUsePassword"

R_Explorer="Software\Microsoft\Windows\CurrentVersion\Explorer"
R_RecentDocs="RecentDocs"
R_OpenSaveMRU="OpenSaveMRU"
R_RunMRU="RunMRU"
R_MapNetworkMRU="Map Network Drive MRU"
```

 TIP Earlier, you learned about LDIDs, which represent directories on the computer. The LDID 10 is *SystemRoot*, for example. Windows 2000 defines strings for each LDID, so you can use them anywhere in an INF file by enclosing them in percent signs. This makes using paths in an INF file easier because you don't have to know the actual path, just the LDID. Try putting the path to the current user's documents in a value without using LDIDs as strings! Here's how that looks: HKLM,Subkey,Value,,%16389%.

Choosing Your Poison

Scripts are complex. They're better to use if manipulating the Registry is part of a larger task, such as connecting users to the network or maintaining security settings.

If your needs are simple, and all you need is to change or add a value, use REG files. They're easy to create by using Regedit's Explorer Registry File command. The one drawback to REG files is that you can't use them to remove subkeys or values from the Registry. If that's your requirement, move on to INF files or use Reg in a batch file.

INF files are the ultimate method for editing the Registry, especially if you need to remove subkeys or values. They are easier to read than REG files, in my opinion, but are harder to create. The ultimate benefit of using INF files is that it works well with all the data types in the Registry. None of the other methods you learn about in this chapter work well with binary data, for example. A smaller benefit is that the default command for an INF file is not to install, so Windows 2000 doesn't install the INF file when you double-click it.

The following table summarizes these details for your convenience:

Feature	REG	Batch	Script	INF
Access OS Features	No	Yes	Yes	No
Add subkeys/values	Yes	Yes	Yes	Yes
Change values	Yes	Yes	Yes	Yes
Delete subkeys/values	No	Yes	Yes	Yes
Easy to learn	Yes	Yes	No	No
Install by default	Yes	Yes	Yes	No
Stable and reliable	Yes	No	Yes	Yes
Works with all types	Yes	No	No	Yes

Changing the Registry During Installation

Unattended installation allows you, an administrator, to automate the installation of Windows 2000, completely or partially. The setup program uses a script, an *answer file*, which provides answers for questions that the setup program normally asks users. Building an answer file isn't always trivial, but *Microsoft Windows 2000 Resource Kit* includes Setup Manager. Setup Manager, which is also in Windows 2000 Resource Kit Support Tools (see "Editing the Registry Within Batch Files," earlier in this chapter), generates answer files from a variety of questions that it asks.

Answer files contain multiple sections that describe how to install Windows 2000. Unattend.txt is a typical name for an answer file, but you can call it anything. The answer file in Listing 10.18 is an example that provides enough information to install Windows 2000 Professional with no user intervention. It names the computer, sets the resolution and color depth of the display, and configures the computer's network connection.

Part
III

Ch
10

Listing 10.18   Sample Answer File

```
;SetupMgrTag
[Unattended]
    UnattendMode=FullUnattended
    OemPreinstall=No
    TargetPath=Windows

[GuiUnattended]
    AdminPassword=password
    TimeZone=20

[UserData]
    ProductID=111111-111111-111111-111111-111111
```

continues

Listing 10.18   Continued

```
        FullName="Jerry Honeycutt"
        OrgName="Jerry Honeycutt"
        ComputerName=WIN2000DSK01

[Display]
        BitsPerPel=16
        Xresolution=800
        YResolution=600
        Vrefresh=72

[LicenseFilePrintData]

[TapiLocation]
        AreaCode=972

[RegionalSettings]

[OEM_Ads]

[GuiRunOnce]
        Command0="rundll32 printui.dll,PrintUIEntry /in /n
\\WIN2000SRV01\LaserJet"

[Identification]
        JoinDomain=CAMELOT
        CreateComputerAccountInDomain=Yes
        DomainAdmin=Administrator
        DomainAdminPassword=password

[Networking]
        InstallDefaultComponents=No

[NetAdapters]
        Adapter1=params.Adapter1

[params.Adapter1]
        INFID=*

[NetClients]
        MS_MSClient=params.MS_MSClient

[params.MS_MSClient]
        RPCSupportForBanyan=No

[NetServices]
        MS_SERVER=params.MS_SERVER

[params.MS_SERVER]

[NetProtocols]
        MS_TCPIP=params.MS_TCPIP
```

```
[params.MS_TCPIP]
    DNS=Yes
    EnableLMHosts=Yes
    AdapterSections=params.MS_TCPIP.Adapter1

[params.MS_TCPIP.Adapter1]
    SpecificTo=Adapter1
    DHCP=Yes
    WINS=Yes
    WinsServerList=192.168.0.1
    NetBIOSOptions=0
```

The following list describes the command that runs the setup program with an answer file as its guide:

Syntax:

```
winnt[32] /unattend:answerfile /s:source [/syspart:targetdrive]
```

Options:

`answerfile`	Name of the answer file
`/s: source`	Path of the installation files
`/syspart: targetdrive`	Disk on which to install Windows 2000

Answer files don't make special provisions for changing the Registry during or after installation. They do allow you to specify a list of commands that run after the setup program finishes, however, so you can put a number of registry changes in a REG file, batch file, script, or INF file and run it after installation finishes:

1. Create the file that's going to change the Registry. It can be a REG file, batch file, Windows Script Host script, or INF file.

2. In the directory that contains the installation files—usually a network share if your users install Windows 2000 from the network—create a subdirectory called oem.

3. In the oem directory, create a text file called `Cmdlines.txt` and add the command that runs the file containing your registry changes. Make sure to enclose the command in quotation marks. To run an INF file, use the following command line:

   `rundll32.exe setupapi,InstallHinfSection DefaultInstall 132 filename.inf`

4. Copy the file containing the Registry changes to the same directory as the `Cmdlines.txt` file.

5. Add the `OEMPreInstall` entry to the answer file's `[Unattended]` section, setting it to Yes (see the top of Listing 10.18).

   ```
   [Unattended]
   OEMPreInstall=Yes
   ```

Part

III

Ch

10

TIP If you allow Setup Manager to create the installation share and copy the source files to the share, it creates the `$oem$` directory and `Cmdlines.txt` file, too. It also sets the `OEMPreInstall` entry to Yes.

Troubleshooting

Diagnosing Registry Errors

Using *Regedit.exe*

Most of the error messages you see while editing the Registry have two causes. The most likely cause is that you're trying to do something with a subkey or value that another process has open or has already removed. If you're viewing a particular branch in the Registry, for instance, and another program removes a subkey in that branch, you'll still see the subkey in Registry Editor even though it doesn't exist anymore. When you try to do something with that subkey, Registry Editor displays an error message. To make sure the subkey still exists, press F5 to update the Registry Editor display. Another likely cause is that you're trying to do something with a dynamic key or value. The only thing I can tell you about editing dynamic keys and values is this: *don't*.

N O T E Registry Editor sometimes allows you to remove an entire subkey containing dynamic data. In most cases, Windows 2000 rebuilds this information after you restart your computer. ■

Cannot create key: error message.

The cause of this error depends on the rest of the message:

- ■ `Error while opening the key` *name*. Either you don't have permission to edit this particular subkey, or you're trying to add a subkey to a key that another program deleted in the background. Refresh Registry Editor by pressing F5 so that you can tell if a program did indeed remove the key.

- ■ `Error writing to the Registry`. If you try to create a new subkey underneath one of the dynamic keys, you'll get this error message. Remember that you can't edit dynamic keys.

- ■ `Unable to generate a unique name`. I would be surprised if you ever see this message. It means Registry Editor wasn't able to create a unique name for the subkey, such as **New Key #1**.

Cannot create value: error message.

This error message is similar to the one you get when creating a new subkey. *Error message* is `Error writing to the Registry` if you're trying to create a value in a subkey that no longer exists or that is dynamic. If you're not trying to create a value in a dynamic subkey, refresh the Registry by pressing F5 to make sure the subkey still exists. As far as `Unable to generate a unique name`, the same goes for values as it does subkeys: Registry Editor wasn't able to create a unique name for the value, such as **New Value #1**.

Cannot edit name: error message.

The meaning of this error depends on the rest of the message:

- **Error reading the value's contents.** This error message indicates that a subkey is in use by another process. To avoid this message, close the process that's using the subkey. Another likely possibility is that another process has removed the subkey, in which case you can refresh the Registry by pressing F5.

- **Error writing the value's new contents.** This message implies that you're trying to write to one of many dynamic values. Don't do that.

Cannot open name: Error while opening key.

The most likely cause is that you're trying to open a subkey that another process has removed. Remember that just because you see a subkey in Registry Editor doesn't mean that another process might not have removed it. To make sure, press F5 to refresh Registry Editor's display. Another possibility is that the subkey you're trying to open is corrupted. No easy solution exists to repair a corrupt subkey; you can try exporting the subkey to a REG file, removing it, and importing the REG file back into the Registry.

Cannot rename name: error message.

The reason behind this message depends on the rest of the message:

- **Error while renaming key.** or **Error while renaming value.** These messages generally mean you're trying to rename a dynamic subkey or value. Don't do that.

- **The specified key name already exists. Type another name and try again.** This message means you're using a name that already exists. Each subkey name within a key must be unique. Likewise, the message The specified value name already exists. Type another name and try again. means you're using a value name that already exists within that same subkey.

- **The specified key name contains illegal character.** This message implies that you're using a backslash (\) somewhere in the subkey's name. Don't do that.

- **The specified key name is too long. Type a shorter name and try again.** This error means you're trying to use a name longer than 255 characters. Use a shorter name. Remember also that creating a subkey with no certainty that a program will use it is as senseless as it is useless.

Cannot delete name: Error while deleting key.

Remember that you can't remove dynamic subkeys from the Registry. You also see this error message if you try to remove a subkey after another process has already beaten you to it. Press F5 to refresh the display, verifying that the subkey does or doesn't exist. Unable to delete all specified values. is a reminder that you can't delete the default value for any subkey. You can delete the default value's contents or, if the default value is the only item remaining for the subkey, remove the subkey itself. You can't delete dynamic values either.

Cannot print: error message.

The reason behind this message depends on the rest of the message. In either of the following cases, follow the instructions the error message gives you to solve the problem:

- ▪ `Insufficient memory to begin job. Try closing down some applications, and try again. If you still see this message, try restarting Windows.`

- ▪ `An error occurred during printing. Check your printer and your printer's settings for problems, and try again.`

Registry editing has been disabled by your administrator.

The system administrator has disabled Registry Editor using policies.

 TIP How did I figure out all the possible error messages? I didn't create errors to see what would happen; I'd never discover all the possible messages. Instead, I used a nifty program called Programmer's Assistant to display a list of all the text messages contained in EXE and DLL files such as Regedit.exe and Regedt32.exe. You can download a copy of Programmer's Assistant from `http://www.hotfiles.com`.

Using Regedt32.exe

The following list describes the error messages you may run across in Regedt32.exe:

- ▪ `Registry Editor cannot create a value entry without a name. Please enter a value name.` You must give new values a proper name. Otherwise, you see this error message.

- ▪ `Cannot create a value entry without data. Please enter the data.` This error indicates that Regedt32 expected you to assign data to the new value. Do so.

- ▪ `Registry Editor could not create the value entry. The value entry already exists. Please enter a new name.` If you try creating a new value using a name that already exists, you see this error message. Either use a unique name or, if you intend to replace the value, edit the old value. Alternatively, you can remove the old value and create a new one with the same name.

- ▪ `The decimal value entered is greater than the maximum value of a DWORD. Registry Editor will truncate the value entered.` Values larger than 65,535 don't fit in a DWORD. Allowing Regedt32 to truncate the value is probably not what you expected, so you might double-check it and create a binary value if necessary.

■ **Data of type MULTI_SZ cannot contain empty strings. Registry Editor will remove the empty string found.** Regedt32 doesn't allow **MULTI_SZ** values to have empty strings in them. Its solution is to remove the empty string from the list; however, if that's not what you intended, you should double-check the value.

■ **Data of type MULTI_SZ cannot contain empty strings. Registry Editor will remove all empty strings found.** This error message is similar to the previous. It indicates that Regedt32 found more than one empty string in the **MULTI_SZ** value. As in the previous case, Regedt32 removes all blank strings from the list, which is possibly not what you expected. Double-check the value.

■ **The binary data entered does not represent a whole number of bytes. Registry Editor will pad the binary data with 0s.** Binary data must have enough digits to be a whole number of bytes. Remember, there are two digits for every byte. Leave off one of the digits and Regedt32 adds a 0 to the end. Most likely, this isn't what you expected, so you should definitely check the value to make sure it looks right.

■ **Registry Editor cannot create a key without a name. Please enter a key name.** Regedt32 requires a unique name for each subkey. Provide one and you won't see this error message.

■ **Registry Editor could not create the key. The key already exists.** Each subkey within a key must have a unique name. You see this error message if you try to use a name that already exists. This doesn't mean you can't use the same name in two different parts of the Registry, however.

■ **The key name specified is not valid. A key name cannot contain \.** Backslashes are not valid in subkey names. Remove all backslashes from the name and try again.

■ **Insufficient privilege to perform requested operation. Registry Editor could not accomplish the requested operation. Registry Editor could not create the subkey.** If you don't have privileges to create a subkey under the current key, you'll see this error message. Generally, the administrator has privileges to add subkeys just about anywhere in the Registry. Users might not, however. In either case, this message usually means you're treading where you shouldn't.

■ **The key currently selected does not give you access to create a subkey. Registry Editor could not create the subkey.** This message means the same thing as the previous message. You don't have sufficient privileges to create a subkey under the current key.

■ **The key, or one of its subkeys does not give you DELETE access. Registry Editor could not delete the key currently selected.** You must have the appropriate privileges to delete the selected subkey. If not, you see this error message. Try logging on as Administrator and then delete the subkey. Note that this error message usually indicates that you're trying to delete a subkey that you shouldn't delete.

■ **The key currently selected does not give you access to create a value entry. Registry Editor could not add the value entry.** You don't have privileges to add a value to the current subkey. Try logging on as Administrator before adding the value.

■ **The key currently selected does not give you access to delete a value entry. Registry Editor could not delete the value entry.** You don't have privileges to delete the selected value. You can try logging on as Administrator before deleting the subkey. This error message usually indicates that you're trying to delete a value that you shouldn't delete.

■ **The key currently selected is marked for deletion. Registry Editor could not save the value entry.** This error indicates that the subkey in which you're saving a value is in the process of being deleted by another program. Regedt32 won't let you add the value. Wait a few seconds and then press F5 to update Regedt32. The subkey will probably disappear.

■ **The key currently selected does not give you access to set a value entry. Registry Editor could not save the value entry.** You don't have privileges to change the selected value. Try logging on as Administrator before changing the value.

■ **The key currently selected does not give you access to retrieve such information. Registry Editor could not retrieve the security information.** Administrators have sufficient privileges to display security information for each subkey in the Registry. Users might not, depending on how the administrator configures security in the Registry. If you don't have appropriate privileges to display security information, you see this error message. There isn't much you can do about it other than logging on as Administrator first.

■ **The key currently selected does not give you access to save such information. Registry Editor could not save the security information.** Administrators have sufficient privileges to change security information for each subkey in the Registry. Users might not, depending on how the administrator configures security in the Registry. If you don't have appropriate privileges to save security information, you see this error message. There isn't much you can do about it other than logging on as Administrator.

Importing and Exporting REG Files

Most of the problems you encounter when importing and exporting the Registry come from two sources. First, the path and filename might be invalid. Second (and more likely), the REG file might be invalid, especially if you create it by hand. Look for these two problems when you get any error message during an import or export operation.

Cannot import filename: error message.

The meaning behind this error depends on the rest of the message:

- **Error accessing the Registry.** For some reason, Registry Editor is unable to access the Registry. Make sure that if you're editing a remote Registry, you have permission to do so, and make sure the Registry files are in place if you're working with a local Registry. Otherwise, open Registry Editor and inspect the Registry to make sure it is indeed OK.

- **Error writing to the Registry.** This means you're trying to import data into a corrupt or dynamic Registry subkey.

- **Error opening the file. There may be a disk or file system error.** First, double-check the filename. If you're importing a filename that contains spaces from an MS-DOS command line or the Run dialog box, you'll see this error message when you forget to surround the filename with spaces. If the filename isn't the problem, try opening the file in Notepad. Also run Chkdsk to check the file system for errors. You might have to use a stronger utility to fix this problem, particularly if Chkdsk doesn't fix it.

- **Error reading the file. There may be a disk error or the file may be corrupt.** This error is similar to the preceding one, except that Registry Editor can open the file; it just can't read it. Try reading the REG file in Notepad. Can you see its entire contents in the editor window? Also run Chkdsk to check the file system for errors. If you can read the file using Notepad, but you can't import the file into the Registry, you have a more serious problem.

- **The specified file is not a Registry script. You can import only Registry files.** This means you're trying to import a REG file that's invalid. If you're definitely importing a REG file, make sure it's not damaged. Double-check Chapter 10, "Scripting Customizations," to make sure you're using the correct format for REG files. Also make sure you have REGEDIT4 on the very first line of the file and that the second line is blank.

Part

IV

Ch

11

Cannot export filename: Error writing the file. There may be a disk or file system error.

Again, double-check the path and filename that you're specifying. Also make sure you have enough space on the disk to create the file. Other than that, this error usually indicates a more serious problem that involves the file system. Run Chkdsk to look for errors in the file system.

 TIP If you suspect that a particular Registry branch is corrupt, try removing that branch from the Registry. Back up the Registry first. If you can export that branch to a REG file before removing it, that's even better. That way, you can restore the REG file after removing the branch. This and other creative techniques can usually help you salvage a damaged Registry, but in most cases you're better off restoring a recent backup copy.

Using Registry Editor's Options

The error messages in this section occur when trying to use Registry Editor on the command line by typing **regedit** *options* at the MS-DOS command prompt. For more information about using Registry Editor on the command line, see Chapter 3, "Editing with Regedit."

Cannot open filename.

The REG file you're trying to import doesn't exist or doesn't contain valid information. Make sure the format of the REG file is correct, starting with REGEDIT4 followed by a blank line. Also make sure you're not missing any brackets ([]). Last, make sure you double-check the filename. If the path contains spaces, enclose it in quotation marks.

Cannot import filename: error message.

The meaning of this error depends on the rest of the message. The messages you see when importing a REG file using Registry Editor's command-line options are the same as when you're using Registry Editor's window. The preceding section describes these messages and tells you what to do about them.

Cannot export filename: error message.

The meaning of this error depends on the rest of the error message. The following two messages are unique to Registry Editor's command-line options. (The preceding section, "Importing and Exporting REG Files," describes any remaining error messages you might see.)

- ▓ `Error creating the file.` This error message suggests that you should double-check the filename, making sure you enclose paths that have spaces in quotation marks. Also, make sure you have enough disk space for the REG file.

- ▓ `The specified key name does not exist.` This message means you're trying to export or delete a key that doesn't exist. Double-check the command line.

Error accessing the Registry: The file may not be complete.

Registry Editor's command-line options report this message if you try to import a REG file that's too big. There might not be enough memory available to import the file. Try freeing additional conventional memory by starting the computer with a minimal configuration. Optionally, split the REG file into multiple REG files using a text editor, and then import each REG file separately.

Registry Editor reports a variety of error messages if you don't get the command line just right:

- Invalid switch
- Parameter format not correct
- Required parameter missing
- Too many parameters

In all of these cases, check Chapter 3, "Editing with Regedit," or type **regedit /?** at the command prompt to make sure you're using the correct command line.

Data Is Missing from the Registry

It's a common complaint: "I imported a REG file, but the data is missing from the Registry." The leading cause of this problem is a REG file that isn't using the correct format or has syntax errors. Refer to Chapter 10, "Scripting Customizations," to make sure you're using the correct format.

Here are some other notes to help you locate problems in a REG file. Make sure you're not missing any brackets around key names: **[HKEY_LOCAL_MACHINE\SOFTWARE]**. Make sure you enclose each value name in quotation marks. Use @ to indicate the default value entry. Check the format used for string, binary, and DWORD values. Enclose string values in quotation marks, and prefix DWORD values with **DWORD:**.

Working with Remote Registries

When working with remote Registries, you might see any of the following error messages:

- **You cannot connect to your own computer.** This error message is self-explanatory. If you want to edit the local Registry, you don't need to try connecting to it by choosing <u>R</u>egistry, <u>C</u>onnect.

- **Error Connecting Network Registry.** The Registry Editor reports this error message when it can't connect to the remote computer's Registry. This error is vague and applies to situations in which the other error messages don't apply. In general, double-check the same old things. Make sure you have permission to connect to the remote computer's Registry. Double-check that remote administration is enabled on the remote computer. Also make sure computers running Windows 98 are using the Microsoft Remote Registry Service.

- **Unable to connect to** *name***. Make sure that this computer is on the network, has remote administration enabled, and that both computers are running the remote Registry service.** Follow the instructions in this error message to fix the problem. Beyond that, make sure your own network connection is working properly.

- **Unable to connect to all of the roots of the computer's Registry. Disconnect from the remote Registry and then reconnect before trying again.** This is an indication that you don't have permission to connect to one or more of the root keys in that Registry.

■ **Unable to connect to** *name*. **Make sure you have permission to administer this computer.**   As this message states, you probably don't have permission to connect to the remote computer's Registry. Double-check the remote administration settings on the remote computer. You might also double-check that you're a member of the appropriate administrative groups on the server.

Repairing Damaged Registries

Using Proper Interfaces

Avoid editing the Registry whenever possible. It's a good rule to live by, because human errors made in the Registry have greater effects and consequences than if the errors were made elsewhere. Simple changes that you make via the Windows 2000 user interface ripple throughout the Registry. The simple act of enabling Active Desktop causes Windows 2000 to write data to over 30 values that are scattered across three areas of the Registry. Which way do you prefer to perform the task: the hard way or the easy way?

Windows 2000 fixes some errors before you even know they exist, and you can fix the remaining problems using the variety of tools that Windows 2000 provides. Let Device Manager and the Add/Remove Hardware Wizard deal with hardware problems, and let the Folder Options dialog box in Windows Explorer handle problems with file associations. Instead of trying to fix an application's corrupted settings, run the application's setup program and allow it to restore its own settings. You'll learn about these solutions in the remainder of this section.

 TIP You can change most of the useful settings in the Registry via the icons in Control Panel.

Don't Reinstall Windows 2000

After a support technician ventures beyond his level of competence, he'll usually tell you to reinstall Windows 2000 to fix a problem, even if the problem is clearly with the application. This is a favorite line of support technicians around the globe, even at Microsoft. This answer is certainly easier than helping you fix the problem, at least from the support person's perspective.

What happens when you reinstall Windows 2000 depends on how you do it. If you start the setup program from within Windows, it migrates your settings from the existing Registry, redetecting plug-and-play devices. If you start the setup program from MS-DOS, it installs a new copy of the operating system, also redetecting all devices. You lose in both cases. In the first case, the same settings are lying around and so reinstalling Windows 2000 gives you no relief. In the second case, you lose all your settings and must start over.

Reinstalling Windows 2000 just isn't necessary, as you can see from the preceding explanation. The only benefit you might receive by doing so is that the setup program will redetect your hardware, possibly rebuilding that portion of the Registry. Even that is questionable, however, because you can do the same thing yourself, as described in the next section.

Devices

If your hardware configuration is behaving strangely, you won't be able to fix it using Registry Editor. Figure 12.1 shows a portion of the Registry that contains configuration data for the display adapter. This branch isn't the only portion of the Registry connected to the display, and sorting it all out is a real nightmare. The bottom line is that the hardware settings in the Registry are far too complicated to do anything other than delete hardware profiles.

FIGURE 12.1
Settings for a single device are scattered.

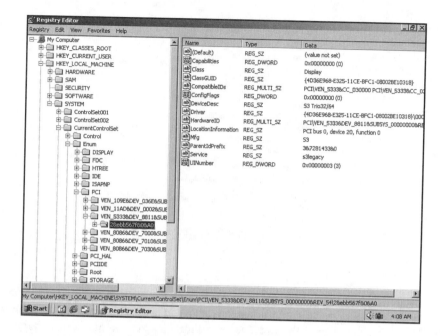

I suggest that you rely on the Add New Hardware Wizard or Device Manager to work with your hardware configuration. If you're changing the resources allocated to a device, use Device Manager. If you're trying to fix a configuration problem, use a combination of both. The following list describes a few different approaches:

- **Reconfiguring a device** Use Device Manager to change the resources for a device. To open Device Manager, in Control Panel, double-click the System icon, click the Hardware tab, and then click Device Manager. Double-click the device to open it, and click the Resources tab, shown in Figure 12.2. Device Manager warns you when you're setting up a device conflict and automatically programs plug-and-play devices to use the resources you assign.

- **Troubleshooting a device** Run the Add/Remove Hardware Wizard from Control Panel. The wizard presents a list of devices that aren't working properly. If you see the device you're troubleshooting, select it so that the Add New Hardware Wizard can help you figure out the problem.

- **Reloading a device** Open Device Manager, and remove the device you're having trouble with. Restart the computer to see if Windows 2000 automatically detects the device. If it doesn't, run the Add/Remove Hardware Wizard.

Part
IV

Ch
12

FIGURE 12.2
Deselect Use
Automatic Settings if
you want to override
Windows 2000's
default resource
settings.

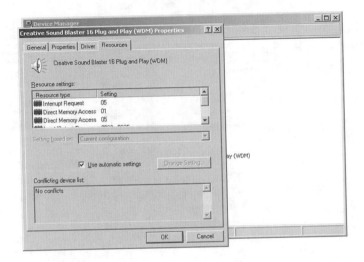

Don't assume that Device Manager represents the extent to which you can configure the hardware on your computer. Device Manager enables you to shuffle resources and set some low-level settings, but it doesn't enable you to specify preferences or higher-level settings. For that, turn to the variety of icons in Control Panel. Allocate memory regions to a display adapter in Device Manager, for example, but set its scan rate and resolution using the Display Properties dialog box. The same goes for multimedia devices, input devices, power management, and so on. Use Control Panel for higher-level settings.

> **N O T E** Windows 2000 provides a number of troubleshooters in Windows 2000 Help that help you diagnose and fix common hardware problems. These troubleshooters aren't just for novices, however. They include help for modems, display adapters, hardware conflicts, and more. ■

Associations

The portion of the Registry that loses its wits most often is **HKCR**. Not surprisingly, this is also the single largest branch in the Registry. The order in which you install programs affects file associations. Shockingly, some programs disregard your preferences altogether and change associations that have extremely loose ties to it. Microsoft Internet Explorer 5 is one of the worst culprits, taking associations for most image files for itself. One other scenario exists in which a particular file extension remains unassociated with any program. You'll notice one of the following two symptoms:

  ■ You double-click a document, and Windows 2000 opens it in the wrong program.

  ■ You double-click a document, and Windows 2000 opens the Open With dialog box, which prompts you for the program in which you want to open the document.

Some programs are good about detecting that they're no longer associated with a particular file extension. Internet Explorer 5 and Nico Mak WinZip are examples. In these cases, you can let the program fix the problem automatically. In other cases, you'll have to manually associate the program with a particular program:

1. Open Windows Explorer, and select a file that has the extension that you want to associate with a program.

2. Hold down the Shift key, and click Open With on its shortcut menu. You see the Open With dialog box, shown in Figure 12.3.

FIGURE 12.3
This list shows the programs with which you can open files.

3. Choose the program you want to associate with the file extension, and select Always Use This Program to Open These Files. Alternatively, click Other to locate an unregistered program.

N O T E   Remember that program identifiers and file extensions are separate entities. Program identifiers include information about a program, such as actions that you can perform on a file. In the Registry, file extension subkeys associate a file's extension with a program's identifier. Windows 2000 can associate more than one file extension with each program. ▓

Software

If a program's settings are messed up, it's often easier to reinstall the program. You don't have to remove the program first—just install right over it. You'll replace the program's files on the hard drive and the program's settings in the Registry. This is a particularly good way to fix problems with property sheet handlers and other shell extensions that an application installs. Be sure to install over the same folder, or you'll end up with two copies of the application on your computer, and only one will be usable.

Smarter programs know enough to leave your preferences alone while they correctly fix other settings. If you reinstall Netscape Navigator, for example, it preserves all your server settings while it resets all the program's settings in **HKCR**. Internet Explorer 5 isn't as smart, because it trashes many of your personal preferences each time you install the latest service pack.

There are other ways to restore a program's settings. Many setup programs use one or more Registration Entries (REG) files to create their initial settings in the Registry. You might be able to use the REG file again to restore damaged settings without reinstalling the program. Look in the program's installation folder and carefully inspect the REG files. If it looks like it will fix the problem, merge it into the Registry. If you want to merge only a portion of the REG file, make a copy of it, remove the extraneous content, and merge it into the Registry. REG files aren't nearly as common as Setup Information (INF) files, however. They're a bit harder to understand but contain similar information for adding, removing, and changing values in the Registry. Again, look in the program's installation folder for its INF file and examine it carefully to determine what portions you want to merge with your configuration.

Removing Program Artifacts

Most programs are rather predictable, storing the same types of information in the same types of places. They store program files in C:\Program Files and file associations in **HKCR**. They put per-user and per-computer configuration data in **HKCU\SOFTWARE** and **HKLM\SOFTWARE**, respectively. Last, they sprinkle some settings in places such as the uninstall list and the installed components list.

Take advantage of this information to remove an application that doesn't provide an uninstall program. Back up your computer, including the Registry. Then make a list of the Dynamic Link Library (DLL) and Executable (EXE) files you find in the program's installation folder, and delete them. You'll probably find them in a folder under C:\Program Files. After removing the program's folder, open Registry Editor to search for any entries belonging to the program, and remove them. Here are some suggestions for the types of things you should search for:

- Search the Registry for each of the program's installation paths. If the program has two paths, C:\Program Files\Company and C:\Program Files\Company\Program, search for both paths in the Registry. Delete any keys or value entries that contain this path. Use a bit of common sense here, and don't remove a key that another application obviously uses.

- Search the Registry for the program's name. If you're removing a program called "Elvis is a Purple Dinosaur," search the Registry for any key or value that contains "Elvis" or "Elvis is a." Search for the program's executables, too. Within reason, delete any keys or value entries that contain the name of the program or the filename of the executable.

- Search the Registry for the EXE and DLL files that you recorded earlier. Delete the key or value entry containing the reference to the file. Again, use common sense and don't remove keys that other programs obviously use.

Borrowing Subkeys and Values

If you've tried everything you can think of and nothing fixes your configuration, try borrowing the offending subkeys from another computer. Take some precautions before doing so, however. First, make sure you're not overreaching your capabilities and that you're comfortable doing this. Also, don't try borrowing hardware information from another computer, even if it's the same make and model. This technique is fine for repairing file associations but not for repairing your hardware configuration. Last, make sure you back up your own Registry before importing a portion of another computer's Registry into your own.

Follow these steps to borrow a key from another computer, importing it into your computer's Registry:

1. On the source computer, export the key you're borrowing to a REG file.

2. Trim the REG file so that it contains only the information you need and no more. Remember that Registry Editor exports the entire branch below the key. If that's your intention, fine, but inspect the contents of the REG file to make sure you know what you're getting.

3. Back up your Registry. Don't skip this step, no matter how unnecessary you think it is.

4. Copy the REG file to your computer, and merge it into the Registry by double-clicking it.

N O T E The preceding instructions show you how to swap settings using a REG file. If you use *Regedt32*, you can save subkeys to binary hive files, too, which completely replace the subkey contained in the hive file. This is often the better way to replace a subkey with the same subkey from another computer. For more information, refer to Chapter 4, "Editing with Regedt32." ∎

Part

IV

Ch

12

Repairing Computers That Won't Start

Windows 2000 has many new features that help you recover a computer that won't start. Recovery Command Console provides a limited command prompt that you can use to fix the computer if Windows 2000 won't boot to the graphical user interface. The Advanced Options Menu is similar to Windows 98's boot menu and provides a similar Safe Mode option that will often start the computer when the problem is a device that doesn't work. The emergency repair process helps you restore a working copy of the Registry, one that you create by creating an emergency repair disk. The following sections tell you about the first two techniques, and you learned about the third in Chapter 5, "Safeguarding Configurations."

Recovery Command Console

With Windows NT 4.0, if the computer didn't start and the system volume was formatted NTFS, you were out of luck. That's because you couldn't access the volume's files by booting an MS-DOS disk, because MS-DOS couldn't read NTFS volumes. In Windows 2000, you can start Recovery Command Console, which provides limited access to the system volume, even if it's NTFS. Using Recovery Command Console, you can start and stop services, format disks, copy and delete files, and so on. For example, if a corrupt driver file prevents the operating system from starting properly, you can use Recovery Command Console to copy the file from the Windows 2000 CD-ROM.

One way to start Recovery Command Console is using the setup program. The process is similar to restoring an emergency repair disk, a process you learned about in Chapter 5. Run the setup program from the CD-ROM or the setup disks. When setup asks whether you want to install Windows 2000 or repair a current installation, choose to repair the current installation and then choose to start the Recovery Command Console.

The other way, and the most useful, is to install Recovery Command Console on the computer so that it's available on the list of available operating systems. Then, you choose Recovery Command Console when you boot the computer. To install Recovery Command Console, type **d:\i386\winnt32.exe /cmdcons** at the command prompt or in the Run dialog box. From then on, you can run Recovery Command Console by choosing it when the boot loader asks you which operating system you want to run.

Recovery Command Console supports a limited number of commands. For more information about each, type **help** at Recovery Command Console's prompt. You'll find that most of them work just like the same commands in MS-DOS. The following list gives an overview of the commands available in Recovery Command Console:

- **Attrib** Changes a file or directory's attributes.
- **Batch** Executes a batch file.
- **Cd (Chdir)** Changes directories or displays the name of the current directory.
- **Chkdsk** Scans (checks) the disk for errors and optionally repair errors on the disk.
- **Cls** Clears the screen.
- **Copy** Copies a single file to another directory.
- **Del (Delete)** Deletes one or more files.
- **Dir** Displays the contents of a directory.
- **Disable** Disables a service or device driver.
- **Diskpart** Manages partitions on the disk.
- **Enable** Starts a service or device driver.
- **Exit** Exits Recovery Command Console and restarts the computer.

- **Expand**   Extracts a file from a compressed file.
- **Fixboot**   Writes a new partition boot sector on the system partition.
- **Fixmbr**   Repairs the master boot record on the partition boot sector.
- **Format**   Formats a disk.
- **Help**   Displays a list of commands that Recovery Command Console supports.
- **Listsvc**   Lists the services available on the computer.
- **Logon**   Logs on to Windows 2000.
- **Map**   Displays drive letter mappings.
- **Md (Mkdir)**   Creates (makes) a directory.
- **More**   Displays a text file one page at a time.
- **Ren (Rename)**   Renames a single file.
- **Rd (Rmdir)**   Removes a directory.
- **Set**   Displays a list of environment variables or sets an environment variable.
- **Systemroot**   Changes the root of the Windows 2000 installation you're logged on to.
- **Type**   Displays a text file.

N O T E   Recovery Command Console limits access to files in `SystemRoot` and `SystemRoot\Cmdcons`. It doesn't provide access to Program Files or Documents and Settings. Thus, it's only useful for repairing Windows 2000 system files and not other program files. Also, it enables you to copy files *from* a floppy disk but not *to* a floppy disk. ■

Advanced Options Menu

If you can't start Windows 2000, and you suspect the culprit is configuration data in the Registry, start in Safe Mode, which is a special mode that forces Windows 2000 to load without most of its device driver support. It loads the standard VGA, mouse, mass storage, and keyboard drivers only as well as a minimal set of services. Note that most of your other devices won't work properly in Safe Mode because Windows 2000 loaded their device drivers or configuration from the Registry. Starting in Safe Mode is easy. When the boot loader prompts you to choose an operating system, press **F8**. Then, choose Safe Mode from the boot menu.

The boot menu has several other options:

- **Safe Mode**   Starts Windows 2000 with basic drivers and services only, and no network connections.
- **Safe Mode with Networking**   Similar to Safe Mode but also includes network connections.

- **Safe Mode with Command Prompt** Starts Windows 2000 but displays the command prompt instead of the desktop, Start menu, and so on.
- **Enable Boot Logging** Logs the drivers and services that the operating system loads or can't load as it boots, storing the log in a file called Ntbtlog.txt in *SystemRoot*.
- **Enable VGA Mode** Starts Windows 2000 with the basic VGA driver, which is particularly useful if you suspect that a faulty display driver is preventing you from starting the operating system.
- **Last Known Good Configuration** Restores portions of the Registry that were saved the last time Windows 2000 shut down, which is useful if a new device driver prevents the operating system from starting normally.
- **Directory Service Restore Mode** Restores the **SYSVOL** directory and the directory service on a domain controller (Windows 2000 Server only).
- **Debugging Mode** Starts Windows 2000 but sends debugging information through a serial cable to another computer.

N O T E Before problems strike, create one or more disks that contain all the files you think you'll need if things go awry. You can also copy the most important bits of the Windows 2000 CD-ROM to your computer's hard disk, assuming that you have enough space. Think of this as your survival kit. ■

Fixing Other Common Problems

The following sections show you how to fix a variety of common problems in Windows 2000. Some of these problems occur when an errant program messes up your system. Other problems are peculiar to Windows 2000.

Restrictions Are Too Restrictive

Here's the rub: You can't edit the Registry because of policy restrictions, but you can't change the policy restrictions because you can't edit the Registry. There is a solution to this problem that your administrator probably doesn't want you to know about. First, create the INF file shown in Listing 12.1. Click Install on the INF file's shortcut menu. This works because Windows 2000 allows an application to change the Registry via an INF file even though policies prevent the user from editing the Registry. Note also that you can use Group Policy to remove this restriction as long as you have access to the program, which requires administrator rights.

Listing 12.1 The INF File to Remove Restrictions

```
[version]
signature="$CHICAGO$"

[DefaultInstall]
```

```
DelReg=Restrictions

[Restrictions]
HKCU,SOFTWARE\Microsoft\Windows\CurrentVersion\Policies
```

The only problem with this INF file is that Group Policy has a tendency to update itself over the network. Thus, you might have to keep this INF file around and use it anytime you want to access the Registry.

The Wrong Program Runs When You Open a File

This problem is self-explanatory. You double-click a document's filename and Windows 2000 doesn't open it in the program you expect. The solution is to reassociate the file extension with the program in which you want to open the file. You learned how to do this in the earlier section, "Associations."

Fonts Don't Work Properly

The most common cause of fonts not working correctly is that HKLM\SOFTWARE\Microsoft\Windows\CurrentVersion\Fonts is corrupted or missing from the Registry. To rebuild *SystemRoot*\Fonts, follow these steps:

1. Move the contents of *SystemRoot*\Fonts to a scratch folder on your desktop.
2. Delete the contents of *SystemRoot*\Fonts and remove HKLM\SOFTWARE\Microsoft\Windows\CurrentVersion\Fonts from the Registry.
3. Drag each font file from the scratch folder to *SystemRoot*\Fonts. This task might be easier using file cut-and-paste or if you open two different Explorer windows.

Property Sheets Don't Work Properly

Property sheets don't get messed up often, but when they do, they wreak havoc. A value that refers to a missing property sheet handler causes Windows 2000 to not open the property sheet at all. A corrupted property sheet handler might cause Windows Explorer to crash when it tries to display the property sheet.

Your first step to fix this problem is to identify the program or class identifier causing it. If you know that Recycle Bin's property sheet causes Windows Explorer to crash, for example, locate Recycle Bin's subkey in HKCR\CLSID. If Windows Explorer won't open the property sheet for a particular file, locate the extension for that file in HKCR. Then use that subkey's default value to locate the program identifier with which it is associated, and open the program identifier in HKCR. Then again, if the problem affects virtually every document in Windows Explorer, start with HKCR*, which adds features to every file's shortcut menu and property sheet.

N O T E   If you can pinpoint an application that is causing problems with a property sheet, reinstall it. The application's setup program will restore health to the property sheet while maintaining most of your preferences. ■

After locating the problem subkey, which is either a program or class identifier, examine the **shellex\PropertySheetHandlers** subkey underneath it. This subkey contains an additional subkey for each handler that adds tabs to the object's property sheet. Identify the application that owns each subkey in **PropertySheetHandlers** by looking up each class identifier in **HKCR\CLSID**. After gathering this information, the action you take depends on the problem you're having:

- **The property sheet displays tabs it shouldn't**   The property sheet displays duplicate tabs or includes a tab that just doesn't make sense. Either way, the solution is the same. You've already made the connection between each subkey and the application that owns it. Using that information, remove the subkey belonging to that subkey.

- **A tab is missing from the property sheet**   This is a bit more difficult to fix because the problem is likely that the subkey for that tab is missing from the **PropertySheetHandlers** key. You must somehow identify the class identifier of the property sheet handler, which you can do by looking at another computer's Registry or by looking through the application's REG and INF files to see what value it used when you installed the program.

- **Explorer crashes when opening the property sheet**   First, try removing the subkey for each property sheet handler from **PropertySheetHandlers** and test the change in Windows Explorer. If it works, one of the DLL files might be corrupted. Restore each DLL file from the Windows 2000 CD-ROM. If you're still out of luck, try reinstalling the application.

Special Folders Won't Open

This problem isn't too common, but it's frustrating nonetheless. You double-click the Control Panel icon and nothing happens. You can't access Recycle Bin to recover files you deleted. This is easily fixed.

Make sure the class identifier's subkey for each shell folder is correctly configured in the Registry. Table 12.1 shows the class identifier for Windows 2000's shell folders, as well as the name of the DLL file that implements it. You should find a subkey under **HKCR\CLSID** for each class identifier. Each class identifier's subkey should also contain an **InprocServer32** subkey whose default value entry indicates the correct DLL file, as described in Table 12.1. Remember to type the complete path of the DLL file in **InprocServer32** so that Windows can find the file.

Table 12.1   Replacing a Shell Folder's Class Identifier

Name	Class Identifier/DLL File
Control Panel	{21EC2020-3AEA-1069-A2DD-08002B30309D}
	SystemRoot\System32\Shell32.dll
Dial-Up Networking	{992CFFA0-F557-101A-88EC-00DD010CCC48}
	SystemRoot\System32\Rnaui.dll
Printers	{2227A280-3AEA-1069-A2DE-08002B30309D}
	SystemRoot\System32\Shell32.dll
Recycle Bin	{645FF040-5081-101B-9F08-00AA002F954E}
	SystemRoot\System32\Shell32.dll
Scheduled Tasks	{D6277990-4C6A-11CF-8D87-00AA0060F5BF}
	SystemRoot\System32\Mstask.dll
Briefcase	{85BBD920-42A0-1069-A2E4-08002B3039D}
	SystemRoot\System32\Syncui.dll
My Computer	{20D04FE0-3AEA-1069-A2D8-08002B30309D}
	SystemRoot\System32\Shell32.dll
The Internet	{3DC7A020-0ACD-11CF-A9BB-00AA004AE837}
	SystemRoot\System32\Shdocvw.dll
Network Neighborhood	{208D2C60-3AEA-1069-A2D7-08002B30309D}
	SystemRoot\System32\Shell32.dll

Duplicate or Bad Commands on Shortcut Menus

Chapter 7, "Customizing Windows 2000," describes how to customize a shortcut menu two different ways. First, you can add or remove built-in menu commands, which include menu commands such as Cut and Properties, to or from a shortcut menu using the **Attributes** subkey. Second, you can include additional commands in a file's shortcut menu by adding them to the appropriate shell subkey. Use the information you learned in Chapter 7 to help you remove bogus commands on the shortcut menu, add missing commands, or change how the menu works.

Shortcuts Don't Work Properly

When shortcuts stop working, the problem is usually with **HKCR\piffile** or **HKCR\lnkfile**. If MS-DOS–based shortcuts no longer work, import the REG file shown in Listing 12.2, or repair the Registry so that it matches the listing. If Windows-based shortcuts don't work, import the REG file shown in Listing 12.3.

Listing 12.2   The REG File for DOS Links

```
REGEDIT4

[HKEY_CLASSES_ROOT\piffile]
@="Shortcut to MS-DOS Program"
"EditFlags"=hex:01,00,00,00
"IsShortcut"=" "
"NeverShowExt"=""

[HKEY_CLASSES_ROOT\piffile\shell]

[HKEY_CLASSES_ROOT\piffile\shell\open]
@=""

[HKEY_CLASSES_ROOT\piffile\shell\open\command]
@="\"%1\" %*"

[HKEY_CLASSES_ROOT\piffile\shellex]

[HKEY_CLASSES_ROOT\piffile\shellex\PropertySheetHandlers]

[HKEY_CLASSES_ROOT\piffile\shellex\PropertySheetHandlers\
➥{86F19A00-42A0-1069-A2E9-08002B30309D}]
@=""

[HKEY_CLASSES_ROOT\piffile\shellex\IconHandler]
@="{00021401-0000-0000-C000-000000000046}"
```

Listing 12.3   The REG File for Windows Links

```
REGEDIT4

[HKEY_CLASSES_ROOT\CLSID\
➥{00021401-0000-0000-C000-000000000046}]
@="Shortcut"

[HKEY_CLASSES_ROOT\CLSID\
➥{00021401-0000-0000-C000-000000000046}\InProcServer32]
@="shell32.dll"
"ThreadingModel"="Apartment"

[HKEY_CLASSES_ROOT\CLSID\
➥{00021401-0000-0000-C000-000000000046}\shellex]

[HKEY_CLASSES_ROOT\CLSID\
➥{00021401-0000-0000-C000-000000000046}\shellex\
➥MayChangeDefaultMenu]
@=""
```

```
[HKEY_CLASSES_ROOT\CLSID\
➥{00021401-0000-0000-C000-000000000046}\ProgID]
@="lnkfile"

[HKEY_CLASSES_ROOT\lnkfile]
@="Shortcut"
"EditFlags"=hex:01,00,00,00
"IsShortcut"=" "
"NeverShowExt"=""

[HKEY_CLASSES_ROOT\lnkfile\CLSID]
@="{00021401-0000-0000-C000-000000000046}"

[HKEY_CLASSES_ROOT\lnkfile\shellex]

[HKEY_CLASSES_ROOT\lnkfile\shellex\IconHandler]
@="{00021401-0000-0000-C000-000000000046}"

[HKEY_CLASSES_ROOT\lnkfile\shellex\DropHandler]
@="{00021401-0000-0000-C000-000000000046}"

[HKEY_CLASSES_ROOT\lnkfile\shellex\ContextMenuHandlers]

[HKEY_CLASSES_ROOT\lnkfile\shellex\ContextMenuHandlers\
➥{00021401-0000-0000-C000-000000000046}]
@=""
```

Internet Security Settings Aren't Accessible

HKCU\Software\Microsoft\Windows\CurrentVersion\Internet Settings\Zones contains Internet Explorer's security settings. If it becomes damaged, Windows 2000 can't display the Security tab in the Internet Options dialog box. The solution to this problem is to completely remove the key from the Registry and allow Internet Explorer to rebuild it.

Part
IV

Ch

12

Disabling Internet Explorer 5 Integration

Many folks, including me, think Internet Explorer's integration into Windows 2000 is a good thing, just as it was in Windows 98. It doesn't quite blend the Internet into my desktop, as Microsoft claims, because the separation between the two realms is still distinguishable. It *does* add new features. Terrific features. It brings Web-style navigation to the desktop, for instance. It provides powerful scripting capabilities. It lets me customize the look and feel of the desktop and individual folders. Thus, boiling it down to two simple reasons that Internet Explorer integration is good, it makes Windows more customizable and easier to use.

That's just one side of the story, however. Here's the other side. Microsoft has forced end users to accept and use software that they don't want. They'd rather use a different browser. They don't want to be forced to use Internet Explorer to view the contents of their computers or to browse the Internet. The don't like the new features. (Animated menus and flying-paper animations, I'll concede, are annoying.) And, most importantly, they're afraid that Internet Explorer's integration into the Windows operating system gives Microsoft a shot at monopolizing the Internet.

If you're in the first camp, you can skip the rest of this section. If you're in the second camp, you'll be interested to note that you can minimize the integration of Internet Explorer into the operating system. You can't remove Internet Explorer, because Microsoft makes Windows 2000 almost totally dependent on its code. You *can* return Windows 2000 to a look and feel that's closer to classic Windows, however. Doing so is quite easy, too; you change only a few Registry settings. You can pick and choose which of the settings in Table 12.2 that you want to change. All the values you see in the table are in **HKCU\Software\Microsoft\Windows\CurrentVersion\Policies\Explorer** and are therefore policies. The first column indicates the name of the **REG_DWORD** value to add to this key, and the second column describes what it does. In each case, set the value to **1** to enable that policy or to **0** to disable it. Alternatively, you can use the INF file in Listing 12.4 to change these settings. The INF file in Listing 12.5 reverses them, enabling you to switch back and forth.

Table 12.2 Disabling Internet Explorer 5 Integration

Value	Description
ClassicShell	Enables the classic shell, which has the old double-click user interface.
NoActiveDesktop	Disables the Active Desktop, reverting to the classic desktop.
NoActiveDesktopChanges	Removes the Web tab from the Display Properties dialog box.
NoChangeStartMenu	Disables drag and drop on the Start menu, reverting to the old version.
NoFavoritesMenu	Removes the Favorites menu from the Start menu.
NoInternetIcon	Removes the Internet icon from the desktop.
NoSetActiveDesktop	Removes the Active Desktop command from the Start menu's Settings submenu.

The **ClassicShell** value has side effects. Setting **ClassicShell** disables the taskbar's toolbar features and removes the As Web Page command from Windows Explorer's View menu. It also disables the Windows Desktop Update section of Windows Explorer's Folder Options dialog box so that the user can't re-enable the new shell. Likewise, **NoActiveDesktop** prevents the user from using the Active Desktop by removing the Active Desktop command from the desktop's shortcut menu.

Listing 12.4   Disabling Internet Explorer 5 Integration

```
[version]
signature="$CHICAGO$"

[DefaultInstall]
AddReg=Integration

[Integration]
HKCU,Software\Microsoft\Windows\CurrentVersion\Policies\
➥Explorer, ClassicShell,0x10001,01,00,00,00
HKCU,Software\Microsoft\Windows\CurrentVersion\Policies\
➥Explorer, NoActiveDesktop,0x10001,01,00,00,00
HKCU,Software\Microsoft\Windows\CurrentVersion\Policies\
➥Explorer, NoActiveDesktopChanges,0x10001,01,00,00,00
HKCU,Software\Microsoft\Windows\CurrentVersion\Policies\
➥Explorer, NoChangeStartMenu,0x10001,01,00,00,00
HKCU,Software\Microsoft\Windows\CurrentVersion\Policies\
➥Explorer, NoFavoritesMenu,0x10001,01,00,00,00
HKCU,Software\Microsoft\Windows\CurrentVersion\Policies\
➥Explorer, NoInternetIcon,0x10001,01,00,00,00
HKCU,Software\Microsoft\Windows\CurrentVersion\Policies\
➥Explorer, NoSetActiveDesktop,0x10001,01,00,00,00
HKCU,"Software\Microsoft\Internet Explorer\Main",
➥Show_ChannelBand,0,"No"
```

Listing 12.5   Enabling Internet Explorer 5 Integration

```
[version]
signature="$CHICAGO$"

[DefaultInstall]
DelReg=Integration
AddReg=ChannelBand

[Integration]
HKCU,Software\Microsoft\Windows\CurrentVersion\Policies\
➥Explorer, ClassicShell
HKCU,Software\Microsoft\Windows\CurrentVersion\Policies\
➥Explorer, NoActiveDesktop
HKCU,Software\Microsoft\Windows\CurrentVersion\Policies\
➥Explorer, NoActiveDesktopChanges
HKCU,Software\Microsoft\Windows\CurrentVersion\Policies\
➥Explorer, NoChangeStartMenu
HKCU,Software\Microsoft\Windows\CurrentVersion\Policies\
➥Explorer, NoFavoritesMenu
HKCU,Software\Microsoft\Windows\CurrentVersion\Policies\
➥Explorer, NoInternetIcon
```

Part
IV

Ch
12

continues

Listing 12.5   Continued

```
HKCU,Software\Microsoft\Windows\CurrentVersion\Policies\
➥Explorer, NoSetActiveDesktop

[ChannelBand]
HKCU,"Software\Microsoft\Internet Explorer\Main",
➥Show_ChannelBand,0,"Yes"
```

Reference

File Associations

Overview

Remember *aliases* from Chapter 1, "Understanding Registries"? **HKEY_CLASSES_ROOT** is an alias for **HKLM\Software\CLASSES** and **HKCU\Software\Classes**. Windows 2000 merges the contents of **HKCU\Software\Classes** and **HKLM\SOFTWARE\Classes** to create **HKEY_CLASSES_ROOT**. Settings in **HKCU** take precedence over settings in **HKLM**. Associates in **HKCU\Software\Classes** are per-user and are in a special hive file that's stored in the user's profile. The hive file is in `UserProfile\Local Settings\Application Data\Microsoft\Windows\UsrClass.dat`.

Any change you make to **HKEY_CLASSES_ROOT** is actually made in the appropriate **\CLASSES** subkey, depending on its original location. Likewise, **HKEY_CLASSES_ROOT** reflects any changes you make in either of the **\CLASSES** subkeys. The pragmatic reason that this alias exists is for backward compatibility with Microsoft Windows 3.1. Yes, Windows 3.1 did have a Registry, which it used for OLE, DDE, and related settings. As far as you're concerned, however, **HKEY_CLASSES_ROOT** just makes getting to this information quicker because you don't have to click your way to **\CLASSES**.

 TIP When editing associations in the Registry, consider editing them in either **HKLM\SOFTWARE\Classes** or **HKCU\Software\Classes** to ensure that you change the per-machine or per-user association that you intend to change. When you edit an association in **HKEY_CLASSES_ROOT**, you don't know for sure which location you're updating.

HKEY_CLASSES_ROOT is the single largest branch in the Registry. On a test computer, I found that this branch contained over 50% of the Registry's data. You can verify this fact yourself by exporting **HKEY_CLASSES_ROOT** to a REG file called `Classes.reg` and exporting the entire Registry to another REG file called `All.reg`. Divide the file size of `Classes.reg` by the file size of `All.reg` to figure out how much of the Registry is **HKEY_CLASSES_ROOT**. In my case, `Classes.reg` was 2.69MB and `All.reg` was 5.23MB.

HKEY_CLASSES_ROOT contains thousands upon thousands of keys and values that associate file extensions with programs, define COM (Component Object Model) classes, and much more. If you look closely at this branch, you'll notice two different types of subkeys. The subkeys toward the top, with the exception of the * subkey, are called *filename extension subkeys,* and they all begin with a period. They look like normal MS-DOS file extensions: *.ext*. They can contain any number of characters. Examples are **.bat, .doc,** and **.html**. * and the subkeys toward the bottom of **HKEY_CLASSES_ROOT** are *class definition subkeys,* and they include program identifiers and class identifiers:

- *Program identifiers* are subkeys in **HKEY_CLASSES_ROOT** that define the actions a program can perform on a file. Examples are **batfile, docfile,** and **inifile**. Some program identifiers also associate a program with a COM class. These are like aliases that make accessing a class easier. Examples are **Word.Document.8** and **Excel.Sheet.8**.

■ *Class identifiers* uniquely identify a COM class, such as an ActiveX control. **HKCR\CLSID** contains all the class identifiers. Each class identifier is a globally unique 16-byte number. An example is **{3B7C8860-D78F-101B-B9B5-04021C009402}**. Windows 2000 uses class identifiers extensively.

You'll learn much more about filename extension subkeys and class definitions in the following sections. The "Miscellaneous Subkeys" section describes a number of subkeys that you frequently find under both types of keys.

N O T E When you install Windows 2000, it registers a large number of filename extension and class definition subkeys. Also, most applications register filename extensions and class definitions during installation. ■

N O T E Some programs store user preferences in **HKEY_CLASSES_ROOT**. It might seem odd to see **\Software\Progressive Networks\RealAudio Player** in this branch, for instance, but its presence is not necessarily an error. Some vendors, such as Progressive Networks, must create programs that work in earlier versions of Windows as well as Windows 2000. To do that, the vendor writes its configuration data to **HKEY_CLASSES_ROOT**, the only root key that Windows 3.1 provides. In other words, *just live with it.* ■

▶ **See** Chapter 1, "Understanding Registries," **p. 9**, for a description of other aliases in the Registry.

▶ **See** Chapter 3, "Editing with Regedit," **p. 39**, to learn how to export all or part of the Registry to a REG file so that you can compare the size of **HKEY_CLASSES_ROOT** to the entire Registry, as described in this section.

Filename Extension Subkeys

Anytime Windows 2000 accesses a file, whether it's to open the file or display information about it in Windows Explorer, the operating system looks up the file's extension under **HKEY_CLASSES_ROOT**. If you open a DOC file, for example, Windows 2000 looks up **.doc**. The filename extension subkey doesn't contain enough information to tell the operating system much about the file, however, so the operating system looks in the filename extension's default value entry for the name of a program identifier, a class definition subkey, that does contain more information. Look up the default value in **.dll** and you'll see that DLL files are associated with **dllfile**. You find the program identifier's subkey in the same place as the file extension: under **HKEY_CLASSES_ROOT**. Figure 13.1 illustrates the relationship by showing how AVI files are associated with the **avifile** program identifier via the **.avi** file extension subkey.

Part
V

Ch
13

FIGURE 13.1

AVI files are associated with the **avifile** file type via the **.avi** file extension subkey.

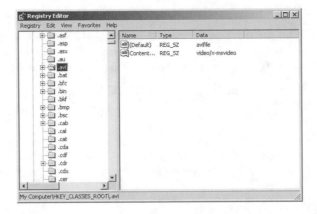

Microsoft really cleaned up the filename extension subkeys for Windows 2000. In a fresh installation of Windows 2000, the only subkeys you find under a filename extension are **shellex** and **ShellNew**. **shellex** describes shell extensions for that particular filename extension. An example is a context menu handler that adds additional items to a file's shortcut menu, which you display by right-clicking the file in Windows Explorer. In earlier versions of Windows, filename extension subkeys contained a strange mix of various **DefaultIcon**, **shell**, **shellex**, and **ShellNew** subkeys, most of which are more appropriate under class definition subkeys. If you upgrade to Windows 2000, you're left with all this clutter in the Registry. Don't forget, too, that many Windows 2000 applications will add these subkeys to the filename extension key when you install them. Even though these subkeys might be misplaced under a file extension rather than in a class definition, they still work for that particular file extension.

TIP

All you need to remember about filename extension subkeys is that they are under **HKEY_CLASSES_ROOT**, they look like *.ext* (where *ext* is a valid file extension), and their default value points to one of the program identifiers that are also defined in **HKEY_CLASSES_ROOT**.

Content Type

Typically, the only value you see in a filename extension subkey is **Content Type**. This value associates the file extension with a *MIME* type (*Multipurpose Internet Mail Extensions*), a standard for specifying data types on the Internet.

A MIME type specifies the type of content embedded in a Web page or contained in the attachments to a mail message. Sometimes the server provides the MIME type of the data it is transmitting, and other times the MIME type is embedded in the document itself. You would think that the server and document could just specify a file extension, but recall that the Internet is platform-neutral. This means that the Internet must support a wide variety of platforms, each of which might have different conventions for naming files.

MIME types look like *type/subtype*. *type* is usually something such as **application, audio, image,** or **text**. **application** specifies that the data is raw and doesn't fit into one of the other MIME types. **audio, image,** and **text** speak for themselves. *subtype* can vary, but there are standards. A subtype for **text** might be **plain** or **rich**, for example, which specifies that the content is either plain text or richly formatted text. A type or subtype that begins with **x-** means that it's a private MIME type that isn't standardized. Just because a MIME type isn't standardized doesn't mean it's not in popular use.

"MIME Types," later in this chapter, contains more information about how Windows 2000 uses **Content Type**. You'll also learn how the operating system cross-references MIME types so that looking them up is quicker than searching each individual filename extension subkey.

Class Definition Subkeys

Class definition subkeys define a particular type of document or object. It might be a file type, which a program can open for editing, printing, and so on. It might be a COM class, such as a compound document or ActiveX control.

Class definition subkeys come in two flavors. *Program identifiers,* which are associated with a filename extension subkey via the extension's default value entry, describe a program and the actions it can perform on a file. You'll learn about program identifiers in the following section. A *class identifier* uniquely identifies a COM class, which can generate objects such as a system folder. Familiar terms associated with COM classes are *object, module,* and *component.* ActiveX and OLE are related technologies that are actually part of COM.

You'll learn about each type of class definition in the following sections. You'll also learn about **HKCR\MIME**, a database that makes cross-referencing a MIME type with a file extension quicker, in "MIME Types," later in this chapter. You'll learn about a variety of subkeys that you might find under class definition keys in "Miscellaneous Subkeys."

N O T E   If the word COM throws you, you might know it better as ActiveX or OLE (Object Linking and Embedding). Let's straighten out these terms for you. *COM* (Component Object *Model*) is Microsoft's technology for allowing applications to interoperate. COM technologies include ActiveX Controls and much more. *ActiveX* controls are COM objects designed for distribution via Web pages. *OLE*, on the other hand, strictly refers to Windows 2000's *Object Linking and Embedding* capabilities, and you'll only see this term used when referring to *OLE drag and drop* or *embedded OLE objects.* ■

Part
V

Ch
13

Program Identifiers

Flexibility—that's the reason Windows 2000 splits information between filename extensions and program identifiers. The operating system *could* store all the information it needs in a filename extension, but doing so would leave the operating system incapable of handling anything but a one-to-one relationship between a file extension and a program. Some documents can have more than one file extension, for instance, as is the case with HTM and HTML files and JPG and JPEG files. Some programs can open more than one file extension, too. For example, Microsoft Word can open DOC, DOT, RTF, and other files. The organization of filename extensions and program identifiers allows the operating system to handle all these cases.

Recall that each filename extension's default value entry refers to a program identifier under **HKEY_CLASSES_ROOT**. The default value entry for **.bat** is **batfile**, for example. Look in **HKCR\batfile**, and you see the information that the operating system requires to open, edit, and print BAT files. Given the way in which the Registry organizes this information, you can associate many different filename extensions with a single program, but you can't associate many different programs with a single file extension. The following table shows you several examples of how a filename extension subkey's default value relates it to a program identifier:

Filename Extension Subkey	File Type/Default Value
.avi	avifile
.dll	dllfile
.exe	exefile
.htm	htmlfile
.lnk	lnkfile
.reg	regfile
.txt	txtfile

Each program identifier can have a number of different values. The default value entry usually contains a plain-English description of the program and the files it can open. You see this description when you view a file's details in Windows Explorer. The mere presence of **AlwaysShowExt**, a string value, indicates whether Windows Explorer will always display the file's extension in a folder, regardless of how the Hide File Extensions for Known File Types option is set on the View tab of Windows Explorer's Folder Options dialog box. **NeverShowExt**, another string value, does the opposite. The presence of **IsShortcut** indicates whether the file is a shortcut and whether the operating system should display the shortcut overlay on top of the file's icon. Table 13.1 summarizes these values, as well as **EditFlags**, another common value in most program identifiers. This is a 4-byte binary value that indicates how much editing you're allowed to do in the File Types tab of Windows Explorer's Folder Options dialog box, shown in Figure 13.2. The following table describes the bits that are used in this 32-bit value; just remember to count the bits from right to left, starting from 0:

Bit	Hex	Description
8	00 00 01 00	Clear Confirm Open After Download
16	00 01 00 00	Disable Description of Type
17	00 02 00 00	Disable Change Icon Button

18	00 04 00 00	Disable the Set Default Button
20	00 10 00 00	Disable Application Used To
21	00 20 00 00	Disable Use DDE Checkbox
23	00 80 00 00	Disable Content Type (MIME)
24	01 00 00 00	Don't Display in Registered File Types
25	02 00 00 00	Do Display in Registered File Types
27	08 00 00 00	Disable the Edit on File Types Tab
28	10 00 00 00	Disable the Remove on File Types Tab
29	20 00 00 00	Disable the New Button
30	40 00 00 00	Disable the Edit Button
31	80 00 00 00	Disable the Remove button

FIGURE 13.2
Choose View, Folder Options from Windows Explorer, and click the File Types tab to view these dialog boxes.

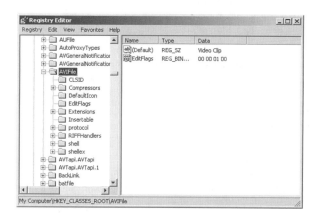

Table 13.1 Common Values for File Types

Value	Type	Description
AlwaysShowExt	String	The presence of this value indicates that Windows Explorer should always display the filename extension in a folder.
NeverShowExt	String	The presence of this value indicates that Windows Explorer should never display the filename extension in a folder.
IsShortcut	String	The presence of this value indicates that the file represents a shortcut, and the operating system displays the shortcut overlay on top of the file's icon.
EditFlags	Binary	This value contains flags that determine how much editing the user can do in the File Types tab of Windows Explorer's Folder Options dialog box.

Part
V

Ch

13

Program identifiers are also an alternative method for identifying COM classes. You'll learn about COM classes in the later section "Significant COM Class Identifiers." Sometimes known as *progids,* program identifiers allow a program to refer to a class without using the nasty class identifiers. Contrast looking up a class under **CLSID** using **{00020906-0000-0000-C000-000000000046}** versus looking up the same class under **HKEY_CLASSES_ROOT** using **Word.Document.8**. The latter makes more sense. In this manner, you can think of program identifiers as aliases.

Program identifiers that represent COM classes are specified using a standard notation: ***vendor.component.version***. An example would be **Microsoft.Word.8**. You'll notice that in the Registry they look more like **Word.Document.8**, which deviates a bit from the standard notation. Regardless, you can also recognize this type of program identifier in one of two ways:

- The name is separated into parts by periods.
- Program identifiers that represent a COM class always have a subkey called **CLSID**, which refers to a class identifier in **HKCR\CLSID**.

> **N O T E** Program identifiers prevent the programmer from having to know the identifier for a class. The programmer can instead use one of the operating system's functions that translate a program identifier into a class identifier, and vice versa. Note that because the program identifier uses some combination of the vendor or application name, component name, and version, there is little chance that two different applications will try to create the same program identifier. ▪

The CLSID Subkey Because a program identifier can refer to a COM class, it must have a way to link itself to a class identifier. It does. Each program identifier can have a subkey called **CLSID** whose default value entry is the class identifier of a COM class.

> **N O T E** You'll notice that the primary perpetrator of program identifiers is Microsoft. Just about every Microsoft Office product that you install creates several program identifiers. ▪

The CurVer Subkey Imagine the following scenario: An application depends on a class labeled **Word.Document.8**. Later, the user installs an upgrade that changes the program identifier to **Word.Document.9**. The application can no longer find the class it needs because the program identifier to which it refers is missing. The solution is version-independent *program identifiers*.

Some program identifiers leave out the version number on the end of their names: ***vendor.component***. Examples are **Excel.Sheet** and **Word.Document**. These are called *version-independent program identifiers*. They allow an application to refer to a class without explicitly specifying a version number in the program identifier. A version-independent program identifier always has a subkey called **CurVer**. The default value of **CurVer** is the complete program identifier, including the current version.

Now change the scenario so that it uses version-independent program identifiers. An application refers to **Word.Document**, whose **CurVer** subkey's default value is set to **Word.Document.8**. When the user installs the upgrade, the application changes the default value entry of **CurVer** in **Word.Document** so that it refers to the new program identifier called **Word.Document.9**. The user got his upgrade, and the application can still find its object.

> **N O T E**   Two subkeys are common in both program and class identifiers: **Insertable** and **NotInsertable**. The mere presence of a subkey called **Insertable** indicates that the class will appear on the Object dialog box of any application that supports it. You open the Object dialog box by choosing Insert, Object from the application. The presence of **NotInsertable** indicates that the class will not appear in the Object dialog box. ∎

COM Class Identifiers

COM class identifiers are like Social Security numbers that uniquely identify people. They identify a COM class using a unique number called a *globally unique identifier* (GUID). A program called Guidgen.exe, which comes with Visual C++ and the WIN32 SDK, generates this number. Don't let **HKCR\CLSID**, the location of all the class identifiers in the Registry, daunt you. Each GUID is really nothing more than a Social Security number for a class. Notice that all these class identifiers have the same peculiar format. They're 16-byte hexadecimal numbers separated into 8-, 4-, 4-, 4-, and 12-digit sections by a hyphen, with curly brackets surrounding the whole mess:

{XXXXXXXX-XXXX-XXXX-XXXX-XXXXXXXXXXXX}

The default value entry for a class identifier describes the class. In most cases, you see a plain-English description of the class. **Microsoft Excel Chart, HTML Thumbnail Extractor,** and **Desktop Task** are examples. In other cases, you see nothing, which leaves you wondering what the class represents. In those cases, you can search the Registry for references to the class identifier. The reference to the class is usually enough to tell you what it does. If you find a class identifier with no name, try these techniques for uncovering its purpose:

- Search the Registry for the class identifier. The location in which the class identifier is used might tell you the purpose of the class.

- Look for a subkey called **ProgID**, which is a link to a related program identifier in **HKEY_CLASSES_ROOT**. The program identifier might provide additional information about the class.

- Look in each of the class identifier's subkeys for a reference to a DLL or other file. View the file's properties by right-clicking it and choosing Properties. Frequently, the Version tab will give you a brief description of the file, indicating its purpose.

Part
V

Ch
13

Class identifiers don't usually contain values. They are defined by their subkeys, as you'll learn in the following sections. One exception is a value called **InfoTip**. You commonly find this value entry in classes that create user interface objects, special system folders, and so on. Windows Explorer displays the contents of **InfoTip** in a small yellow box, also known as a ToolTip, when the user hovers the mouse pointer over the object. This is an additional way that the operating system provides help to the user. When you hover the mouse pointer over My Computer on the desktop, for example, you see a tip that reads `Displays the contents of your computer`. Adding **InfoTip** to classes that don't already define this value doesn't seem to do much good. You can customize **InfoTip** for classes that do include it, however.

N O T E   Anytime you see a GUID elsewhere in the Registry, you can almost always find a matching class identifier in **CLSID**. Exceptions do exist, however. Sometimes programs use a GUID to uniquely name subkeys or values in other parts of the Registry. These don't lead to class identifiers, but they look like them. ■

Generating Class Identifiers: `Guidgen.exe`

Programmers use a program called `Guidgen.exe`, which comes with Visual C++ and the WIN32 SDK, to generate GUIDs. Microsoft guarantees that each GUID that `Guidgen.exe` generates will be globally unique. That is, the program will generate a new 16-byte integer GUID every time it runs—no matter how many times it runs.

It does so using a complex algorithm that uses a combination of data. The current date and time are in the GUID. The clock sequence on the computer is in there. An IEEE machine identifier, which `Guidgen.exe` gets from the network card if available, is in there. If the computer doesn't have a network card, `Guidgen.exe` generates a machine identifier from extremely variable machine data. This quote from the Microsoft Developer Network Library explains it all: "The chance of [`Guidgen.exe`] generating duplicate GUIDs...is about the same as two random atoms in the universe colliding to form a small California avocado mated to a New York City sewer rat."

ShellFolder Subkey   If you see **ShellFolder** underneath a class identifier, it will have a single value called **attributes**. **attributes** indicates the built-in commands that Windows Explorer displays on the object's shortcut menu. **attributes** is a 4-byte binary value with each bit representing a flag that enables or disables a specific command. Table 13.2 describes the bits used by Windows 2000. Setting a particular bit to **0** disables the command, and setting it to **1** enables the command. Remember that you count bits right to left in a binary value, so bit 0 is the first bit on the right, bit 1 is the second bit on the right, and so on. Because the Registry shows **attributes** as a hexadecimal value, you must convert it to binary to figure out which commands are enabled. Work with this value in binary until you're ready to change **attributes**, and then convert it to hexadecimal.

Here's a real-world example. The **attributes** value for the Microsoft Internet Explorer icon is **72000000** in hexadecimal, which is **01110010000000000000000000000000** in binary. Counting from right to left, bits 25, 28, 29, and 30 are 1s. Thus, Windows 2000 displays the Cut, Rename, Delete, and Properties commands on the Internet Explorer icon's shortcut menu. You can remove the Cut command from the shortcut menu by turning off bit 25, which leaves you with a hexadecimal value of **70000000**.

Table 13.2   Bits in the attributes Value

Bit Number	Command
30	Properties
29	Delete
28	Rename
25	Cut
24	Copy
16	Paste
5	Open and Explore for the Recycle Bin

▶ **See** Chapter 7, "Customizing Windows 2000," **p. 107**, for a description of how to use **ShellFolder** to make shortcut menus look the way you want.

The LocalServer and LocalServer32 Subkeys   The default values of the **LocalServer** and **LocalServer32** subkeys specify the path of an EXE that implements the server application. **LocalServer** specifies a 16-bit server application, and **LocalServer32** specifies a 32-bit server application. Local servers run in their own address space.

The InprocServer and InprocServer32 Subkeys   The default values of the **InprocServer** and **InprocServer32** subkeys specify the path of a DLL file that implements the server. **InprocServer** specifies a 16-bit server, and **LocalServer32** specifies a 32-bit server. In-process servers run in the client process's address space.

If an in-process server is multithreaded, you see an additional value entry called **ThreadingModel**. This value can be one of the following:

■ **Apartment**   This represents the *apartment threading model*. Each object exists in only a single thread.

■ **Both**   An object can exist in a single thread, as with apartment threading, or it can exist in multiple threads of a single process—*free threading*.

The InprocHandler and InprocHandler32 Subkeys   The default values of the subkeys called **InprocHandler** and **InprocHandler32** specify the path of a DLL file that handles objects defined by the class identifier. **InprocHandler** specifies a 16-bit handler, and **InprocHandler32** specifies a 32-bit handler. In-process handlers work in conjunction with local or in-process servers. You'll notice that this value almost always contains `Ole32.dll`, which provides COM functionality to the operating system and other applications.

Part

V

Ch

13

N O T E The difference between in-process and local servers is the address space in which they run. *In-process servers* run in the host application's address space. *Local servers* run in their own address space. In-process servers perform better but can crash the client application. Local servers perform worse than in-process servers do, but they don't affect the host application if they crash. ■

The ProgID Subkey   Earlier in this chapter, you learned that a program identifier can be an alias for a class. Each program identifier can contain a subkey called **CLSID** whose default value contains the class identifier of the associated class. Each class identifier also contains a reference to its matching program identifier, if it exists, in a subkey called **ProgID**. The default value entry of **ProgID** is the program identifier or the version-independent program identifier.

MIME Types

In the earlier section called "Filename Extension Subkeys," you learned how the operating system associates a MIME type with a variety of file extensions. These file extensions contain a value called **Content Type**, which defines the MIME type associated with that extension. When a client program, such as Internet Explorer or Outlook Express Mail, needs to associate a program with a bit of data, it searches for the MIME type in the Registry. The search yields a file extension that in turn yields information about the program used to display and edit the data.

Windows 2000 doesn't examine each and every filename extension subkey for a matching **Content Type** value, however, because doing so would make the whole process pathetically slow. It looks up the MIME type in **HKCR\MIME\Database\Content Type** instead. This key contains a subkey for each MIME type registered in the Registry. **Content Type*MimeType*** contains a value called **Extension** that associates the MIME type with a file extension. **Content Type\Text/Plain** contains information about the **Text/Plain** MIME type, for example, and **Extension** contains **.txt**, which associates the **Text/Plain** MIME type with the TXT file extension. The **Extension** value entry for **Content Type\image/gif** contains **.gif**, which associates the **image/gif** MIME type with the GIF file extension.

Underneath some MIME types, you see a subkey called **Bits**. This subkey contains terrific information about the header that begins each type of file. Each value entry—the first being **0**, the second being **1**, and so on—in **Bits** defines a possible file header that identifies a file matching the MIME type. The first 32-bit **DWORD** specifies the length of the file header. The next n bytes, where n is the length of the file header, appear to be a mask that determines which bits of the header to check. This portion is almost always **FF FF FF FF ...**, indicating that the operating system should check every bit of the file header. The next n bytes, up to the end of the binary value entry, is the actual file header. If the operating system encounters a file with an unknown MIME type or file extension, it can sometimes identify the file's MIME type by comparing its header to the values in **Bits**. Likewise, the operating system can test a file's header against the values in **Bits** to make sure that the file is valid.

You see **02 00 00 00 FF FF 42 4D** in the value entry called **0** found under **MIME\Database\Content Type\image/bmp\Bits**, a subkey of **HKEY_CLASSES_ROOT**. This indicates that a BMP file's header has two bytes, **42 4D**, and every bit in each of those bytes is significant. Sure enough, if you view a BMP file in a hex editor, the file starts with **42 4D**.

Miscellaneous Subkeys

Filename extensions and class definitions can contain a number of subkeys that define how they look and behave. It's more common for class definitions to contain such subkeys as **shell** and **DefaultIcon**, but these subkeys are still valid under filename extensions. **shellex** and **ShellNew** subkeys are common under filename extensions, however.

The following sections describe the most common subkeys. Here's an overview of each:

- **shell**   Defines commands that appear on the shortcut menu of the file or object.
- **shellex**   Defines shell extensions for the file or object, such as extensions to the property sheet or shortcut menu.
- **ShellNew**   Defines a template for a new empty file with a particular file extension that the user creates by right-clicking a folder and choosing New.
- **DefaultIcon**   Defines an icon for the file or object.

The shell Subkey

When you right-click a file or object in Windows Explorer, it displays a shortcut menu. Some of the items on the shortcut menu are built into the operating system (Shell32.dll); these appear at the bottom of the menu. You learned how to control these options in the earlier section "ShellFolder Subkey." Other items come from class definitions such as **Unknown** or *, both of which you'll learn about later in this chapter. The remaining items are at the top of the shortcut menu and come from the **shell** subkey of the class definition. **HKCR\txtfile\shell** defines items you see at the top of a TXT file's shortcut menu, for example. In some unlikely cases, a filename extension key might have a **shell** subkey too, which adds items to the file's shortcut menu only if the filename extension subkey is not connected to a program identifier by the subkey's default value entry. All this is a bit much to swallow, so look at the following generalization about how Windows Explorer builds the shortcut menu after the user right-clicks a file:

1. Windows 2000 notes the file's extension and looks up that extension in **HKEY_CLASSES_ROOT**.

2. Windows 2000 notes the default value entry of the filename extension subkey, which is the associated program identifier. If this value is empty, the operating system looks for a **shell** subkey in the filename extension key and adds those commands to the top of the shortcut menu. Otherwise, the operating system adds any commands it finds in the program identifier's **shell** subkey to the top of the shortcut menu.

3. Windows 2000 adds any commands it finds in the * and **AllFilesystemObjects** keys' **shell** subkey to the middle of the shortcut menu. These are commands that apply to all files and all file system objects on the computer.

4. Windows 2000 adds any built-in commands to the bottom of the shortcut menu. These are defined in `Shell32.dll`.

Verb Subkeys   Each subkey under **shell** is a verb. A *verb* shows action in the user interface, just as it does in the English language. "Open `Readme.txt`," "Edit `Budget.xls`," and "Print `Picture.bmp`" all represent examples of verb phrases that contain an action and a direct object. The actions are open, edit, and print. The direct objects are `Readme.txt`, `Budget.xls`, and `Picture.bmp`. The user completes one of these verb phrases by right-clicking a file, which supplies the direct object, and choosing one of the commands on the menu, which supplies the verb. In the Registry, verbs have simple, arbitrary names such as **open**, **edit**, and **print**. The default value of **shell** indicates which verb defines the default command on the menu. Thus, if a **shell** key has two subkeys, **open** and **edit**, and the **shell** key's default value is **open**, the shortcut menu starts with the commands Open and Edit, and Open is the default choice. If the user clicks the file in the single-click user interface or double-clicks the file in the double-click interface, Windows 2000 opens the file using the command defined in **shell\open**.

> **N O T E**   Microsoft documentation refers to some verbs as *canonical verbs*. If you look in the dictionary, you'll discover that *canonical* means official, sanctioned, or approved. **open**, **ope-nas**, **print**, **find**, and **explore** are recognized by and built in to the operating system and are therefore canonical verbs. Canonical verbs are localized by Windows 2000, so the operating system always uses the appropriate language when displaying them on a menu. ■

The default value of each verb contains the text that Windows 2000 displays on the shortcut menu. If the default value is blank, the operating system takes the text for the menu item from `Shell32.dll`, if the verb is canonical, or from the verb's name. Find, Open, Open With, and Print are canonical, so the operating system will look to `Shell32.dll` for the shortcut menu's text if the default value of the verb is empty. If the operating system uses the verb's name, it uses it verbatim, without capitalizing it or adding a hotkey to it. The operating system does maintain the capitalization you use in the verb's default value, and you can indicate a hotkey by prefixing the letter with an ampersand (&). Here are examples of what different values look like on a shortcut menu:

In the Registry	On the Shortcut Menu
open	open
&Open	Open
open in Wordpad	open in Wordpad
open in &Wordpad	open in Wordpad

The command Subkey   Underneath each verb, you see a single subkey called **command** whose default value defines the command line that Windows 2000 executes when you choose that command from the shortcut menu. The command line for different verbs varies. In some cases, you see only the path and filename of the program, allowing the operating system to affix the file or object's name to the end of the command.

In most cases, however, you see commands that explicitly include the file or object's name in the command line using the **%1** placeholder. Windows 2000 substitutes the file or object for **%1** when it executes the command. Using **%1** becomes particularly important when the command line contains switches and you must include the filename in a specific location: **myprog /p /k "%1" /s**, for example. In cases in which the program has trouble with long filenames that include spaces, probably because the program is expecting multiple filenames or options on the command line, you see **%1** surrounded by quotes, like this: **"%1"**. This ensures that the program sees the entire filename as a single unit, such as **filename with spaces.txt**, rather than individual chunks of text, such as **filename**, **with**, and **spaces.txt**.

Some command lines launch `Rundll.exe` or `Rundll32.exe`. This might seem kind of odd when you look at the command line for **cplfile\open**, which opens a dialog box in the Control Panel. Some programs aren't EXE files, however; they're DLL files, and the operating system provides `Rundll.exe` and `Rundll32.exe` to launch a specific function within a DLL file. The command line looks like this: **rundll.exe** *filename,function options*. *filename* is the name of the DLL file, and *function* is the name of the function within the DLL to execute. The remainder of the command line contains options that `Rundll.exe` passes to the function.

TIP

Some command lines contain nothing but **%1**. Recall that Windows 2000 replaces **%1** with the filename when the operating system executes the command. A command line that contains nothing but **%1** treats the file as a program, launching it as a new process. You see this in **scrfile** and **exefile**, for example.

▶ **See** Chapter 7, "Customizing Windows 2000," **p. 107**, to learn how to put the information you learned in this section to practical use. You learn to add, change, and remove items on the shortcut menu.

The Least You Need to Know

All you need to remember about **shell** subkeys is described here:

```
HKCR\Name
    shell
        (default) = default
        verb
            (default) = Name
            command
                (default) = command
```

Name is a filename extension subkey or program identifier. *default* is the name of one the subkeys under **shell**, the verbs, and it identifies the default command on the shortcut menu. *verb* is an arbitrary name, and *name* is the text that the operating system displays on the shortcut menu for that command. The operating system maintains the text's capitalization, and an ampersand (&) precedes a hotkey. *command* is the command line that the operating system executes when you choose the command from the shortcut menu.

The shellex Subkey

The term *shell extension* is almost, but not quite, self-explanatory. A shell extension enhances the user interface beyond its normal capabilities. A shell extension can add a tab to a property sheet, add commands to a shortcut menu, or provide an alternative means for a user to browse the contents of a folder. Other shell extensions provide icons for a file or object, add features to Windows 2000's Drag and Drop functionality, and more. You know you're dealing with a shell extension when you see something called a *handler,* which is a 32-bit in-process server. A *property sheet handler* is a shell extension that adds tabs to a property sheet, for example, and an *icon handler* is a shell extension that supplies icons for an object. Windows 2000 supports a variety of shell extensions:

- Context menu handlers add items to a shortcut menu, which the user opens by right-clicking a file or object.
- Drag handlers provide drag-and-drop support to a file or object.
- Drop handlers provide support for additional commands when the user drops a file or object.
- Icon handlers supply icons for a file or object.
- Property sheet handlers add new tabs to a file or object's property sheet, which you display by right-clicking it and choosing Properties.
- Copy-hook handlers extend the copy, move, delete, or rename operations for a file or object.

Windows 2000 defines shell extensions for a filename extension or class definition in its **shellex** subkey. **shellex** is usually devoid of values, deriving its meaning from its subkeys instead. A handful of filename extension subkeys contain **shellex**, extending the shell just for that particular file extension. **shellex** is more common under class definitions, however, extending the shell for all file extensions belonging to an application or for a particular class. **shellex** will have different subkeys, depending on the types of shell extension registered in it:

- **ContextMenuHandlers**
- **CopyHookHandlers**
- **DataHandler**
- **DragDropHandlers**
- **DropHandler**
- **ExtShellFolderViews**
- **IconHandler**
- **PropertySheetHandlers**

The format of each subkey, **shellex*handler***, can differ a bit. First, the default value of *handler* might contain a class identifier that implements that particular handler. A typical example is **shellex\IconHandler** with its default value entry set to the class identifier of a

COM class that can supply icons for that particular file or object. Second, *handler* might contain a subkey whose name is the class identifier of a COM class, and its default value entry is the plain-English name of the handler. Last, *handler* might contain a subkey whose name is a plain-English name, and its default value entry is the class identifier of a COM class. You'll find all these formats in the Registry. They all work equally well.

Some subkeys under **shellex** have unintelligible names that look like GUIDs. They are in fact GUIDs, but you won't find them defined in **HKCR\CLSID**. That is, they aren't class identifiers. These unknown GUIDs just represent another type of shell extension, or handler, that extends a filename extension or class definition. Most of these oddities are due to Internet Explorer 5, and they represent the first wrinkle in an otherwise flawless design. In a typical installation of Windows 2000, I found the following subkeys under **shellex**, whose default value entries don't refer to an actual class definition under **CLSID**:

- **{BB2E617C-0920-11d1-9A0B-00C04FC2D6C1}** contains the GUID of a thumbnail extractor. It's common in the **shellex** subkeys of images, because Windows Explorer can display a thumbnail of images when you view a folder as a Web page.

- **{00021500-0000-0000-C000-000000000046}** contains the GUID of an InfoTip handler. An InfoTip handler displays help text in a yellow box when the user hovers the mouse pointer over the object.

- **{000214EE-0000-0000-C000-000000000046}** contains the GUID of a shortcut handler for Internet shortcuts. Four other **shellex** subkeys also refer to shortcut handlers: **{000214F9-0000-0000-C000-000000000046}**, **{00021500-0000-0000-C000-000000000046}**, **{CABB0DA0-DA57-11CF-9974-0020AFD79762}**, and **{FBF23B80-E3F0-101B-8488-00AA003E56F8}**.

- **{D4029EC0-0920-11d1-9A0B-00C04FC2D6C1}** contains the GUID of a channel handler.

ExtShellFolderView Is an Odd Bird

ExtShellFolderView is a subkey you frequently see under the **shellex** subkey of folders and classes that act as folders. It's an odd key that contains handlers for displaying a folder as a Web page. In every case, **ExtShellFolderView** contains a single subkey called **{5984FFE0-28D4-11CF-AE66-08002B2E1262}**. You don't find this GUID in **HKCR\CLSID**, however, meaning that this GUID isn't a class identifier.

Discovering how the operating system uses **ExtShellFolderView** took a bit more digging than just looking in **CLSID**. I used Registry Monitor, a utility you learned about in Chapter 9, "Tracking Down Registry Settings," to see what happens when I display a folder as a Web page:

1. Windows Explorer opens **shellex\ExtShellFolderView** in the class definition subkey. If you're viewing a folder, for example, Explorer opens **shellex\ExtShellFolderView** underneath **HKCR\folder**.

continues

continued

2. Windows Explorer enumerates each subkey of **ExtShellFolderView** and makes a note of its name. It also looks for a value called **PersistMoniker** in each subkey, which contains the path to the HTML file that Windows Explorer uses to draw the folder.

3. Windows Explorer displays the folder using the HTML file it found in **PersistMoniker**.

{5984FFE0-28D4-11CF-AE66-08002B2E1262}, which is the subkey that Windows Explorer finds in step 2, is an arbitrary GUID. You can rename this subkey to any valid GUID, and the operating system still finds **PersistMoniker**. The only special significance that this GUID might have is that Windows 2000 creates an identical subkey under **HKLM\Software\Microsoft\Windows\CurrentVersion\ExtShellViews**, which describes the view's menu command, As Web Page, on Windows Explorer's View menu.

▶ **See** Chapter 11, "Diagnosing Registry Errors," **p. 227**, to fix a number of problems that result from incorrect keys and values in **shellex**.

▶ **See** Chapter 12, "Repairing Damaged Registries," **p. 237**, to diagnose and fix problems that relate to orphaned shell extensions in **shellex** keys.

The ShellNew Subkey

Right-click any folder and choose New to display a menu of new documents you can create in the folder. This is a quick way to create a new document. You can then open the new document to edit its contents. If the associated program identifier has a verb called **new**, Windows 2000 automatically opens the file using the command line specified in **new\command**.

Windows 2000 builds this menu of templates by examining each filename extension subkey in the Registry to see if it has a **ShellNew** subkey. This process is why the New menu sometimes takes so long to display. **ShellNew** defines a template for the file extension. If Windows 2000 finds a **ShellNew** subkey, the operating system looks up the program identifier associated with it and displays a description of the file type on the New menu. Four different methods are available for specifying a template within **ShellNew**. Each method involves adding a different value entry to the filename extension's **ShellNew** subkey:

- **Command** This string value entry indicates the command line to execute to create the new file.
- **NullFile** This empty string value entry indicates that the new file will be completely empty.
- **FileName** This string value indicates the filename of a particular template file that the operating system looks for in \Windows\Shellnew.
- **Data** This is a binary value whose contents Windows 2000 uses to create the new file when the user chooses it from the New menu. Windows 2000 just copies the bytes from this value entry directly into the file.

N O T E These three terms are similar, but they mean different things in the Registry. **Shell** defines commands that you can perform on a file or object. **ShellEx** defines shell extensions that enhance how you interact with the object. **ShellNew** defines a template so that you can easily create a new file of a particular type in a folder. ■

▶ **See** Chapter 7, "Customizing Windows 2000," **p. 107,** for step-by-step instructions for customizing the <u>N</u>ew menu using **ShellNew**.

The DefaultIcon Subkey

All filename extension and class definition keys support the **DefaultIcon** subkey, which defines the icon for a file or object. You also see this icon used in folders, on an application's title bar, on the Start menu, and so on.

The default value entry of **DefaultIcon** specifies the location of the icon that Windows Explorer displays for the file. Icons come from EXE, DLL, RES, ICO, and other files. ICO, BMP, and similar files contain a single icon; you specify them by giving the pathname and filename of the image file. EXE, DLL, and RES files can contain any number of icons. You reference a particular icon in such files using the icon's index, starting from 0. The first icon is 0, the second is 1, and so on. You specify an icon in an EXE, DLL, or RES file by giving the file's pathname and filename, followed by the icon's index, like this: *path,index. path* is the full path and filename of the file, and *index* is the index of the icon in the file.

There is one more convention you should be aware of. Windows 2000 allows a programmer to assign a fixed identifier to each icon. This identifier is usually called a *resource ID.* The resource ID is any arbitrary integer value, such as 1037. It provides an easier way for the programmer to reference an exact icon without having to figure out the icon's index. The programmer can assign the integer value to a symbol and then use that symbol in the code. You can also specify an icon using its resource ID, assuming that you know it, by writing a line like this: *path,-resource. path* is the full pathname and filename of the file, and *resource* is the icon's resource ID. The following list shows you an example of both methods for specifying the location of an icon:

Index	`C:\Windows\System\Shell32.dll,9`
Resource ID	`C:\Windows\System\Shell32.dll,-37`

If you see **%1** in **DefaultIcon**, this means that the icon handler will provide the icon. Look for a subkey under **shellex** called **iconhandler**, which you learned about earlier in this chapter. This shell extension will supply the icon specified by the **%1** in **DefaultIcon**. If you don't find an icon handler for the class, the file is probably an image, so Windows Explorer uses a scaled-down copy of the file's contents as the icon.

N O T E Windows 2000 doesn't even look at **DefaultIcon** if it finds the item's icon in the icon cache, `Shelliconcache`. You learned how to work with this file in Chapter 7, "Customizing Windows 2000." ■

Part

V

Ch

13

▶ **See** Chapter 7, "Customizing Windows 2000," **p. 107**, for a description of how to change the icon that the operating system uses for a file or object.

Significant Class Definitions

Many class definitions look like **txtfile**, **docfile**, and **regfile**. These define programs such as a text editor, word processor, or Registry Editor. Other class definitions have names like * and **folder**. These don't define a particular program; they define special-purpose classes and classes for special types of objects. These aren't usually associated with a file extension or COM class. Windows 2000 just knows to look for them by name.

The following sections describe the most interesting of these special class definitions. If you don't find an explanation in this chapter for a class definition that appears to have a special purpose, you can almost always figure out its purpose by examining its contents. If that doesn't help, use a program such as Registry Monitor to see which types of files and objects access that class definition.

▶ **See** Chapter 9, "Tracking Down Registry Settings," **p. 155**, shows you how to observe Registry access in real time using a program called Registry Monitor.

The * Class Definition

Windows 2000 applies the contents of **HKCR*** to every file on the computer. Usually the first subkey of **HKEY_CLASSES_ROOT**, * is a wildcard. Keep in mind that this is not a filename extension, contrary to what you might have read elsewhere. It's a class definition with all the features of any other class definition subkey.

* usually has a single subkey called **shellex** that leads to two other subkeys. **ContextMenuHandlers** adds additional items to every file's shortcut menu. An example is a handler that adds Update to a file's shortcut menu when the file is in a briefcase. **PropertySheetHandlers** adds additional tabs to every file's property sheet, which you open by right-clicking the file and choosing Properties.

The Unknown Class Definition

When you right-click a file for which Windows Explorer doesn't find a matching filename extension, the operating system uses the **Unknown** class definition to build the file's shortcut menu. **Unknown\shell** typically contains a single verb called **openas**, which adds the Open With option to the file's shortcut menu. You can add additional verbs to **Unknown** to provide additional commands for unknown files. Consider adding a verb that opens an unknown file in Notepad, for instance, which allows you to easily open any unregistered file in Notepad. This is a handy feature considering the variety of file extensions that vendors use to name Readme files: Read.me, Readme.txt, Readme.doc, Readme.1st, and so on.

The AllFilesystemObjects Class Definition

AllFilesystemObjects is a special class that applies to every object in the file system, including removable drives, folders, and files. By default, the only thing this class does is add the **Send To** menu to each removable drive, folder, and file's shortcut menu.

The Directory, Drive, and Folder Class Definitions

Directory, **Drive**, and **Folder** are similar class definitions. They extend the user interface for directories, drives, and folders. The distinction lies in which class the operating system uses when you work with different types of folders:

Folder Type	Example	Class Definitions
System folders	Control Panel	**Folder**
Drives	C:\	**Drive** and **Folder**
Normal folders	C:\Windows	**Directory** and **Folder**

> **N O T E**   A *folder* is any container that you can open and browse. This includes normal file system folders and special system folders. Windows 2000 provides a number of system folders. Examples include the Control Panel, Dial-Up Networking, Microsoft Network, My Computer, Network Neighborhood, Printers, and Recycle Bin folders. ▓

The AudioCD Class Definition

Windows 2000 uses this class definition for audio CDs. It adds the **Play** option to an audio CD's shortcut menu.

The AutoRun Class Definition

When you insert a data CD into the CD-ROM drive, Windows 2000 copies several values from the Autorun.inf file in the disk's root folder, if it exists, to **AutoRun**. The following code snippet shows an example of a typical Autorun.inf file. Windows 2000 puts the value assigned to **icon** in the default value of the **DefaultIcon** subkey. It puts the value assigned to **open** in the default value **AutoRun*num*\Shell\AutoRun\command**, where *num* is **0** if the disk is in drive A, **1** if it's in drive B, **2** if it's in drive C, and so on. Windows 2000 automatically executes the program indicated in the disk's **AutoRun\Command** subkey after the user inserts the disk. The user can also right-click the disk in Windows Explorer and choose AutoPlay, defined by the verb **Shell\AutoRun**.

```
_[autorun]
open=autorun.exe
icon=autorun.ico
```

Part

V

Ch

13

For AutoRun to work properly, Auto Insert Notification must be enabled on the Settings tab of the CD-ROM drive's property sheet. Open the Device Manger from the Control Panel, double-click the CD-ROM drive to open its property sheet, and click the Settings tab. Enable Auto Insert Notification, and close the drive's property sheet and the Device Manager to save your changes.

The regfile Program Identifier

regfile is a plain old program identifier. So what is it doing here? I mention it because the Registry Editor has an annoying habit of automatically importing REG files when you double-click them.

The default command for a REG file is to merge the file's contents into the Registry. If you accidentally double-click the file thinking that you're going to edit it, you'll make a mistake. You can avoid this mistake by changing the default command for a REG file. To do so, change the default value of **regfile\shell** to **edit**, which then makes **regfile\shell\edit** the default command on the shortcut menu.

Significant COM Class Identifiers

Some classes have special significance. These are primarily classes that Windows 2000 adds to the namespaces of the desktop and the My Computer folder. The following table provides the names and class identifiers of these significant classes:

Folder	Class Identifier
ActiveX Cache Folder	{88C6C381-2E85-11D0-94DE-444553540000}
Briefcase	{85BBD920-42A0-1069-A2E4-08002B30309D}
Control Panel	{21EC2020-3AEA-1069-A2DD-08002B30309D}
Dial-Up Networking	{992CFFA0-F557-101A-88EC-00DD010CCC48}
Infrared Recipient	{00435ae0-bffb-11cf-a9d8-00aa00423596}
Internet Cache...	{7BD29E00-76C1-11CF-9DD0-00A0C9034933}
Internet Explorer	{FBF23B42-E3F0-101B-8488-00AA003E56F8}
My Computer	{20D04FE0-3AEA-1069-A2D8-08002B30309D}
My Documents	{450D8FBA-AD25-11D0-98A8-0800361B1103}
Network Neighborhood	{208D2C60-3AEA-1069-A2D7-08002B30309D}
Printers	{2227A280-3AEA-1069-A2DE-08002B30309D}
Recycle Bin	{645FF040-5081-101B-9F08-00AA002F954E}
Scheduled Tasks	{D6277990-4C6A-11CF-8D87-00AA0060F5BF}
Shell Favorite...	{1A9BA3A0-143A-11CF-8350-444553540000}

Subscription Folder	{F5175861-2688-11d0-9C5E-00AA00A45957}
The Internet	{3DC7A020-0ACD-11CF-A9BB-00AA004AE837}
URL History Folder	{FF393560-C2A7-11CF-BFF4-444553540000}

TIP The best way to search for special class identifiers (those that you can insert into the desktop's namespace) is to search **CLSID** for any keys that contain a subkey called **ExtShellFoldersView**. Doing so uncovers only those shell folders that can actually display content in a folder.

▶ **See** Chapter 7, "Customizing Windows 2000," **p. 107**, to learn how to use the special class identifiers you learned about in this section to customize the operating system in a variety of ways.

GUIDs in Memory

The binary representation of a GUID in memory is a bit different from the string definition you see in the Registry. The first four bytes are stored as a **DWORD**, so the bytes are reversed. (Refer to Chapter 10, "Scripting Customizations," to learn how the computer stores **DWORD** values in memory.) The next four bytes are stored as two words, again with their bytes reversed. The remaining bytes are stored as single bytes, so the order is not reversed. Thus, when you're looking for **{5984FFE0-28D4-11CF-AE66-08002B2E1262}** in memory, you're actually looking for a binary string like **e0,ff,84,59,d4,28,cf,11,ae,66,08,00,2b,2e,12,62**.

This is good information to know if you're trying to track down how Windows 2000 is using a particular class identifier. You find class identifiers referenced in a surprisingly large number of binary value entries. These aren't obvious until you export the entire Registry to a REG file and start examining each binary value. After doing so, you start to see patterns emerge. Therefore, if you're trying to figure out how the operating system uses a particular class identifier, search a complete REG file for the binary representation of it. A REG file might split a large binary value across multiple lines, by the way, so search for a portion of the GUID. In the preceding example, searching for **D4,28** (remember that the fifth and sixth bytes are stored as a single word with the bytes reversed) yields the desired result.

Part
V

Ch
13

Per-User Settings

HKCU\AppEvents

In Microsoft Windows 2000, an *application event* is any event to which you can assign a sound. The operating system plays the sound when that event occurs. Maximizing a window is an event for which Windows 2000 plays a sound, for instance. So is a critical error. You assign sounds to events by double-clicking the Sounds and Multimedia Properties icon in the Control Panel.

Windows 2000 and each application you install define the events with which you can associate sounds, so inventing events out of thin air does you little good. That is, Windows 2000 and applications only recognize events that they register themselves. They register events by listing them in the following two subkeys of **HKCU\AppEvents**:

EventLabels	Defines the label for each event
Schemes	Associates sounds with each event

N O T E It doesn't make sense to customize sound events in the Registry, although you can do it. First, trying to register new events for an application is useless, because each application only looks for events that it registers. Second, the Sounds and Multimedia Properties dialog box makes choosing sound themes or associating sound files with particular events much easier than doing the same task in the Registry. ∎

EventLabels

Figure 14.1 shows the relationship between the Sounds and Multimedia Properties dialog box and the two subkeys you see under **AppEvents**: **EventLabels** and **Schemes**. **EventLabels** defines the name of each event. The name of each subkey under **EventLabels** is the internal name of the event, and the default value of each is the label for the event as you see it in the Sounds and Multimedia Properties dialog box. Thus, the subkey called **Close** describes an event whose label is Close program. Table 14.1 describes the event labels you typically find in **EventLabels**.

FIGURE 14.1
The Sounds and
Multimedia Properties
dialog box retrieves its
information from the
subkeys under
AppEvents.

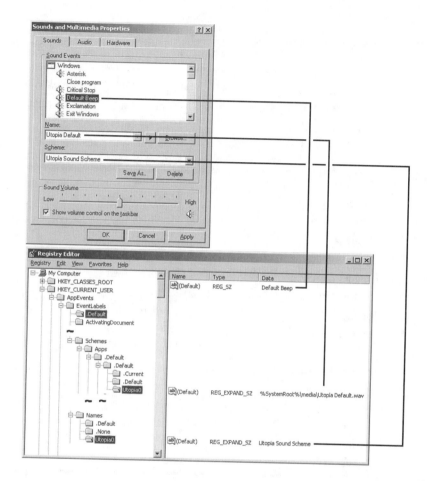

Table 14.1   Typical Sound Events

Subkey	Event Label
Windows	
.Default	Default beep
AppGPFault	Program error
CCSelect	Select
Close	Close program
InfraredBeginCommunication	Infrared: Begin Communication
InfraredBeginDeviceInRange	Infrared: Begin Device(s) In Range

continues

Part
V

Ch
14

Table 14.1   Continued

Subkey	Event Label
InfraredEndCommunication	Infrared: End Communication
InfraredEndDeviceInRange	Infrared: End Device(s) In Range
InfraredInterrupted	Infrared: Interrupted
InfraredNewFiles	Infrared: New Files Notification
MailBeep	New Mail Notification
Maximize	Maximize
MenuCommand	Menu command
MenuPopup	Menu popup
Minimize	Minimize
Open	Open program
RestoreDown	Restore Down
RestoreUp	Restore Up
RingIn	Incoming Call
RingOut	Outgoing Call
ShowBand	Show Toolbar Band
SystemAsterisk	Asterisk
SystemExclamation	Exclamation
SystemExit	Exit Windows
SystemHand	Critical Stop
SystemQuestion	Question
SystemStart	Start Windows

Windows Explorer

ActivatingDocument	Complete Navigation
EmptyRecycleBin	Empty Recycle Bin
Incoming-Fax	Incoming Fax
MoveMenuItem	Move Menu Item
Navigating	Start Navigation
Outgoing-Fax	Outgoing Fax

Media Player

Close	Close program
Open	Open program

Subkey	Event Label
Power Management	
CriticalBatteryAlarm	Critical Battery Alarm
LowBatteryAlarm	Low Battery Alarm
Sound Recorder	
Close	Close program
Open	Open program
Microsoft Office	
Office97-AddItemtoView	Add Item to View
Office97-Alert	Alert
Office97-AutoCorrect	AutoCorrect
Office97-BestFit	Best Fit
Office97-Clear	Clear
Office97-Cut&Clear	Cut & Clear
Office97-Delete	Delete
Office97-DeleteRow	Delete Row
Office97-DialogCancel	Dialog Cancel
Office97-DialogOk	Dialog Ok
Office97-Drag	Drag
Office97-Drop	Drop
Office97-Expand/Collapse	Expand/Collapse
Office97-FolderSwitch	Folder Switch
Office97-GroupScopeSwitch	Group Scope Switch
Office97-GroupSwitch	Group Switch
Office97-InsertRow	Insert Row
Office97-ModeSwitch	Mode Switch
Office97-NewItem	New Item
Office97-PlyScroll	Ply Scroll
Office97-PlySelect	Ply Select
Office97-ProcessComplete	Process Complete
Office97-Redo	Redo
Office97-ScrollArrow	Scroll Arrow
Office97-ScrollBar	Scroll Bar

Part
V

Ch
14

continues

Table 14.1   Continued

Subkey	Event Label
Office97-ScrollThumb	Scroll Thumb
Office97-Send	Send
Office97-Sort	Sort
Office97-ToolbarClick	Toolbar Click
Office97-ToolbarClose	Toolbar Close
Office97-ToolbarDock	Toolbar Dock
Office97-ToolbarDrop	Toolbar Drop
Office97-ToolbarFocus	Toolbar Focus
Office97-ToolbarUndock	Toolbar Undock
Office97-Undo	Undo
Office97-ViewSwitch	View Switch
Office97-ZoomIn	Zoom In
Office97-ZoomOut	Zoom Out

Wireless Link

InfraredInRange	Device In Range
InfraredInterrupt	Communication Interrupted
InfraredOutOfRange	Device Out Of Range

Schemes

Schemes\Apps associates sounds with the events registered by Windows 2000 and each application. Underneath this subkey is a single subkey for each application. **.Default** contains events that Windows 2000 registered; for example, **MPlay32** contains the events that Media Player registered. Look to the default value for each **Schemes\Apps*AppName*** key to see the actual name of the application that registered the events. In a typical installation that includes Microsoft Office, *AppName* would be the following subkeys:

AppName	Application Name
.Default	Windows
Explorer	Windows Explorer
MPlay32	Media Player
Office97	Microsoft Office
PowerCfg	Power Management
SndRec32	Sound Recorder

Each subkey under **Schemes\Apps***AppName*, which we'll call *Event*, is one of the events you learned about in the preceding section. In other words, each is a registered event whose label can be found in **EventLabels***AppName**Event*. Underneath each event, you see a subkey called **.Current** whose default value contains the path and filename of the sound file associated with the event. You might see several other subkeys that associate sound files with sound themes, too, such as **Jungle0** and **Utopia0**. The default value of **Schemes** indicates the current sound theme, and Windows 2000 looks up that name in **Schemes\Names**. For instance, if the current sound theme is **Utopia0**, Windows 2000 looks in **Schemes\Names\Utopia0** to find that the name of this sound theme is "Utopia Sound Theme."

To help you sort all this out, take a look at what happens when an event occurs. The application looks up **HKCU\AppEvents\Schemes\Apps***AppName*, where *AppName* is the name under which the application registered the event. Underneath that subkey, the application looks up *Event***.Current**, where *Event* is the name of the registered event, and plays the sound file indicated by the default value entry of **.Current**. Also, look at what happens when the Sounds and Multimedia Properties dialog box displays information about the events registered in **AppEvents**:

- In the <u>S</u>ound Events list, you see one category for each subkey of **AppEvents\Schemes\Apps**. The label you see comes from the subkey's default value.
- Underneath each category, you see an event for each subkey of **AppEvents\Schemes\Apps***AppName*. The label you see comes from **AppEvents\EventLabels***Event*, where *Event* is the same under both branches.
- The sound file you see in <u>N</u>ame comes from the default value entry of **AppEvents\Schemes\Apps***AppName**Event***.Current**.

N O T E   Some applications don't register sound events in their own category. They add events to the Windows category, **Apps\.Default**. ■

HKCU\Console

Anytime you customize console windows (MS-DOS command prompts), Windows 2000 stores their settings in **Console**. Click <u>D</u>efaults on the system menu, change settings in the Console Windows Properties dialog box, and the operating system stores those settings in **HKCU\Console**. Change settings by clicking <u>P</u>roperties on the system menu, and the operating system prompts whether you want to use those settings for the current window or for all windows with that same title. When you choose to save those settings for all windows with that same title, the operating system stores them in **HKCU\Console***Title*. The only time this really applies is when you run a console by typing **cmd** in the Run dialog box, because the operating system stores settings for console windows that you start from a shortcut in the shortcut file.

HKCU\Control Panel

Table 14.2 describes each interesting subkey of Control Panel and indicates the Control Panel icon that sets the configuration data in it. I've divided the table into sections, each of which describes a single Control Panel icon. The third column indicates the tab on which you configure the options found in each subkey. Keep in mind that only a handful of the icons in the Control Panel store configuration data in this branch of the Registry. Other Control Panel icons store configuration data in **HKLM**, especially per-computer settings, or in other branches within **HKCU**.

Although Table 14.2 helps you determine which Control Panel icon sets configuration data in each subkey of **Control Panel**, the following sections help you make sense of the data you find in each of these subkeys. Some are completely uninteresting, so their descriptions are brief, but others contain very useful information.

N O T E Of all the subkeys in **Control Panel**, the most interesting is **Desktop**. This subkey contains a variety of settings that determine how Windows 2000 looks and feels. You learn more about these settings in Chapter 7, "Customizing Windows 2000." ■

Table 14.2   Control Panel Subkeys

Subkey	Tab
Accessibility Options	
Accessibility\HighContrast	Display
Accessibility\KeyboardPreference	Keyboard
Accessibility\KeyboardResponse	Keyboard
Accessibility\MouseKeys	Mouse
Accessibility\SerialKeys	General
Accessibility\ShowSounds	Sound
Accessibility\SoundSentry	Sound
Accessibility\Stickykeys	Keyboard
Accessibility\TimeOut	General
Accessibility\ToggleKeys	Keyboard
Display	
Appearance	Appearance
Appearance\Schemes	Appearance
Colors	Appearance
Desktop\WindowMetrics	Appearance

Subkey	Tab
Desktop	Screen Saver
Desktop	Background
Desktop	Effects
Mouse	
Cursor	Pointers
Cursor\Schemes	Pointers
Infrared	
Infrared	Options
Infrared\Monitor	Preferences
Regional Options	
International	General
International	Numbers
International	Currency
International	Time
International	Date
International	Input Locales
Power Options	
PowerCfg	Power Schemes
PowerCfg\GlobalPowerPolicy	Power Schemes
PowerCfg\PowerPolicies	Power Schemes

Accessibility

This subkey defines the accessibility settings you set by double-clicking the Accessibility Options icon in **Control Panel**. Table 14.2 showed you how each subkey matches up to each tab on this dialog box. Each value you find in these subkeys is self-explanatory. Although you can configure the accessibility options using Registry Editor, stick with the Accessibility Options dialog box, because it makes the task much easier.

Appearance

HKCU\Control Panel\Appearance\Schemes contains values for each scheme you see in the <u>S</u>cheme list of the Display Properties dialog box's Appearance tab. Each entry in this list

Part

V

Ch

14

corresponds to each value name under this subkey. The format of each value's binary data is almost indecipherable, so you're better off defining themes using the Display Properties dialog box.

In **HKCU\Control Panel\Appearance**, the **REG_SZ** value **Current** contains the name of the current scheme.

Appearance does contain one interesting value, however. When you define custom colors by clicking the Color button on the Appearance tab, you have to define those colors in decimal notation or use the color wheel. Both are difficult to use because most people are accustomed to defining RGB values in hexadecimal notation, as is common in HTML. The binary value **CustomColors** defines these custom colors; they're in hexadecimal notation. The first 4 bytes define the first color in RGB notation followed by 0x00, the second 4 bytes define the second color, and so on. Thus, if you want to set the first color to the khaki color that Microsoft is fond of on their Web pages, type **CC CC 99 00** in the first 4 bytes of **CustomColors**. Figure 14.2 shows the relationship between these values and the Color dialog box.

FIGURE 14.2
Defining custom colors in the Registry is frequently easier than using the Color dialog box.

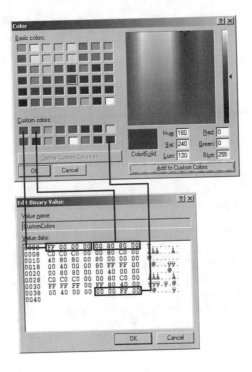

Colors

The values in **Colors** define the color for each element in the user interface. **ActiveTitle** defines the color of each window's active title bar, for example, and **Window** defines the background color for each window. Each value entry uses the RGB notation, but it does so in decimal, not hexadecimal. This is one of those cases in which changing these values on the Appearance tab of the Display Properties dialog box is easier than changing them in the Registry. If you like to use the same odd colors every time you install Windows 2000, you might consider saving this branch to a Registration Entries (REG) file so that you can import your colors the next time you install the operating system.

Cursors

Each value in **Cursors** indicates the path and filename of a .cur file for that particular pointer. The value's name indicates the name of the pointer, which isn't necessarily what you see in the Pointers tab of the Mouse Properties dialog box. Note that this key's default value entry contains the name of the current scheme.

Cursors\Schemes defines the pointer schemes you see in the Schemes list of the Mouse Properties dialog box. Each value is named after a particular theme, and its string contents contain a comma-separated list of .cur files for each pointer in the theme. The order of this comma-separated list is as follows:

- Arrow
- Help
- AppStarting
- Wait
- Crosshair
- IBeam
- NWPen
- No
- SizeNS
- SizeWE
- SizeNWSE
- SizeNESW
- SizeAll
- UpArrow

Part

V

Ch

14

Desktop

Desktop is one of the most interesting subkeys in **Control Panel**. It contains a variety of settings that control how Windows 2000 looks and feels. You define most of these settings using the Display Properties dialog box. Also note that you can define any settings you don't find in a traditional Windows 2000 dialog box via Microsoft Tweak UI (see Chapter 8, "Using Microsoft Tweak UI"). With the exception of **SmoothScroll** and **UserPreferenceMask**, which are **REG_DWORD** values represented as binary values, all the settings described here are **REG_SZ** values. The following table describes the most useful settings for customizing the operating system:

Value	Description
DragFullWindows	Determines whether you see the full window or its outline as you move it around the desktop: 0 = drag window outline 1 = drag full window contents
FontSmoothing	Determines whether Windows 2000 smoothes fonts when it displays them onscreen: 0 = don't smooth screen fonts 1 = smooth screen fonts
MenuShowDelay	Time in milliseconds that the user must hover the mouse pointer over a submenu's name before Windows 2000 opens the menu (500ms equals 1/2 second).
PaintDesktopVersion	Determines whether Windows 2000 displays the operating system version in the lower-right corner of the desktop: 0 = don't display version 1 = display version number
UserPreferenceMask	See the following discussion.

UserPreferenceMask is the most interesting value in **Desktop** and is in fact one of the most useful values in the Registry for customizing the look and feel of Windows 98. **UserPreferenceMask** is a **REG_DWORD** represented in binary. You only care about the first two bytes of this value, however, which are bit masks. Each bit is a flag that enables or disables an option. Table 14.3 describes what each bit represents. If you want to prevent menus, combo boxes, and list boxes from animating when you open them, turn off bits 1, 2, and 3 of the first word in **UserPreferenceMask**. Turn off bit 5 if you don't want Windows 2000 to underline hotkeys in menus. Bit 6 controls whether windows come to the foreground when you hover the mouse over them, and bit 7 controls whether you see those tips in yellow boxes when you hover the mouse over the minimize, maximize, and close buttons in a program's title bar. Here are some examples:

Old Value	Old Binary	To Do This	New Binary	New Value
0x2e	00101110	Disable menu hot keys	00001110	0x0e
0x2e	00101110	Enable X-mouse effects	01101110	0x6e
0x20	00100000	Enable mouse tracking	10100000	0xa0
0x20	0010000	Enable animations	00101110	0x2e

Table 14.3   UserPreferenceMask

Bit	Mask	Hex	Description
0	00000001	0x01	Unused
1	00000010	0x02	Menu animation
2	00000100	0x04	Combo box animation
3	00001000	0x08	List box animation
4	00010000	0x10	Unused
5	00100000	0x20	Menu hot keys
6	01000000	0x40	X-mouse effects
7	10000000	0x80	Mouse tracking effects

The two subkeys of **Desktop** are **ResourceLocale** and **WindowMetrics**. The default value in **ResourceLocale** contains the locale for the version of Windows 2000 that you purchased. This value is set when you install Windows 2000, and you can't change it. You see a definition of this value in the Locale.inf file that you find in *SystemRoot***Inf**. Note that the value used for the United States is 409, which is defined as "English (United States)." Versions of Windows 2000 sold in other regions might have a different value. The remaining subkey, **WindowMetrics**, defines various characteristics of icons, menus, and so on. Most of these values are uninteresting, except for **MinAnimate**, which controls whether Windows 98 animates windows as they minimize to the taskbar and restore to the desktop.

Bit Masks for the Binary-Illiterate

If you don't understand binary or hexadecimal notation, you'll have difficulty working with bit masks in the Registry. I won't teach you everything you need to know about these notations. I'll teach you just enough so that you can work with masks.

First, understand that each digit in a hexadecimal byte (there are two digits) has a 4-bit binary equivalent. Thus, the hexadecimal numbers 0xAC, 0x01, and 0xF3 are bytes that have two *nibbles* that are 4 bits each. To translate a hexadecimal byte into an 8-bit binary number, look up each nibble in the following table and combine (concatenate) them. If you were to translate 0xFA to binary, you would find that F is 1111 and A is 1010, so 0xFA must be 11111010. Likewise, 0x93 is 10010011. Refer to Table 14.3 to translate bit numbers into masks.

Part
V

Ch
14

continues

continued

Digit	Nibble	Digit	Nibble
0	0000	8	1000
1	0001	9	1001
2	0010	A	1010
3	0011	B	1011
4	0100	C	1100
5	0101	D	1101
6	0110	E	1110
7	0111	F	1111

Now that you know the binary representation for the byte, you need to figure out which bit you want to enable or disable. If you're working with bit 6, counting from 0, 1, 2, 3, 4, 5, 6 from the right, your mask is 01000000. Working with bit 3, your mask is 00001000. This mask helps you determine which bit you need to tweak in your 8-bit binary number. Line up your mask with the binary number so that you can identify the bit. Then turn that bit off in the number to disable the option, or turn that bit on to enable the option. After you've tweaked the bit in the mask, translate the number back to hexadecimal by reversing the procedure. For example, if you're left with 01111110, the first four digits represent a 7, and the second four represent an E. Thus, the hexadecimal number is 0x7E.

Here are some examples:

Hex	To Binary	Mask	Leaves Binary	To Hex
0x7E	01111110	Disable bit 3	01110110	0x76
0x2D	00101101	Enable bit 7	10101101	0xAD
0xFF	11111111	Disable bit 0	11111110	0xFE
0xB2	10110010	Enable bit 3	10111010	0xBA
0x25	00100101	Enable bit 4	00110101	0x35

don't load

This is a simple subkey. Windows 2000 looks at the values in **don't load** to determine whether it displays an icon in Control Panel. It looks for a value whose name is the same as the icon's filename and then uses its **REG_SZ** value to determine whether to load the icon. If the value is **no**, it doesn't load it; if the value is **yes**, it does load it. Of course, if the operating system doesn't contain a value corresponding to the Control Panel icon, the operating system goes ahead and loads it.

Infrared

This subkey defines configuration data set by the Infrared Monitor dialog box in the Control Panel. Most of these settings are uninteresting because they're easier to configure in the dialog box than in the Registry.

International

In most cases, **International** contains a single value entry called **Locale**, which is similar to the **ResourceLocale** defined in the **Desktop** subkey. Locale.inf in *SystemRoot*\Inf defines each of the possible settings. You control this setting in the General tab of the Regional Options dialog box. If you further customize the computer's international settings, you'll see several other values. These define things such as the currency symbol, date format, list separator, and so on. I don't recommend that you change this value in the Registry, because you'll miss a variety of related settings in the Registry that the Regional Settings dialog box changes.

PowerCfg

PowerCfg defines the schemes you see in the Power Schemes list in the Power Schemes tab of the Power Options dialog box. **CurrentPowerPolicy** is a **REG_SZ** value that contains the name of the current scheme. **PowerCfg\PowerPolicies** contains a subkey for each default scheme: **0**, **1**, **3**, and so on. Thus, if **CurrentPowerPolicy** is **1**, **PowerCfg\PowerPolicies\1** contains the current power management settings. Each subkey contains the following value entries to describe the power scheme: **Description**, **Name**, and **Policies.**

> **N O T E**   So far in this chapter, you've seen three different cases in which Windows 2000 stores schemes in the Registry: colors, pointers, and power. You might have noticed that Windows 2000 doesn't use the same organization for any of these. That's the usual case for data stored in the Registry: The same type of data is seldom stored using the same organization or data types. ▪

Sound

The **Sound** subkey has a single value called **Beep**. This string value indicates whether Windows 2000 beeps on errors. **Yes** means it will beep. **No** means it won't.

HKCU\Environment

Environment contains a subkey for each per-user environment variable. Users define environment variables by double-clicking the System icon in Control Panel and then clicking Environment Variables on the Advanced tab.

HKCU\InstallLocationsMRU

Control Panel\InstallLocationsMRU contains a value for each location from which you've installed components into Windows 2000. This includes times when you've added components using the Add/Remove Programs dialog box or when you've clicked the Have Disk button in Add New Hardware Wizard. The first value name is **a**, the second is **b**, and so on. Because the order of these values changes over time, Windows 2000 stores the order in **MRUList**, which is a **REG_SZ** value that indicates the order in which Windows 2000 displays these paths in history lists. For instance, if **MRUList** contains **ebcad**, the value in **e** is first in the list, the value in **b** is second, and so on.

History Lists

Windows 2000 stores history lists in a consistent manner throughout the Registry. The subkey with the history list contains a number of values, all named **a** through **z**. The data for each value depends on how the operating system uses the list.

You also find a value called **MRUList**, or something similar. This value indicates the order of the items in the history list. It's a string value that contains a single character for each item **a** through **z**, and the order of the characters determines the order of the list. If **MRUList** contains **feabcd**, **f** is first, **e** is second, **a** is third, and so on. You'll also notice that **MRUList** contains as many characters as the key contains entries.

HKCU\Keyboard Layout

Keyboard layout\preload contains a numbered subkey for each keyboard language you install via the Language tab of the Keyboard Properties dialog box. The default value entry of each subkey contains the locale ID of the keyboard language as defined in Local.inf and Multilng.inf, which you find in *SystemRoot*\Inf.

Keyboard layout\substitutes contains a value that defines substitutes for many of the keyboard layouts defined in **preload**. The default value for a subkey called **00000809** might be **00010409**, indicating that the keyboard language defined by **00010409** is a viable substitute for **00000809**.

The last subkey, **toggle**, indicates whether the user can toggle between each keyboard layout using the shortcut keys Ctrl+Shift and Alt+Shift. You set this and the other options in the Languages tab of the Keyboard Properties dialog box.

> **NOTE** As with similar locale-type settings, changing **Keyboard layout** in the Registry is senseless. You're better off changing these values using the appropriate Control Panel icon, because you're likely to miss related values or mess things up completely. ▪

HKCU\Network

Network contains one subkey for each network connection. The name of each is the drive letter to which you've mapped the network drive. The values under each connection describe the type of connection, the network provider, and the username used to connect to the share.

If you permanently map a drive by checking Reconnect at Logon, you see a subkey under **Persistent** for the drive to which you mapped the network share. Merely the presence of **Persistent***Drive* is enough to indicate that the connection is persistent.

HKCU\RemoteAccess

RemoteAccess describes the dial-up connections you've configured in the Network and Dial-Up Connections folder. You see a binary value entry under **RemoteAccess\Addresses** for each connection you create. The content of this value is indecipherable.

RemoteAccess\Profile*Connection* contains additional information about each connection if necessary. If you configure a connection to use a script, for example, you see information about that script in *Connection*. Likewise, if you configure a connection to use Multilink, you see information about the additional devices to use for that connection. The format of the values in **RemoteAccess** is indecipherable, so don't try creating connections using the Registry.

TIP

Dial-Up Networking connections aren't files. You can't copy them from computer to computer like you can files. At least not quite. You can export **HKEY_CURRENT_USER\RemoteAccess** to a REG file and then copy the file to another computer and import it into the Registry. This has the same effect as copying the connection between both computers. This is also a great way to back up your connections so that you can re-create them after reinstalling a fresh copy of Windows 2000.

HKCU\Software

Most applications store per-user configuration data in **HKCU\Software**. They do so using organization similar to *Company\Product\Version*. *Company* is the name of the company that produces the application, *Product* is the name of the application, and *Version* is the version of the application whose settings you find in that branch. Thus, **Honeycutt\Monster\1.0** contains preferences for version 1.0 of a program called Monster developed by a company called Honeycutt. Some companies use the name **CurrentVersion** instead of an actual version number, as Microsoft does for Windows.

Microsoft is generally the most interesting subkey of **HKCU**. Aside from containing the per-user settings for Windows 2000 in **Windows\CurrentVersion**, it also contains a plethora of settings that govern Internet Explorer. This branch is so interesting that it is covered all by itself in the following sections.

Part
V

Ch
14

N O T E   If you find a key or value that seems out of place, it probably is. Windows 2000, more than any previous version of Windows, even Windows 98, stores data in the Registry where it shouldn't be located. This problem is most likely due to human error—probably too many programmers with their hands in the cookie jar. ■

HKCU\Software\Microsoft\Windows\CurrentVersion

CurrentVersion contains varieties of settings that control users' experiences:

- ■ **Applets**   Contains settings for Windows 2000's accessories, including Registry Editor.
- ■ **Explorer**   An interesting subkey that configures Windows Explorer. You learn about this later.
- ■ **Internet Settings**   Contains users' Internet configurations, including proxy settings.
- ■ **NetCache**   Where Synchronization Manager stores settings for offline files and folders.
- ■ **Policies**   Contains Registry-based group policy. You learn more about this subkey later.
- ■ **Run** and **RunOnce**   Contain the names of programs that the operating system runs when it first starts.

HKCU\Software\Microsoft\Windows\CurrentVersion\Explorer is one of the most important Registry branches for customizing Windows 2000. You can add objects to the desktop's name space, clear the history lists, and relocate shell folders via this branch.

Advanced contains settings that you change in the Advanced tab of the Folder Options dialog box. In Windows Explorer, choose Tools, Folder Options and click the Advanced tab. Each setting in this tab reflects a value entry in **Advanced**. The names are—you guessed it— self-explanatory. **AutoComplete**, **BrowseNewProcess**, and **SmallIcons** come from the Advanced tab of the Internet Options dialog box, not Folder Options.

Some of the subkeys under **Windows\CurrentVersion\Explorer** are indecipherable, but you can make an educated guess as to their functions. **CabinetState**, **DeskView**, **ExpView**, **StreamMRU**, **Streams**, and **StuckRects** are among that elite group of subkeys. They mostly contain settings that reflect the current state of the desktop and Windows Explorer. These are mostly bit masks. Uncovering what each bit means is difficult, however.

Explorer\MenuOrder

MenuOrder*Menu*, where *Menu* can be **Favorites** or **Start Menu**, indicates the sort order for the specified menu. Underneath *Menu*, you find a subkey for each submenu. Thus, under **Start Menu**, you'll find **&Documents**, **&Programs**, and so on. You'll also find a value called **Order** that indicates the sort order of each command on the menu. Go one level down, and you'll notice that this whole structure repeats itself. Look under the key for one of the submenus, and you'll notice more subkeys, one for each command on the submenu.

Explorer\Recent Docs

These subkeys contain history lists:

Map Network Drive ...	Contains a list of the network paths you've typed while mapping them
Recent Docs	Contains the list of recently opened documents that you see on the Start menu's <u>D</u>ocuments submenu
RunMRU	Contains the list of recently run documents that you see in the Run dialog box

Editing these history lists is senseless. **Recent Docs** stores each entry as a binary value that contains the document's name and the filename of the shortcut in Windows\Recent, for example. The only reason you should really care about these lists is if you want to clear them, in which case you can simply remove the entire subkey that contains the list you want to delete. The earlier "History Lists" sidebar described how Windows 2000 stores history lists in the Registry. In this case, all three history lists use this format.

Explorer\Shell Folders

These two subkeys contain paths for Windows 2000's shell folders. When the operating system or some other program wants to know the location of the Favorites folder, for instance, the operating system looks in these keys to find it.

Shell Folders contains string values for every shell folder Windows 2000 supports. Each value contains the fully qualified path to the folder. **User Shell Folders** contains similar values for each folder you customize. Note that in most cases, the operating system recognizes when you move a shell folder to a new location and updates these values automatically.

Policies

Many of the best customizations are actually policies that you can set with Group Policy. If you don't want to hassle with Group Policy, or you want to create a Setup Information (INF) file that you can use to import the same policies repeatedly, you should know how each policy translates to values in the Registry.

Table 14.4 describes the majority of per-user policies you can set in Windows 2000. I've divided the table into sections. The title of each section indicates the subkey under **Windows\CurrentVersion\Policies** in which you create the **REG_DWORD** value named in the first column. To enable a particular policy, set the **REG_DWORD** value to **0x00000001**. To disable the policy, remove the value or set it to **0x00000000**. For example, if you want to remove the My Network Places icon from the desktop, create a new

Part
V

Ch
14

REG_DWORD value called **NoNetHood** under **HKCU\Software\Microsoft\Windows\CurrentVersion\Policies\Explorer** and set its value to **0x00000001**. If you want to disable all items on the desktop, create a new **REG_DWORD** value called **NoComponents** under **ActiveDesktop** and set its value to **0x00000001**.

N O T E   In general, setting policies is easier using the Group Policy. You can think of this program as another customization tool rather than an administrative tool. ■

Table 14.4   Policies and Values

Value	Policy
Explorer	
NoSaveSettings	Don't save settings at exit
NoActiveDesktop	Disable Active Desktop
NoActiveDesktopChanges	Do not allow changes to Active Desktop
NoInternetIcon	Hide Internet Explorer icon
NoNetHood	Hide Network Neighborhood icon
NoDesktop	Hide all desktop items
NoFavoritesMenu	Remove the Favorites submenu from the Start menu
NoFind	Remove the Find submenu from the Start menu
NoRun	Remove the Run submenu from the Start menu
NoSetActiveDesktop	Remove the Active Desktop item from the Settings submenu
NoChangeStartMenu	Disable drag-and-drop context menus on the Start menu
NoFolderOptions	Remove the Folder Options menu item from the Settings submenu
NoRecentDocsMenu	Remove the Documents submenu from the Start menu
NoRecentDocsHistory	Do not keep a history of recently opened documents
ClearRecentDocsOnExit	Clear history of recently opened documents
NoLogoff	Disable logoff
NoClose	Disable the Shut Down command
NoSetFolders	Disable changes to Printers and Control Panel settings
NoSetTaskbar	Disable changes to the Taskbar and Start menu settings

Value	Policy
NoTrayContextMenu	Disable the context menu for the taskbar
NoStartMenuSubFolders	Hide custom Programs folders
ClassicShell	Enable the Classic Shell
NoFileMenu	Disable the File menu in Shell folders
NoViewContextMenu	Disable the context menu in Shell folders
EnforceShellExtensionSecurity	Only allow approved Shell extensions
LinkResolveIgnoreLinkInfo	Do not track Shell shortcuts during roaming
NoDrives	Hide floppy drives in My Computer
NoNetConnectDisconnect	Disable network connections and disconnections
NoPrinterTabs	Hide the General and Details tabs in Printer Properties
NoDeletePrinter	Disable Deletion of Printers
NoAddPrinter	Disable Addition of Printers
RestrictRun	Run only specified Windows applications

ActiveDesktop

NoComponents	Disable *all* desktop items
NoAddingComponents	Disable adding *any* desktop items
NoDeletingComponents	Disable deleting *any* desktop items
NoEditingComponents	Disable editing *any* desktop items
NoClosingComponents	Disable closing *any* desktop items
NoHTMLWallPaper	No HTML wallpaper
NoChangingWallPaper	Disable changing wallpaper
NoCloseDragDropBands	Disable dragging, dropping, and closing *all* toolbars
NoMovingBands	Disable resizing *all* toolbars

WinOldApp

NoRealMode	Do not allow the computer to restart in MS-DOS mode
Disabled	Disable the MS-DOS prompt

System

DisableRegistryTools	Disable Registry editing tools
NoDispCPL	Disable the Display Control Panel
NoDispBackgroundPage	Hide the Background page

Part
V

Ch
14

continues

Table 14.4   Continued

Value	Policy
NoDispScrSavPage	Hide the Screen Saver page
NoDispAppearancePage	Hide the Appearance page
NoDispSettingsPage	Hide the Settings page
NoSecCPL	Disable the Passwords Control Panel
NoPwdPage	Hide the Change Passwords page
NoAdminPage	Hide the Remote Administration page
NoProfilePage	Hide the User Profiles page
NoDevMgrPage	Hide the Device Manager page
NoConfigPage	Hide the Hardware Profiles page
NoFileSysPage	Hide the File System button
NoVirtMemPage	Hide the Virtual Memory button

Network

NoNetSetup	Disable the Network Control Panel
NoNetSetupIDPage	Hide the Identification Page
NoNetSetupSecurityPage	Hide the Access Page
NoEntireNetwork	No "Entire Network" in Network Neighborhood
NoWorkgroupContents	No workgroup contents in Network Neighborhood

Per-Computer Settings

HKLM\HARDWARE

Unlike other hives in the Registry, Microsoft Windows 2000 does not store **HARDWARE** in a hive file. Instead, the hive is volatile, meaning the operating system rebuilds the hive every time it starts and does not save it between sessions. In **HARDWARE**, Windows 2000 stores information about the hardware it detects during the hardware detection phase of the boot process. The contents of this hive are a bit cryptic, containing a mixture of **REG_FULL_RESOURCE_DESCRIPTOR**, **REG_DWORD**, **REG_BINARY**, and **REG_SZ**.

The hive file **HARDWARE** provides no opportunities for customizing the computer, for two reasons. First, the settings in this hive are more than a little cryptic. Second, changes users make are not persistent; the operating system rebuilds **HARDWARE** the next time it starts. I explain each of this hive's subkeys in the following sections primarily for your information. The most interesting values are the **REG_SZ** values under **HARDWARE\DESCRIPTION** and its subkeys. These values contain English descriptions of some of a computer's hardware, such as the CPU.

DESCRIPTION

When Windows 2000 starts, the hardware recognizer stores information about the hardware it finds in **HARDWARE**. In **HARDWARE\DESCRIPTION\System** there are three subkeys (possibly more in some configurations). The first, **CentralProcessor**, contains a subkey for each CPU that the hardware recognizer detects. Values that describe the CPU's speed, components, and so on are found in **CentralProcessor\N**. The second, **FloatingPointProcessor**, contains a subkey for each FPU that the hardware recognizer detects. Each contains similar information as **CentralProcessor\N**.

The third, **MultifunctionAdapter**, contains a subkey for each bus that the hardware recognizer detects. In each subkey, the **REG_SZ** value **Identifier** contains the friendly name of the bus: PCI, ISA, and so on. **Component Information** and **Configuration Data** further describe each bus and aren't decipherable. Below each bus's subkey you might find more subkeys that describe devices attached to the bus. For example, **MultifunctionAdapter\4\ DiskController** describes a disk controller that's connected to the fourth bus, which is the ISA bus on my computer. Drill down even farther, and you'll find subkeys for devices connected to the various controllers, including these:

- Disk controllers
- Keyboard controllers
- Other controllers
- Pointer controllers
- Serial controllers

N O T E The information in **HKLM\HARDWARE** does not describe all the hardware in the computer. You don't find information about network and sound cards in **HARDWARE**, for example. You find bare-bones information about basic hardware, and that's all. Because Windows 2000 is now a Plug and Play operating system, you find better hardware information in other parts of the Registry. ▓

DEVICEMAP

As the name implies, subkeys in **DEVICEMAP** map devices to the services that enable them.

Each subkey contains one or more values. The names of the values are device names, such as keyboard. The data for these values reference another subkey that describes the service behind the device. For example, **DEVICEMAP\KeyboardClass** might contain the value **\Device\KeyboardClass0** whose value is **\REGISTRY\ MACHINE\SYSTEM\ControlSet001\Services\kbdclass**. This means the service that enables the keyboard is in **HKLM\SYSTEM\ControlSet001\Services\kbdclass**. **REGISTRY** just means to look in the Registry. **MACHINE** means to look in **HKLM**. Why Microsoft couldn't just put the name of the subkey and uses this cryptic notation instead is beyond me.

RESOURCEMAP

Values in **RESOURCEMAP** associate the computer's resources with each device. The following are the resources that each value associates with a device:

- Bus number
- DMA Channels
- Interrupt vectors
- Memory ranges
- I/O ports

Of particular interest is **PnP Manager\PnPManager**, which contains a value of **REG_RESOURCE_LIST** for each device and bus. Open the value in the **Resource Lists** dialog box to see the bus to which it's associated. Click the bus and then click Display to display the actual resources the device uses by displaying them in the Resources dialog box. Figure 15.1 shows an example.

FIGURE 15.1
Device Manager is the best way to view this information.

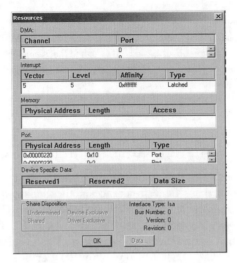

HKLM\SAM

HLKM\SAM is a link to **HKLM\SECURITY\SAM**, which you learn about in the section following this one. That means it's a duplicate copy of **SECURITY\SAM**, and any change that Windows 2000 makes to **HKLM\SAM** reflects automatically in **HKLM\SECURITY\SAM**. **SAM** contains the Security Account Manager's (SAM's) security database for the local computer. If the computer also manages a domain, **SAM** contains the security database for the domain as well as the local computer.

The contents of **SAM** are purposefully cryptic; it does contain security information after all. Users have no reason to edit settings in this subkey, nor can they unless they change its subkeys' permission using *Regedt32* or run *Regedt32* using AT by typing **at** *time* **/interactive "%sytsemroot%\system32\regedt32.exe"** at the MS-DOS command-prompt. For *time*, use a time that's only a few minutes in the future so *Regedt32* will launch soon. This command runs *Regedt32* in the System account so you can see the full contents of **SAM**, something no user account has permission to do.

Domains doesn't contain any values, but it has two subkeys that describe the computer's accounts and groups as well as its built-in accounts and groups. **Account** contains information about accounts and groups that administrators added by double-clicking the Users and Passwords icon in Control Panel or using the Local Users and Groups node of Computer Management. **Builtin** contains information about the built-in users and groups, the users and groups that Windows 2000 defines and users can't remove. Built-in groups include Administrators and Users, and built-in users include Administrator and Guest.

Account and **Builtin** have the same three subkeys: **Aliases**, **Accounts**, and **Groups**. More information about each is given here:

- **Aliases**   Defines local groups on the computer.
- **Groups**   Defines domain groups on the computer.
- **Users**   Defines local user accounts on the computer.

HKLM\SECURITY

This subkey, **SECURITY**, stores Windows 2000's security information. It includes **SAM**, the subkey you learned about in the previous section. SAM stores security data for local and network users and groups in the **SAM** subkey. **SECURITY** contains one additional subkey, **Policies**. The same trick you learned about in the previous section to view **SAM** works to view the contents of **SECURITY**: run *Regedt32* under the System account so you can view its contents. Alternatively, replace the permissions on **SECURITY** and all its subkeys so you can view them, a process that requires administrator rights on the computer. Do this on scratch computers only, however, because you don't want to tamper with the security on a production computer.

Policy defines local policy for users and groups. **Accounts** is one example. The remaining subkeys contain policies that administrators define in Computer Management. **HKLM\ SECURITY\Policy\Accounts** contains subkeys for all SIDs defined on the computer. Each subkey is named after the SID and has four subkeys that further define it. Those subkeys are listed here:

- **ActSysAc**   Defines the access to the operating system allowed for that SID.
- **Privilgs**   Defines the privileges for that SID.
- **SecDesc**   Contains the SID's security descriptor.
- **Sid**   Defines the groups to which SID belongs.

HKLM\SOFTWARE

SOFTWARE contains a variety of per-computer software settings. That is, the settings you find in this branch apply to every user who logs on to the computer. **HKCU** has a similar key, which you've learned about in Chapter 14, "Per-User Settings," but those settings apply to individual users. Applications such as text editors and graphics programs tend to store settings in the **Software** subkey in **HKCU**, although hardware and utility vendors tend to store settings in **HKLM\SOFTWARE**. Seagate and Symantec are examples of vendors that store settings in **HKLM**.

Within **SOFTWARE**, applications use an organization similar to *Company\Product\Version*. *Company* is the name of the company that produces the application, *Product* is the name of the application, and *Version* is the version of the application whose settings you find in that branch. Thus, **Honeycutt\MyProg\1.0** contains preferences for version 1.0 of a program called MyProg developed by a company called Honeycutt. Some companies use the name **CurrentVersion** instead of an actual version number, as Microsoft does for Windows.

Clients

Clients is an oddball; it doesn't conform to those rules. Within **Clients**, you find a single subkey for each type of client you can configure on the Programs tab of Microsoft Internet Explorer 5's Internet Properties dialog box, shown in Figure 15.2. In other words, you can associate mail, news, conferencing, calendar, and contact list clients with Internet Explorer. When you click a news link, for example, Internet Explorer knows the correct program in which to open the newsgroup. Click a mail link, and Internet Explorer knows which mail client you want to use.

FIGURE 15.2
By adding a program to **Clients**, you can associate it with different types of links in Internet Explorer.

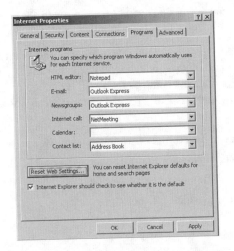

Clients contains five subkeys: **Calendar**, **Contacts**, **Internet Call**, **Mail**, and **News**. The default value for each subkey names the application currently chosen and points to one of the subkeys one level below. Thus, the default value for **Clients\Mail** is *Client*, and **Clients** **Mail***Client* describes that application. The organization of each client's subkey is virtually the same as for programs in **HKCR**. For example, under **Outlook Express**, the subkey **shell\open\command** contains the command line that starts the program. **Protocols** **mailto\shell\open\command** contains the command line that Internet Explorer launches when you click a mail link on a Web page. Other types of clients have the same two subkeys, **shell** and **Protocols**.

Program Groups

Program Groups indicates whether Windows 2000 has converted any existing group files, which Windows 3.1 used. If the **REG_DWORD** value **ConvertedToLinks** is **0x0001**, it has already converted existing groups. If it's **0x0000**, it hasn't. Unless you're upgrading from a version of Windows earlier than Windows 95, this subkey and its values are of little use.

HKLM\SOFTWARE\Microsoft

Microsoft, immediately under **HKLM\SOFTWARE**, contains per-computer settings for Microsoft products such as Office 2000 and, more importantly, Windows 2000. The settings in this portion of the Registry are useful for troubleshooting and customizing the operating system. The following sections describe the most interesting of its immediate subkeys.

Command Processor

This subkey contains settings that control the command processor in console windows, the window that contains the MS-DOS command prompt. Several values are particularly interesting:

- **AutoRun**   Each time you start a command prompt, whether by opening a new console window or by typing `Cmd.exe` in an existing console window, MS-DOS executes the commands it finds in this subkey. This value can be a **REG_SZ** or **REG_MULTI_SZ** value. If it's a **REG_MULTI_SZ** value, which you must create using *Regedt32*, MS-DOS executes the command represented by each string in the value.

- **CompletionChar**   Filename completion at the MS-DOS command prompt is not enabled by default. You can enable it by putting the ASCII code of the completion character you want to use in the **REG_DWORD** value **CompletionChar**. For example, to use a Tab to automatically complete filenames, put **0x0009** in this value.

- **DefaultColor**   This is the default color of the console window, which is usually **0x0000**, black.

- **DelayedExpansion**   This **REG_DWORD** value controls whether the command prompt expands environment variables when you surround them with exclamation points (!) as well as percent signs (%). Set it to **0x0001** to enable delayed expansion or **0x0000** to disable this feature.

- **EnableExtensions**   This **REG_DWORD** value is a simple flag that enables or disables the command extensions. Set to **0x0001**, the default, to enable extensions or set to **0x0000** to disable them. Command extensions add new features to the following commands: **Del**, **Color**, **Cd**, **Md**, **Prompt**, **Pushd**, **Popd**, **Set**, **Setlocal**, **Endlocal**, **If**, **For**, **Call**, **Shift**, **Goto**, **Start**, **Assoc**, and **Ftype**. To learn more about what those extensions are for each command, type *command* /? at the MS-DOS command prompt, where *command* is one of the commands that have extensions.

■ **PathCompletionChar**   This value is similar to **CompletionChar** except that it only applies to directory names, not filenames. It gives you a way to quickly fill in a path without having to cycle through all the files in each directory. You might put **0x0004** in this **REG_DWORD** value, which causes the command prompt to complete what you've typed with the next matching directory each time you press Ctrl+D.

DrWatson

The subkey **DrWatson** contains the settings for the Dr. Watson program, which you can use to log details about application failures. To change these settings, type `drwtsn32.exe` at the MS-DOS command prompt or in the Run dialog box. Figure 15.3 shows its window. The settings you see in its window correspond to the **REG_DWORD** values you find in **DrWatson**:

- **AppendToLogFile**
- **CreateCrashDump**
- **DumpAllThreads**
- **DumpSymbols**
- **Instructions**
- **Maximum Crashes**
- **NumberOfCrashes**
- **SoundNotification**
- **VisualNotification**

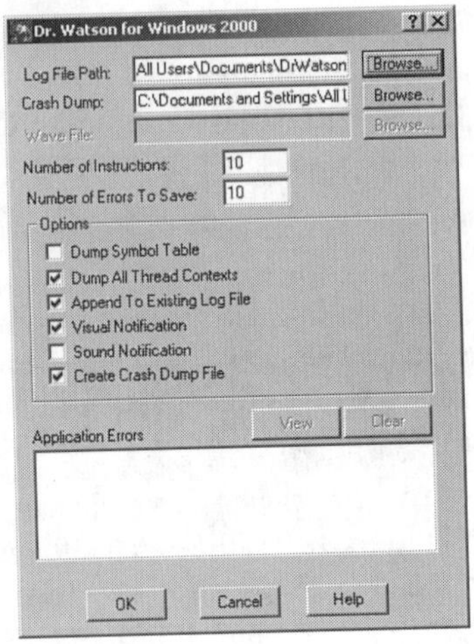

FIGURE 15.3
Dr. Watson for Windows 2000 has many new features over earlier versions of Dr. Watson.

InternetExplorer

InternetExplorer contains browser settings that apply to every user who logs on to the computer. For example, **AboutURLs** has a number of values that point to HTML files for certain errors. **Advanced Options** contains templates that Internet Explorer uses to display the options on the Advanced tab of the Internet Options dialog box. **Main** is the most interesting subkey of **InternetExplorer**. It contains settings such as the default search URL, the amount of disk spaced used for the cache, and the size of placeholders used for images on a Web page.

HKLM\SOFTWARE\Microsoft\Windows\ CurrentVersion

Windows\CurrentVersion contains a plethora of values, most of which the setup program created when you installed Windows 2000. You find some of the most interesting settings under **Windows\CurrentVersion**. This is where the operating system stores its per-computer settings, such as application paths and setup parameters. The following sections describe the most interesting of these subkeys and values.

App Paths

Immediately under **CurrentVersion** is a subkey called **App Paths**. This is how you can run a program from the Run dialog box or MS-DOS command prompt just by typing its name, even though the program isn't in the path.

The default value for **App Paths***filename*, where *filename* is the name of the executable file including the .exe file extension, contains the command line that executes the program. An optional value called **Path** might contain a path that describes where to find other files, perhaps .dll flies, which the program might require. For example, if you want to be able to run a program called Myprog.exe without putting the program in the path, add a subkey to **App Paths** called **Myprog.exe** and set the default value to the program's path and filename.

Applets

Windows 2000 accessories store per-computer settings in **Applets**. The actual data each accessory stores is different, but in most cases you'll see things such as most recently used lists, paths, or any other per-computer data that the accessory requires. Most of the settings in these subkeys are self-explanatory, so you can easily customize them.

Detect

This subkey contains values that Windows 2000 stores, and it also describes the computer's BIOS. Windows 2000 examines the BIOS to see whether it's ACPI-compliant and, in the process, it stores the BIOS' timestamp in the **REG_SZ** value called **TimeStamp** and stores the detection date in **ACPICheckDate**. The **REG_BINARY** value **Version** contains version information about the BIOS.

Explorer

The subkey **Explorer** contains settings that mostly affect Microsoft Windows Explorer but sometimes affect the desktop. In reality, the similar key you find in **HKCU** is more customizable than this one, but there are still a few opportunities.

Explorer\Desktop\Namespace contains subkeys whose names reflect class identifiers. For each subkey under **Namespace**, Windows Explorer puts the corresponding object on the desktop. The default value entry for the key contains the name of the object, which you'll see under its desktop icon. **MyComputer\Namespace**, **Internet\Namespace**, **RemoteComputer\Namespace**, **NetworkNeighborhood\Namespace**, and **Control Panel\Namespace** are similar to **Desktop\Namespace**, but each subkey in these represents objects that Windows Explorer will add to the My Computer, Internet, Remote Computer, Network Neighborhood, and Control panel folders, respectively.

When you choose Start, Search, you find that the submenu contains a number of commands that let you search in various places. Windows Explorer gets these from **Explorer\FindExtensions**. If you see an extension on the Search menu that you want to remove, remove its corresponding subkey from **FindExtensions**.

Explorer\Shell Folders and **Explorer\User Shell Folders** work similar to the same branches in **HKCU**. The versions in **HKLM** define the location of shell folders for all users who log on to the computer.

Run

A popular question on the Internet is "Why does such-and-such a program automatically start when I boot Windows 2000?" If you don't see the program in the Start menu's Startup group, the answer must be one of the **Run** keys.

Each time you start the operating system and possibly before the user closes the login dialog box, Windows 2000 starts any application it finds in **Run**. This subkey contains a value, whose name is arbitrary, for each application the operating system runs at startup. The string data in each value is the command line that the operating system uses to launch the program. Windows 2000 starts the programs it finds in **Run Once** and then removes the value for it. That way, the program runs only once. An example of a program that you would run only one time is one that completes a program's installation after you restart the computer.

SharedDLLs

Immediately under **CurrentVersion** is a subkey called **SharedDLLs**. This subkey contains a value for each .dll file installed on the computer. The name of the value is the path and file-name of the .dll file. The value assigned to this **REG_DWORD** is the number of applications using it. If you see a .dll in this subkey that's assigned the value of 2, that means two different applications are using it.

SharedDLLs is how uninstall programs know when it's safe to remove a .dll file from the computer and when it's not. When a file's value under **SharedDLLs** is 0, removing it is safe. That's the theory, but here's the rule: Because some programs don't use this subkey prop-erly, you can't rely on this method.

Uninstall

Uninstall is another interesting subkey of **CurrentVersion**. Each subkey, **Uninstall** *Application*, contains information about an application's uninstall program. The Add/Remove Programs dialog box uses the value of the string **DisplayName** to fill its list, and **UninstallString** contains the command line that starts the application's uninstall program.

Some programs store additional information in **Uninstall**. For example, Adobe Acrobat Reader stores extra information that helps its uninstall program do its job.

If you manually remove a program from your computer as described in Chapter 12, "Repairing Damaged Registries," make sure you remove the program's entry in **Uninstall**. That way, you won't see an entry for the program in the Add/Remove Programs dialog box when the program no longer exists.

With Windows 2000, **Uninstall** gets a bit more complicated than in earlier versions of Windows. The Windows Installer Service stores varieties of information in **Uninstall**, including help desk information, links to a Web page where users can get help, and version numbers. The values are mostly self-explanatory.

 TIP Removing an application's uninstall program from **Uninstall** is a good way to prevent users from accidentally removing a program. Group Policy is a better way to do the same thing.

HKLM\SOFTWARE\Microsoft\Windows NT\ CurrentVersion

This subkey is similar to **Windows\CurrentVersion**. Although Windows 98 provides a subkey similar to **HKLM\SOFTWARE\Microsoft\Windows**, **Windows NT** is unique to Windows 2000 and Windows NT Workstation 4.0. This subkey contains a handful of interesting values:

- **CurrentBuildNumber** This value describe the version of Windows 2000 that you're using, which is a better indicator than the value in **CurrentVersion**.

- **RegisteredOrganization** This value contains the name of the organization that you provided when you installed Windows 2000. If the computer you're using came with Windows 2000 preinstalled on it and you want to change the organization, change this **REG_SZ** value to reflect its name.

- **RegisteredOwner** This value is similar to **RegisteredOrganization** and it contains the name of the user who owns the computer. Like the other value, you can change this **REG_SZ** value if the computer came with Windows 2000 and you don't want the registered owner to say something stupid like "Valued Customer."

- **SourcePath** This value is the path to the installation files.

- **SystemRoot** This value is the path in which you install Windows 2000. It's usually something like **C:\Winnt** and is the same value as is in the environment variable **SYSTEMROOT**.

Compatibility, Compatibility2, and **Compatibility32** contain values for different programs. The name of each value is the same as the program's filename. The **REG_DWORD** data assigned to each value is a flag that indicates any compatibility issues with that program.

HotFix contains a subkey for each hotfix you installed. You download hotfixes from Microsoft's Web site. When you install a hotfix, it adds a subkey to this subkey and, in that subkey, it adds a **REG_DWORD** value called **Installed** that indicates the hotfix is installed on the computer.

HKLM\SYSTEM

SYSTEM leads to a handful of subkeys called **CurrentControl00N** (N is 0, 1, 2, and so on) and one subkey called **CurrentControlSet**. **CurrentControlSet** is a link to one of the subkeys called **CurrentControl00N**.

A *control set* contains information that describes how to start and configure the computer. These are all per-computer settings, of course. Each control set has four subkeys, **Control**, **Enum**, **Hardware Profiles**, and **Services**. You learn more about each in the following sections.

CurrentControlSet\Enum

Enum contains configuration data for every device installed on the computer. Even if a device isn't present at the moment, you still see it listed in this branch. Needless to say, the contents of **Enum** are different from computer to computer, because each computer's configuration is different. Not only that, each hardware vendor has certain twists to how it stores configuration data in the Registry. If you want to get a glimpse of how a vendor configures the Registry for a certain device, take a look at the Setup Information (INF) files you used to install the device's drivers. You'll find them in *SystemRoot*\Inf.

Enum leads to a number of subkeys, one for each type of enumerator. Following each enumerator is a subkey—whose name represents a *device ID*—for each specific device installed on the computer. Thus, the subkey **Enum***Enumerator**Device* represents a device that is or once was present. The name used for *Device* is different within different types of enumerators. Under **Root**, for example, *Device* looks like **PNPXXXX*. This is called the *EISA format*. It starts with an asterisk (*) and is followed by a three-letter manufacturer code, a three-digit identification number, and a one-digit revision number. If the device is generic, you'll typically see **PNP** used for the manufacturer code. In other enumerators, *Device* looks like *VENDOR&DEVICE&SUBSYS&REV*, which contains vendor and device codes as well as a revision number.

Enum*enumerator**Device**Instance* represents an actual instance of the device and is therefore called an *instance ID*. You might see two or more instances under a device ID if there are two or more devices of that type on the computer. For example, if you have two communications ports, you'll see two instances under the device ID. The name used for *Instance* is typically one of three types: a sequence number, a device number as assigned on the bus, or a combination of the bus, device, and function numbers that looks like *BUS&DEVICE&FUNCTION*. In cases in which a device has a parent device (a serial mouse's parent device is the serial port), an instance ID might look like *BUS&DEVICE&INSTANCE*, allowing you to find the parent device by opening **Enum***BUS**DEVICE**INSTANCE*. This gets a bit complicated when the parent device and instance IDs are *VENDOR&DEVICE&SUBSYS&REV* and *BUS&DEVICE&FUNCTION*, because you end up with instance IDs that look like *BUS&VENDOR&DEVICE&SUBSYS&REV&BUS&DEVICE&FUNCTION*.

Enum*Enumerator* and **Enum***Enumerator**Device* are usually devoid of any values. Windows 2000 frequently infers meaning from the name of *Device*, however, particularly in the case of devices listed under **Enum\PCI** or when a device has a parent listed elsewhere within **Enum**. The instance subkey, **Enum***Enumerator**Device**Instance*, contains the actual configuration data for each device, and it usually contains all of the following values and then some:

- **Capabilities**
- **CompatibleIDs**
- **ClassGUID**
- **Class**
- **ConfigFlags**
- **Driver**
- **DeviceDesc**
- **FriendlyName**
- **HardwareID**
- **Mfg**

Some of these values are interesting, but none of them are useful for configuring the Registry. **Class** contains a name that describes the device's hardware class. The string value in **Class** refers you to a branch under **HKLM\System\CurrentControlSet\Services\Class** for the class's plain-English description. The string value in **Driver** refers you to a branch under the same key that contains information about the device's driver, including its filename, date, INF file and section, provider, and so on. **DeviceDesc** is the device's description as you see it in Device Manager.

> **N O T E** Within each device's subkey, you see a value called **Driver**. This string value indicates the path to the device's driver, starting from **HKLM\System\CurrentControlSet\Services\Class**. Thus, if you see **MODEM\0001** in a device's **Driver** value, look up **Class\MODEM\0001** to find more information about that device's driver and INF file. ■

The following list describes the different enumerators you typically find in **Enum**:

- ■ **ACPI** ACPI standards for *Advanced Configuration and Power Interface*. Windows 2000 stores power-management devices in this enumerator subkey. In my experience, the device ID is a plain-English name, and the instance number is just a sequence number.

- ■ **BIOS** You see this enumerator subkey on computers that have a Plug and Play-compliant BIOS. It contains a variety of devices that are embedded in the computer's motherboard. The BIOS reports them to the operating system. Each device ID is in the EISA format (for example, ***PNP0001**), and each instance ID is a hexadecimal sequence number. Microsoft assigns certain ranges of device IDs to certain types of devices, as described in the following table:

Range	Description
PNP0000-PNP0004	Interrupt controllers
PNP0100-PNP0102	System timers
PNP0200-PNP0202	DMA controllers
PNP0300-PNP0313	Keyboard controllers
PNP0400-PNP0401	Printer ports
PNP0500-PNP0501	Communication ports
PNP0600-PNP0602	Hard disk controllers
PNP0700	Standard floppy disk controller
PNP0800	System speaker
PNP0900-PNP0915	Display adapters
PNP0930-PNP0931	Expansion buses
PNP0940-PNP0941	Expansion buses
PNP0A00-PNP0A04	Expansion buses

Range	Description
PNP0B00	CMOS real-time clock
PNP0C01	System board extension
PNP0C02	Reserved
PNP0C04	Numeric data processor
PNP0E00-PNP0E02	PCMCIA controllers
PNP0F01	Microsoft Serial Mouse
PNP0F00-PNP0F13	Mouse ports
PNP8000-PNP8FFF	Network adapters
PNPA030	Mitsumi CD-ROM controller
PNPB000-PNPB0FF	Other adapters

■ **EISA** You see this enumerator subkey on computers that have an EISA bus. Each subkey represents a device installed on that bus. You will see at least one subkey called `*PNP0A00` under **EISA** that represents the ISA Plug and Play bus. Note that this subkey isn't common on newer computers that don't use this bus. And, of course, the device IDs are in the EISA format.

■ **ESDI** You see this enumerator subkey on computers that have an ESDI device installed—notably hard disks. The device IDs are plain-English names that usually indicate the type of disk, and the instance IDs look like *BUS&DEVICE&INSTANCE*, allowing you to find the parent device by following the path to **Enum***BUS\DEVICE\INSTANCE*. Each instance's subkey contains additional values not found for other devices, such as **CurrentDriveLetter**, which indicates the drive letter assigned to the device. If you partitioned the drive, this string value entry will contain a letter for each drive, such as "CD".

■ **FLOP** Most computers contain this enumerator subkey because it describes the floppy drives installed on the computer. Each device and instance ID is named similarly to those in **ESDI**. As with the subkeys of **ESDI**, you see additional values such as **CurrentDriveLetter**, which indicates the drive letter assigned to the floppy drive.

■ **HTREE** This subkey doesn't contain any devices. **HTREE\RESERVED** maintains a list of resources that you reserve via Device Manager.

■ **ISAPNP** You see this enumerator subkey on computers with ISA or EISA buses when the computer doesn't have a Plug and Play BIOS. Each subkey describes a device installed on that bus and uses the EISA name format without the asterisk (*).

■ **INFRARED** Some computers, particularly newer portable computers, have infrared ports. You see a subkey under **INFRARED** for each virtual device attached to this port. In particular, you'll see **COM** and **LPT**.

■ **LPTENUM** **LPTENUM** exists only if you install a Plug and Play printer on the parallel port.

■ **MF** MF contains a subkey for each multifunction device installed on the computer. Because most modern computers have a primary and secondary IDE controller, you'll see two device IDs: **CHILD0000** and **CHILD0001**. The devices in **MF** have parent devices that are listed elsewhere in **Enum**. Like devices in ESDI, the instance IDs look like *BUS&DEVICE&INSTANCE*, allowing you to find the parent device by opening **Enum*BUS\DEVICE\INSTANCE***.

N O T E When you see an instance ID that begins with the name of an enumerator in **Enum**, that's a good indication that the ID refers to a parent device. Follow the path given in the instance ID, beginning with **Enum**. Thus, if you see the instance ID **BIOS&*PNP0700&0800**, open **BIOS** under **Enum**, followed by ***PNP0700** and **08**. ■

■ **MONITOR** MONITOR usually contains a single subkey: **DEFAULT_MONITOR**. If you're using two monitors, a new feature for Windows 2000, you might see additional subkeys. Below the monitor's subkey, you see additional subkeys called **0001**, **0002**, and so on, one for each hardware profile. The only time you'll see more than one key is in cases where you might be using different monitors at different times, such as docked and undocked configurations. While a portable is docked, the computer might use a regular monitor, but while it's undocked, the computer might use the LCD panel. To see which monitor Windows 98 is using, you must look in **HKEY_DYN_DATA\ Config Manager\Enum**.

■ **PCI** On computers that have a PCI bus, you see a subkey under **PCI** for each device on it. **VEN_*XXXX*&DEV_*YYYY*&SUBSYS_*ZZZZZZZZ*&REV_*NN*** is the way each device ID resembles. *XXXX* is a vendor code, and *YYYY* is a device code. Each instance looks like **BUS_*XX*&DEV_*YY*&FUNC_*ZZ***, where *XX* is a bus code, *YY* is a device code, and *ZZ* is a function code.

■ **PCMCIA** PCMCIA contains a single subkey for each PC Card device installed in the computer. When you remove a PC Card from the computer, Windows 2000 retains its settings under **PCMCIA**. The device IDs used in **PCMCIA** seem to be plain-English values queried from each PC Card device. The instance ID can be a simple device number, or it can be in the form *BUS&DEVICE&INSTANCE*, which refers to the parent device within **Enum**.

■ **Root** This enumerator subkey contains a subkey for each legacy ISA and VLB device installed on the computer. These devices include those detected via the Add New Hardware Wizard. You find a combination of names used for device IDs in this key. Device IDs that use the EISA format are actual legacy devices. Device IDs that have names such as **SwEnum** and **Net** are virtual Windows devices. **Net** represents the Dial-Up Networking adapter, for example.

■ **SCSI** This enumerator subkey contains a single subkey for each SCSI device installed on the computer. Note that the host adapter is installed under the **PCI** key, not **SCSI**. SCSI uses naming conventions similar to **ESDI** and **FLOP**.

- **SERENUM** SERENUM contains a single subkey for each device attached to a serial port. For example, if you plug a mouse into a serial port, you see a subkey for that mouse under **SERENUM**. The instance ID is *BUS&DEVICE&INSTANCE*, allowing you to find the serial port to which the device is attached by opening **Enum***BUS\DEVICE\INSTANCE*.

- **USB** You see a single subkey for each device connected to the Universal Serial Bus. You also see a subkey that represents the USB hub called **ROOT_HUB**. The instance ID is *BUS&DEVICE&INSTANCE*, allowing you to find the root hub by opening **Enum***BUS\DEVICE\INSTANCE*.

- **VPOWERD** This enumerator subkey leads to additional subkeys that contain configuration data for Windows 2000's power management devices. One such example includes the APM Battery Slot. The device IDs in this enumerator use plain-English names.

CurrentControlSet\Hardware Profiles

The subkey **Hardware Profiles** contains a subkey for each hardware profile that users define by double-clicking the System icon in Control Panel. Each profile is named **0001**, **0002**, and so on. **Current** is a link to the current hardware profile.

CurrentControlSet\Services

Services leads to a series of subkeys that define the services that Windows 2000 loads. Every subkey has similar values, which correspond to the controls on the *Name* Properties dialog box for a service. These include **ErrorControl**, **Group**, **Start**, **Tag**, and **Type**. These values are all self-explanatory. Many services have additional subkeys that are interesting, however:

- **Enum** This subkey contains **REG_SZ** values that reference a subkey in **HKLM\Enum**. By looking at this subkey in **Enum**, you can find additional information about additional devices or drives associated with the service.

- **Linkage** This subkey is more common on network services. The values in this subkey define how different network services bind or link together.

- **Parameter** This subkey contains additional settings that the service requires. Many service subkeys have this subkey, but each service puts the settings it requires here. For example, **lanmanserver** puts settings in **lanmanserver** that you can use to fine-tune its performance.

- **Security** This subkey contains security information for the service. In particular, it defines the account under which the service runs.

HKLM\SYSTEM\CurrentControlSet\Control

Control contains a seemingly random group of settings that configures the computer. Most of these settings apply to the computer as Windows 2000 starts. The operating system refers to other settings throughout the session. Some subkeys are more interesting than others, and you learn about the more interesting ones in the following sections.

BackupRestore

BackupRestore has two subkeys, both of which apply to Microsoft Windows Backup:

- **FilesNotToBackup** This subkey contains a list of files that Windows Backup will not back up.
- **KeysNotToRetore** This subkey contains a list of subkeys that Windows Backup uses when it restores the Registry from a backup copy.

Class

Subkeys under **Class** look like COM class identifiers (**{4D36E964-E325-11CE-BFC1-08002BE10318}**). You find one for every device class. The IDs are new to Windows 2000 and provide a method for accessing devices that's similar to how Windows 2000 accesses other objects. Each ID has at least one value: **Class**. **Class** is the friendly name of the device class. A couple different values are typically in each device class' subkey:

Icon	Indicates the icon that Windows 2000 displays in Device Manager. This is an index or resource ID. The icon comes from the DLL file given by **Installer32**.
Installer32	Indicates the program file that's responsible for installing the device. This is also where Device Manager gets the icon you see in the list.

Each instance ID under **HKEY_LOCAL_MACHINE\Enum** contains a value entry called **Driver** that points to one of the branches under **Class**. For example, **Enum\Root\ *PNP00400\PnPBIOS_11** contains a value called **Driver** whose string value is **{4D36E978-E325-11CE-BFC1-08002BE10318}\0000**. Look up this value in **Class** to find more information about the device's driver, INF file, and so on. If you don't see any numbered subkeys under a device class, a device of that class is not installed on the computer. Otherwise, you see those familiar subkeys numbered **0000**, **0001**, and so on. Each subkey under a device class typically has the same types of values. You might find values and subkeys unique to a particular device, however, particularly in the case of more-complex devices such as modems and network adapters. Here's a description of the typical values you find for **\Class*ClassName*\Device**:

DriverDate	Contains the date the device driver was released from the vendor.
DriverDesc	Contains a brief description of the device driver. You see this description in the Device Manager.
InfPath	Contains the filename of the INF file used to install the device. You find this INF file in *SystemRoot*\Inf.
InfSection	Contains the section name within the INF file that was used to install the device.
MatchingDeviceId	Contains the device ID of the device as you find it in **Enum**.
ProviderName	The name of the device driver vendor.

ComputerName

ComputerName in **ComputerName\ComputerName** contains the name of the computer as provided on the Identification tab of the Network dialog box, which you open from the Control Panel.

FileSystem

FileSystem contains a number of settings that control how the Windows 2000 file system works. You can disable long filenames, for example, by changing **Win31FileSystem** from **00** to **01**. You can change how Windows 2000 creates 8.3 aliases for long filenames by adding a binary value called **NameNumericTail** and setting it to **00**. This means the operating system will try to create filenames that use eight full characters of the long filename (if doing so doesn't create a duplicate filename) instead of adding a tilde (~) followed by a number. The following table describes a variety of other settings you can change in **FileSystem**:

Value	Description
AsyncFileCommit	00 = enable synchronous buffer commits 01 = enable asynchronous file commits
LastBootPMDrvs	Contains the number of the last boot driver
ReadAheadThreshold	Read-ahead optimization
DriveWriteBehind	00 00 00 00 = disable write-behind caching FF FF FF FF = enable write-behind caching
PreserveLongFilenames	00 00 00 00 = disable preservation FF FF FF FF = enable preservation
ForceRMIO	00 = use protected mode disk I/O 01 = force real mode disk I/O

continues

Value	Description
VirtualHDIRQ	0 = disable protected mode HD interrupts
	1 = enable protected mode HD interrupts
SoftCompatMode	00 = disable file-sharing semantics
	01 = enable file-sharing semantics

SessionManager

SessionManager leads to a series of subkeys that don't really relate to the name of this key. In fact, most of the subkeys in **SessionManager** help Windows 2000 keep track of various .dll files or help it determine whether an application can run in Windows and what is necessary for the application to run.

AppPatches leads to additional subkeys, each of which leads to the name of a program. Windows 2000 can make these programs work by patching them after it loads them into memory. The subkeys under each application describe each patch. **KnownDLLs** contains a value entry for each 32-bit DLL that Windows 98 knows about. ●

Index

Other Related Titles

DATE DUE	
NOV 2 6 2003	